New Managerialism, New Welfare?

New Managerialism, New Welfare?
This Reader provides some of the set readings for a 16 week module (D861
Managerialism and Social Policy) which is offered by The Open University
Masters Programme in the Social Sciences.

The Open University Masters Programme in the Social Sciences
The MA/MSc Programme enables students to select from a range of modules
to create a programme to suit their own professional or personal
development. Students can choose from a range of social science modules to
obtain an MA in the Social Sciences, or may choose to specialize in a particular
subject area by studying modules in one of the offered study lines. D861
Managerialism and Social Policy is a module for both the MA in Social Policy and
the MA in Social Policy and Criminology.

OU Supported Learning
The Open University's unique, supported ('distance') learning Masters
Programme in the Social Sciences is designed to facilitate engagement at an
advanced level with the concepts, approaches, theories and techniques
associated with a number of academic areas of study. The Social Sciences
Masters Programme provides great flexibility. Students study in their own
environments, in their own time, anywhere in the European Union. They
receive specially prepared course materials, benefit from structured tutorial
support throughout all the coursework and assessment assignments, and have
the chance to work with other students.

How to apply
If you would like to register for this programme, or simply find out more
information, please write for the Masters Programme in the Social Sciences
Prospectus to The Open University, Course Reservations Centre, PO Box
625, Milton Keynes, MK7 6ZW, UK (Telephone +44 (0)1908 858585) (E-mail:
ces-gen@open.ac.uk)

New Managerialism, New Welfare?

edited by
John Clarke, Sharon Gewirtz and Eugene McLaughlin

The Open
University

in association with

SAGE Publications
London • Thousand Oaks • New Delhi

First published 2000. Reprinted 2001

SAGE Publications Ltd
6 Bonhill Street
London EC2A 4PU

SAGE Publications Inc
2455 Teller Road
Thousand Oaks, California 91320

SAGE Publications India Pvt Ltd
32, M-Block Market
Greater Kailash – I
New Delhi 110 048

British Library Cataloguing in Publication data

A catalogue record for this book is available
from the British Library

ISBN 0 7619 6756 7
ISBN 0 7619 6757 5 (pbk)

Library of Congress catalog record available

Typeset by Mayhew Typesetting, Rhayader, Powys
Printed in Great Britain by The Cromwell Press Ltd,
Trowbridge, Wiltshire

Contents

Preface

This collection has been prepared as a text for an Open University course: *Managerialism and Social Policy* (D861), one of the courses in the Open University's Master's programmes in Social Policy and Criminology. The course is concerned with the role that managerialism has played within the remaking of the welfare state in the UK. This book explores these processes in the social and political contexts of the 'New' Labour government elected in 1997 and its commitment to modernize the state and public services.

The book has been developed from papers presented at a workshop held in May 1999 at the Open University and was completed in the Spring of 2000. We are grateful to the Social Policy discipline for funding the event and to the participants both for their initial enthusiasm and for delivering the worked up chapters that now form this book. Although we are named as the editors of the book, its development has depended on the other members of the course team that forms the Open University's 'collective teacher'. Thanks to Penny Bennett, Hilary Canneaux, Donna Collins, Ross Fergusson, Pauline Hetherington and Sue Lacey.

Finally, we are grateful to Sage – and Karen Phillips in particular – for their continuing enthusiasm for this work.

John Clarke
Sharon Gewirtz
Eugene McLaughlin

1

Reinventing the Welfare State

John Clarke, Sharon Gewirtz and Eugene McLaughlin

This book examines the continuing reconstruction of the welfare state in the United Kingdom. Although reform of welfare has long been a central part of the British political agenda, the changes begun in the 1980s by the Conservative governments of Margaret Thatcher inaugurated a period of 'permanent revolution' that has affected the scale, purposes, forms and social relationships of welfare. Subsequent reforms, initiatives and modernization programmes have been directed at the 'reinvention of welfare'. The New Labour government elected in 1997, following eighteen years of Conservative rule, proved to be just as enthusiastic about the reconstruction of welfare as a major political task, seeing it as a means through which a distinctively 'modern' British people might be constructed. Almost all of the reforms since 1979 have placed questions of organizational design, structure, culture and co-ordination at their centre. Hardly any reform has avoided attempting to redesign the systems of provision, the forms of organizational control and direction, and the relations between 'leaders', 'staff' and 'customers' involved in the production and delivery of welfare outcomes. This process of reconstruction has been a compound one – involving more than just 'policy' changes. Rather new policy directions have been bound up with new system designs, new funding and financial arrangements, new relationships between centre and periphery, and new relationships between state and citizen. This book is concerned to make sense of such compound changes by drawing together studies that explore different dimensions of welfare reconstruction and different sites of welfare. In this introduction we set out three contexts that are significant for the studies that are presented in the following chapters. We explore how social welfare in the UK was re-imagined and reconstructed by successive New Right governments; the emergence and significance of managerialism in public services; and the emergence of 'New Labour' as a political formation. The intersection of these three strands forms the main focus of this book.

Whilst the main emphasis of this volume is on the UK (although see Chapter 2 by Flynn) it is important to note at the outset that aspects of the policy developments described here have unfolded internationally and were not produced exclusively by UK-specific forces. We find across a variety of welfare regimes the emergence of public sector reform movements which have in common a belief that bureaucratic institutions and practices impede government performance. Despite differences in national circumstances, public sector traditions and the balance of local political forces, in broad terms at least, a remarkably similar set of arguments is presented (Pollitt and Bouckaert, 2000). In particular, these movements have advocated the need to reappraise the rationale for state intervention and restructure the organizational basis for the delivery of public services (Organization for Economic Co-operation and Development, 1995). In doing so, they are also seeking to reinvent the relationship between the nation state and the citizen.

1   Re-imagining and reconstructing social welfare

The last two decades of the twentieth century saw a shift way from the form of welfare state constructed in many of the advanced capitalist nations after the Second World War. In the UK – as in the USA – the initial process of reconstruction was largely driven by New Right political forces and ideologies that combined anti-welfarism and anti-statism (Clarke and Newman, 1997; Hughes and Lewis, 1998; Jones and Novak, 1999), although it is important to note that it was a leading Labour politician who first said 'The party is over', and that the deepest public expenditure percentage cuts occurred in 1977–78. It was the belief that there were unsustainable demographic and expenditure trends which helped convince a number of governments (including a Labour New Zealand, a coalition Netherlands and a Social Democratic Sweden) that some measure of privatization and curbing of welfare state programmes was necessary.

The anti-welfarist element of the New Right treated welfare spending as economically unproductive (a drain on the 'real economy') and as socially damaging (producing a dependency culture). The anti-statist element treated the free market as the normative mechanism for allocating resources, goods and services. From this starting point, 'the state' was seen as an interference in the natural workings of market processes – a distorting intrusion.

The effects of these anti-welfarist and anti-statist politics could be seen in the two privatizing patterns of reform associated with Conservative governments in the 1980s and 1990s. In one, the anti-statism of the New Right drove 'marketizing' reforms of welfare provision – opening up service provision to competition and encouraging corporate (for-profit) and voluntary (not-for-profit) providers. At the same time, public sector providers were increasingly required to engage in contracting and competitive forms of relationship, acting like small and medium sized businesses (Hoggett, 1996). This privatizing project juxtaposed the 'private sector' – equated with the market – and the 'public sector' – equated with the state – and wore down some of the boundaries separating the two (see, *inter alia*, Bartlett et al., 1998; Johnson, 1995).

This tendency intersected with a second form of 'privatization': the shift of responsibility for welfare from the 'public sphere' to the 'private sphere' – the world of individuals and the family. In part, this was justified as the process of placing choice in the hands of 'individuals and their families' (e.g. in parental choice of schooling). In part, it was a means of making the family the site of responsibility for issues ranging from childhood delinquency to care for elderly or disabled kin. Together, these privatizing shifts both diminished the scale and significance of public provision and celebrated the value of the private (in both senses) over the public.

As others have noted, the British 'welfare state' was an imaginary entity rather than an organizational whole – but it was a national social construction that played a significant role in public and political discourse (Hughes, 1998; Hughes and Lewis, 1998). In that context, the New Right's project of reconstructing the welfare state needs to be seen as directed at the meanings of welfare and the state as well as to the policy and organizational structures to which they refer. It is important to look on the New Right assault on the 'welfare state' as endeavouring to change public understandings and expectations of both 'welfare' and 'the state' as well as the relationships between them. Levels of benefits and services were reduced and tougher access conditions were attached to them, although demographic, economic, social and technological change tended to ensure that overall patterns of spending did not fall (Department of Social Security, 2000). Publicly provided welfare also became increasingly stigmatized and in certain important respects criminalized through the linkage of US representations of 'welfare dependency' and 'demoralization' with UK images of 'scrounging' and 'undeserving' (see, *inter alia*, Clarke, 1991; Katz, 1995; Mink, 1998). At the same time, both the meaning and structure of 'the state' have been changed. Where the post-war 'welfare consensus' had conceptualized 'the state' as the embodiment of the collective or public interest, the New Right identified it as a power exercised over individuals that inhibited and constrained them. The restructuring of the state involved the centralization of control and direction at the same time as the decentralization or dispersal of service provision or delivery (so the National Curriculum went alongside the 'self-management' of schools). The scale and reach of the public sector reduced while the state brought more and more organizations into 'sub-contracting' forms of relationships to provide services (ranging from home help to prison management). Debates about the changing fortunes of the 'welfare state' have often concentrated on one dimension of the changes. Different analyses have focused on the levels of benefits or services; the conditions of access to benefits and services; the levels of public spending; the organizational integrity of public services; the scale or scope of 'privatization' and so on. Given the complexity of the construction of the welfare state in post-war political discourse, it remains important to trace the different dimensions along which it has been reconstructed.

One further important dimension is highlighted by the New Right's attempts to reconstruct – or reinvent – the relationship between public services and the public in a 'consumerist' pattern. Aiming to overthrow the monopoly power of the old welfare producers (which treated the public as passive recipients), the New Right argued that competition between producers would create empowering conditions of 'consumer choice'. In the years since 1997, the public's relationship to welfare and the state has been continually reimagined (Hughes, 1998). We have seen the public identified as a passively dependent collectivity; as an aggregate of actively choosing consumers; as 'active citizens' promoting their own well-being; as communities engaged in partnerships with other agencies; and as the modern nation of 'sceptical citizen consumers' envisaged in the New Labour government's first Green Paper on welfare reform (Secretary of State for Social Security, 1998).

In terms of outcomes, the reforms introduced in the 1980s and 1990s brought about major shifts in the 'organizational settlement' of social welfare in the UK. They dismantled some of the old professional bureaucracies of public provision, or at least subjected them to new pressures that were intended to make them behave in more 'business like' ways (Clarke and Newman, 1997). Commentators have pointed to three main dimensions of this reorganization:

- The creation of 'mixed economies' of welfare, in which providers come from public, private, voluntary, and informal sectors and networks. Mixed economies marked the diminution of public sector monopolies or dominant roles in welfare provision (Butcher, 1995; Rao, 1996).
- The increasing use of market or market-like mechanisms for co-ordinating the provision of services (see, *inter alia*, Bartlett et al., 1998; Clarke, 2000; Mackintosh, 1998). Distinctions between purchaser and provider roles were constructed within services and even

within organizations, in both internal and external markets. Competition between providers was encouraged (e.g. between hospital trusts or schools). New providers were encouraged to enter areas of service provision (e.g. in social care). Such changes were supposed to introduce the disciplines of competition and contracting into the business of social welfare.

- The organizational forms of government were tilted increasingly towards what Skelcher (1998) has called 'quasi-government': the growth of non-elected agencies directing or overseeing the spending of public money and the provision of public services (see also Flinders and Smith, 1999).

Not all areas of the welfare system experienced all of these processes – they were unevenly distributed across welfare institutions. But each of these processes of reform created the conditions for the far-reaching impact of managerialization. By this we mean the process of subjecting the control of public services to the principles, powers and practices of managerial co-ordination (Clarke et al., 1994; Clarke and Newman, 1997; Pollitt, 1993; Cutler and Waine, 1998). The imagery of new 'business like' organizations and the more dispersed or fragmented network of organizations playing different roles in welfare provision led inexorably to the conclusion that 'more and better management' was a necessary condition for efficient, effective and economical services to the public. We will explore these issues further in the next section.

The Conservative governments of the 1980s and 1990s did not and could not fulfil some of the central rhetorical claims and demands of New Right ideology. The New Right legacy of welfare reform was, therefore, an ambiguous and contradictory one:

- it had a limited impact on controlling overall public spending;
- it shifted, rather than reduced, the tax burden, away from income and corporate taxation;
- it did not 'roll back the state' in any simple sense – though it certainly changed the capacities of the state and some of its relationships to the market and civil society;
- it 'set the people free' in some limited ways but 'rolled the state forward' through the expansion of policing powers, criminalization and the number of people in prison;
- it increased the scale and gradients of inequality in the UK while refusing to recognize the link between poverty and social problems;
- it attempted to change the meaning of welfare and the role of the state but had to go to considerable lengths to assure the public that cherished welfare provisions were 'safe in our hands'.

However contradictory and limited its outcomes were, the New Right did create a new ideological, political and organizational landscape in which 'New Labour' thinking and schemes for further welfare reform were developed. They also produced a complex set of tensions and contradictions – the 'unfinished business' of welfare reform – that was a central part of New Labour's inheritance. We return to these issues in section 3.

2　Coming to terms with managerialism and managerialization

One significant dimension of the reconstruction of the welfare state has been the process of managerialization: the shift towards managerial forms of organizational coordination. Public sector management was one of the significant growth areas of employment and education during the 1980s and 1990s (Ferlie et al., 1996). A whole range of studies have discussed the emergence or rise of a New Public Management (NPM) (e.g., Butcher, 1995; Dunleavy and Hood, 1994; Ferlie et al., 1996; Flynn and Strehl, 1996; Hood, 1991; Pollitt and Bouckaert, 2000). The NPM is usually taken to refer to some combination of processes and values that was developed in the 1980s as a distinctively different approach to the co-ordination of publicly provided services. The NPM is characteristically contrasted with forms of bureaucratic administration in public service organizations. Butcher, for example, argued that

> A system dominated by central government departments, local authorities and the NHS, and based upon the values and practices of public administration . . . is being replaced by a new set of practices and values, based upon a new language of welfare delivery which emphasizes efficiency and value for money, competition and markets, consumerism and customer care. (1995, p. 161)

Although there are variations, features typically ascribed to the NPM include:

- attention to outputs and performance rather than inputs;
- organizations being viewed as chains of low-trust relationships, linked by contracts or contractual type processes;
- the separation of purchaser and provider or client and contractor roles within formerly integrated processes or organizations;
- breaking down large scale organizations and using competition to enable 'exit' or 'choice' by service users;
- decentralization of budgetary and personal authority to line managers. (Adapted from Dunleavy and Hood, 1994)

Such features are seen as differentiating the NPM from older bureaucratic and administrative methods of co-ordinating public services.

Although helpful as a way of marking a set of changes, such views of the NPM have some significant limitations. Among these is a tendency to a rather over-unified or over-coherent view of the NPM as a form of co-ordination. For example, Ferlie and his colleagues have suggested that a singular view of the NPM disguises the existence of four overlapping, but separate, models of the NPM. They distinguish between the 'Efficiency Drive', 'Downsizing and Decentralization', 'In Search of Excellence' and 'Public Service Orientation' models of the NPM (1996, pp. 10–15). These distinctions emphasize both different sources and different focal points of elements within the NPM. There are other difficulties, too. The NPM is too often treated as a coherent whole of global significance and force despite the fact that comparative studies have tended to show wide national divergences in reform programmes, albeit often utilizing the language – or discourse – of New Public Management as a means of legitimation and institutionalization (see, *inter alia*, OECD, 1995; Flynn and Strehl, 1996; Flynn, Chapter 2 in this book; and Pollitt and Bouckaert, 2000).

However, we would argue that one of the key problems of studying the NPM is a degree of confusion about its status. Many examinations of the NPM conflate the politics and practice of public service reform treating the NPM as though it has been installed as the only mode of co-ordination in public services. They also conflate the descriptive and normative aspects of the concept treating the claims of NPM advocates as though they describe new realities. For example, in the above list based on Dunleavy and Hood (1994), what does it mean to say that organizations are viewed as chains of low-trust relationships? Is that *all* organizations are viewed as – or are they seen as having other significant features? Whose view is it – and are there other views? Does it mean that all actions are governed by this view of what organizations are like? It is certainly the case that many of the reforms of the 1980s and 1990s built on this view of organizations – and tried very hard to persuade the public that trust in public services was misplaced. Nevertheless, it seems overstated to treat this as an unequivocal, and completely accomplished, change in the co-ordination of public services. We would suggest that the impact of these ideas has been more uneven, contested and complex than can be accounted for in a view of a simple shift from public administration to New Public Management or from hierarchies to markets or networks (Stoker, 1999).

More troublingly, accounts of the New Public Management tend to focus attention on an activity – 'management' – and an occupational group – 'managers' – in ways that miss more complex social, political and organizational changes. For example, Farnham and Horton begin from a generic view about managing as involving 'a complex set of human and technical activities which take place within specific organizational settings and environments' (1996, p. xiii). We think Flynn provides a more productive starting point in his argument that

'Management is not a neutral, technical activity. Management techniques and styles are themselves political . . .' (1997, p. 41). Indeed,
managing is often presented as a neutral, technical set of activities,
performed by neutral technical experts, in pursuit of goals defined by
others – and that invocation of neutrality is at the core of 'managerialism' as an ideology. Flynn's highlighting of the political dimension of
management enables several lines of critical inquiry.

- It opens up the politics of viewing 'specific organizational settings' as
  places for 'management' – the political process of defining public
  services as in need of 'more and better management'.
- It allows attention to the choices involved in making organizational
  relationships, processes and decisions subject to managerial
  authority and principles (rather than other modes of coordination).
  In that process, it is not just the existence of 'managers' (or even
  those with managerial responsibilities) that is seen to be necessary,
  but the process of engaging everyone into the habits of thinking and
  behaving 'managerially'.
- It obliges us to think about the contested character of managerialism
  and the macro- and micro-politics of organizations through which
  managerialism has been introduced, adopted, adapted and resisted.

Although we have reservations about the use of the term NPM, it has
been extensively used as convenient shorthand for a set of shifts in
organizational beliefs and practices, including in some of the chapters in
this volume. However, in this book, we have tended, on the whole, to
explore processes of *managerialization* and the cluster of beliefs and
orientations best described as *managerialism*. These two terms can be
thought of as equivalent to the concepts of professionalization and
professionalism. These terms refer to processes by which an occupational
group claims to be the possessor of a distinctive – and valuable – sort of
expertise, and uses that expertise as the basis for acquiring organizational
and social power. They also indicate the ways in which topics of public
and political concern become colonized – owned, even – by particular
types of knowledge in ways that organize power relations. For example,
it is difficult to think of the social organization of health care without
taking note of the impact of medical professionalization. One distinctive
dimension of that professionalization has been the domination of official
knowledge about health and illness by medical discourses.

Managerialization refers to similar social and organizational processes
linked to the establishment of a claim about who possesses the right to
direct, co-ordinate or run organizations. Pollitt (1993) and others have
demonstrated how public services in the UK (and the USA) were subjected to managerializing processes – in which such services were defined
as lacking 'proper management'. As we noted earlier in this chapter, the
control and coordination of public services has been a constant source of

concern in British politics. However, the period after 1979 saw a distinctive shift. As Cutler and Waine have argued, what was different about this period 'was the systematic introduction of managerialism. . . . In a general sense, public sector managerialism is characterized by the belief that the objectives of social services . . . can be promoted at lower cost when the appropriate management techniques are applied' (1998, p. xiv). The most visible effect of this shift towards managerialism is a growth in the numbers of public sector managers and in their power relative to other organizational groups. However, managerialization extends beyond such consequences. It involves changes to the ways in which other organizational actors are expected to think and behave (what we might call devolved managerialism); to how relationships between different organizations are understood and co-ordinated (forms of competitive and collaborative management); and to how social policy, politics and service provision are understood.

Managerialism – like professionalism – defines a set of expectations, values and beliefs. It is a normative system concerning what counts as valuable knowledge, who knows it, and who is empowered to act in what ways as a consequence. Indeed, a central issue in the managerialization of public services has been the concerted effort to displace or subordinate the claims of professionalism. It can no longer be assumed that 'professionals know best'; rather we are invited to accept that managers 'do the right thing' (Newman, 1998). Like others, we see managerialism both as a 'general ideology' (Pollitt, 1993) that legitimizes and seeks to extend the 'right to manage' and as composed of overlapping, and sometimes competing, discourses that present distinctive versions of 'how to manage'. Its natural home has been the corporate capitalist organization that provides the reference point for claims about 'behaving in a businesslike way'. There too, successive waves of innovation in how to manage have provided a changing repertoire of demands on, and possibilities for, public sector managerialism (Clarke and Newman, 1993).

What have been the consequences of managerialization? It brings about changes in power, knowledge and calculation within organizations, between organizations and in the organization of social welfare. Within organizations, managerialization has tended to subordinate other forms of power, and other forms of knowledge, to managerial authority. Public service organizations have come to 'think' managerially about themselves, their 'business' and their relationships with others. Within this dominant tendency, there has been a range of resistances, adaptations and co-options, particularly around strong centres of professionalism (Clarke and Newman, 1997; Ferlie et al., 1996). Between organizations, relationships have tended to shift towards the contractual, competitive and calculative (in relation to each organization's calculation of its 'business interests') in ways that have fragmented both service areas and notions of collective or public interest. Within government, managerialism has changed the dynamics of power between senior managers and politicians, enlarging the power and scope of those deemed to be 'strategic', but also offering politicians new means of control 'at a distance'. Finally, managerialism has linked the internal regimes of welfare organizations to the public realm of debates about social welfare. In both settings managerialism has tended to subordinate other principles of judgement to the managerial calculus of economy and efficiency. National debates about 'the future of welfare' have been framed by questions of cost and the managerial agenda of 'driving down costs', concentrating on the 'core business' and providing 'value for money' (Clarke and Newman, 1997). This process – what Jones and Novak (1999, p. 146) have called 'retooling the State' – has formed a significant part of New Labour's political and organizational inheritance from the New Right.

3 New Labour or hard labour?

One central issue for this book concerns how the processes of welfare state reconstruction and managerialization have developed and will further develop in the changing political conditions associated with the return of a New Labour government in 1997. Much effort has already been spent on trying to identify the distinctive political configuration of New Labour and, to a large extent, the existing commentary is dominated by questions of difference and continuity in relation to 'Old Labour' (or social democracy) and to the New Right (or Thatcherism or neo-liberalism).

Part of the difficulty in drawing up a balance sheet arises from the fact that New Labour tells stories for itself about difference and continuity that emphasize how it seized the political initiative through transcending or moving beyond both Old Left and New Right (Blair, 1998a; Giddens, 1998; Gould, 1998; Anderson and Mann, 1997; Mandelson and Liddle, 1996). For example, Tony Blair's depiction of the Third Way (1998a) contrasts the ideological commitments of the Left (pro-state/anti-market) and the Right (pro-market/anti-state) between which a modern and modernizing, pragmatic route can be constructed. The route is similar to that mapped out by Anthony Giddens in the movement 'Beyond Left and Right' (1994, 1998). Such imagery is central to the self-promotional representations of New Labour as ushering in a new era in domestic and international politics. Its spokespersons are conscious of the need to construct a guiding political philosophy and to imprint 'brand identity' and 'product differentiation' in the realm of 'post-ideological politics'. Nevertheless, such self-assessments should not be accepted as the only possible frame of reference. For example, in the caricaturing of Left and Right on which the Third Way rests there are some striking omissions and acts of amnesia. The equation of the New Right with neo-liberalism and markets overlooks the vital role that neo-conservatism played in the formation of that transatlantic political project (Clarke, 1991). Similarly, the equation of the 'Old' Left with statist socialism forgets the 'New Left' and its complex mixture of feminisms, anti-racist and anti-colonial movements, and its 'anti-oppressive' struggles mixed with varieties of libertarian socialism (see also Andrews, 1999). Finally, there is little acknowledgement of the fact that the notion of a 'third way' in politics has a long history. In many respects all European social democratic political parties have their historical roots in the notion of a 'third', 'middle' or 'centre' way between communism and capitalism. Through 'forgetting', the 'Third Way', with both its European and North American genealogies, can function as a rhetorical figure that proclaims its own historical inevitability and political necessity in the face of discredited, outdated and failed alternatives (Clarke and Newman, 1998).

A second part of the difficulty stems from the problem of the relationship between ideology and policy, sometimes described as the problem of distinguishing 'rhetoric and reality'. What New Labour – like other political parties – says is not necessarily what it does. The gap between rhetoric and reality is conventionally viewed in two ways. On the one hand, 'reality', the practice of policy enactment, is seen as falling short of the rhetorical claims of politicians: reality suffers from the 'implementation gap'. On the other, rhetoric provides a 'smokescreen', concealing the 'real intentions' of the political project. While both views may involve significant truths in general and about New Labour in particular, both treat the 'rhetoric' as insignificant and insubstantial – by contrast with the 'real thing' of policy and practice. Nevertheless, we also need to recognize that what political parties say matters – politics is about ideology as well as policy. Rhetoric – the articulation of identities, trajectories and projects – is never 'mere rhetoric'. It is part of the political processes of building, cementing and mobilizing alliances – and demobilizing actual or potential opposition (Clarke and Newman, 1998). In those terms, the distinction between New and Old Labour has provided a potent rhetorical resource for demobilizing potential alternative conceptions of policy and direction within and around the party.

Nevertheless, there are clearly important issues about the relationship between New Labour and the legacy of the New Right, and the political project represented by 'Blairism', 'New Labour' and the 'Third Way' has attracted considerable attention from critics and commentators. The crucial question raised here is whether and in what ways the 'new' in New Labour marks a distinctive move beyond the social, political and economic landscape of the New Right. Some have stressed the essential differences between New Labour and the New Right. In particular, they have pointed to:

- New Labour's pragmatism (as between state and market);
- its reassertion of the social and communal over the individual, particularly in social policy;
- its commitment to modernize the institutions of government and public service;
- the different intellectual and political resources out of which its ideology is constituted;
- its more 'European' orientation in contrast to the US-centred neo-liberalism of the New Right (see, for example, Giddens, 1998; Driver and Martell, 1997, 1998; Corrigan and Joyce, 1999).

Others have placed more emphasis on the continuities with both the neo-liberal and neo-conservative strands of the New Right, noting that New Labour cannot break free from the endemic contradictions that are constitutive of the 'post-Thatcherite' terrain (Hay, 1996; see also Fitzpatrick, 1998; Jones and Novak, 1999; King and Wickham Jones, 1999; Marquand, 1998). As evidence of continuity, they have pointed to:

- New Labour's legacy of public spending control and limited conceptions of social reform;
- its promotion of 'low tax/high choice' images of the enterprising consumer-citizen to be freed from state paternalism, articulating a US-derived version of the 'Third Way';
- the shared assumptions of the New Right and New Labour about the global and national economy and the claimed impotence of governments to do anything but improve the competitiveness and 'market position' of the national economy;
- New Labour's 'communitarian' concern to restore forms of traditional morality and authority (Lavalette and Mooney, 1999).

It is not surprising that many of the attempts to define or pin down the ideological character of New Labour have involved paradoxical designations, e.g. Andrews' 'neo-liberal humanism' (1999); Driver and Martell's 'liberal conservatism' (1997); or even Fitzpatrick's 'post-social communitarianism' (1998). Such paradoxes register the problem of tracing both the continuities with the New Right and the differences or peculiarities that New Labour adds to the mix. They also try to capture the unevenness between different elements of the political project that contrasts:

- radical constitutional change with forms of authoritarian moralism;
- an emphasis on the dynamics of economic, social and cultural transformation paralleled by a regressive familialism;
- a neo-liberal view of the global economy tempered by a concern with social inclusion;

- a democratizing and decentralizing programme alongside a profoundly centralist view of party and political discipline.

Such paradoxical designations of New Labour's programme are helpful to the extent that they interrupt the search for New Labour's 'essential' character. The chapters in this book indicate that there is no reason to think that New Labour is a single, coherent and unified project – rather than an unstable attempt to reconcile and manage economic, social and political contradictions. Nor are there any grounds to assume that there is any specific 'Third Way'. It is worth remembering that the defining features of 'Thatcherism' only emerged gradually and at no time could it be described as a fully-fledged or uni-dimensional ideological formation. This is why it attracted paradoxical designations such as Hall's (1988) concepts of 'authoritarian populism' and 'regressive modernization' (1988) and Gamble's (1988) 'free economy, strong state'. More generally, the Anglo-American axis of the New Right combined strands of neo-liberalism and neo-conservatism in complex and volatile ways.

New Labour's relationship to social welfare has itself been a distinctive focus of attention and controversy and again there has been a tendency to look for continuities and breaks with the New Right (e.g. Clarke and Newman, 1998; Dwyer, 1998; Jones and MacGregor, 1998; Jones and Novak, 1999; Lister, 1999; Powell, 1998). In studying the reconstruction of social welfare under New Labour we have found it useful to distinguish different types of 'settlement' that underpinned the creation and development of the post-war welfare system in the UK: political-economic, social and organizational (Clarke and Newman, 1997; Hughes and Lewis, 1998). One way of approaching New Labour may be to ask to what extent it shares the main tendencies around which the New Right attempted to construct new 'settlements'. In many respects, there appears to be a common political-economic alignment. There is a shared view of the primacy of economic competitiveness; of the subordination of public and social policy to promoting a competitive national economy; of the reduced or limited scope for government intervention or direction; of the significance of controlling public spending and, possibly, of the 'incentivizing' effect of economic inequality. Jones and Novak have argued that

> In the third way capitalism is not challenged, rather it is embraced. New Labour's acceptance of the market differs little from that of the new right, echoing its predecessor's claim that 'there is no alternative'. . . . The global market is seen as the final, and unchallengeable arbiter in economic – and ultimately in social – life. But the market is not only accepted as setting the agenda and imposing constraints which national governments are powerless to resist. It is also embraced as the main provider. (1999, p. 180)

In a similar vein, Dwyer (1998) has sketched some of the elements of an emerging new 'welfare consensus' obsessed with cost containment and promoting 'conditional citizenship'. He highlights two linked processes: 'Many of the welfare provisions once regarded as rights are evolving into market commodities. . . . Other provisions are becoming increasingly dependent on recipients of benefits and services agreeing to meet compulsory duties or standards of behaviour' (1998, p. 513). 'Work' – in the narrow sense of paid employment – is the critical hinge that articulates the economy, welfare and New Labour's view of social opportunity, responsibility, solidarity and inclusion.

Around the 'social settlement', however, the alignment of New Right and New Labour looks less clear. In part, this may be because the New Right's uneasy alliance of neo-liberalism and neo-conservatism never quite produced a settled vision of the 'people' and their 'way of life' that commanded popular support. Indeed, the oscillations between the individualism of neo-liberalism and moral authoritarianism of neo-conservatism were a recurrent source of tension in New Right politics and ideology (Clarke and Newman, 1997). New Labour has attempted to address, possibly even exploit, some of these failings – insisting that there 'is such a thing as society' and that what Blair has called 'social-ism' is to be valued. The attention to social exclusion, to (some) forms of discrimination and to (some) aspects of 'diversity' marks out a degree of difference from the neo-liberal individualism of the New Right. Giddens, for example, argues that the Third Way is being built at the conjunction of concerns for 'social justice' and attention to 'lifestyle diversity' (1998, p. 43). Nevertheless, some of the concerns with respectability, order, discipline and responsibility that inform New Labour approaches to the social have more in common with the moral authoritarian strands of neo-conservatism (if not all of its 'little Englander' orientation). There are also strong echoes of a much older, puritanical and authoritarian 'Old Labour' in its views of the work ethic, welfare and the disciplines of respon-sibility. It may be that New Labour is – or even has become – more attentive to 'diversity' but its preferred solution for social inclusion is a remarkably narrow one: the acquisition of paid employment (Lister, 1999; Clarke and Newman, 1998).

> In the New Labour imagination, employment is the route to full membership of society and performs a variety of other valuable social functions too. It overcomes social isolation, provides role models for children and is an independence-promoting and fulfilling experience. Nevertheless, in other respects, the 'social settlement' continues to look remarkably unfinished. Gender relations are poised uneasily between opportunity and responsibility, as New Labour moves towards a 'universal breadwinner model'. (Lister, 1999)

Racialized divisions fluctuate between highly intense visibility (the Lawrence inquiry and its aftermath) and repressed invisibility (in most welfare policy proposals); while New Labour can live with (and even celebrate) the diversity of a multi-ethnic culture, it finds it hard to recognize the intersection between differentiation and inequality.

Finally, the New Right's 'organizational settlement' appears to have been accepted and even enhanced by New Labour. As Flynn has suggested,

> From the mid-1990s the Labour Party's themes about the public sector were similar to those of the Conservatives: the need to control public expenditure in order to keep taxation levels down, the importance of a mixed economy of private, individual provision and state services and benefits, the need for efficiency. A new consensus seems to have emerged, which is at least as strong, if not stronger, than the supposed post-war one. (1997, p. 41; see also Butcher, 1998)

The critique of Old Labour's 'statism' has meant a consistent emphasis on 'no going back' to models of public service provision predicated on integrated professional bureaucracies. Certainly, New Labour sees itself as the inheritor of the New Right's populist relationship to public service providers. The Labour government has consistently positioned itself on the side of the 'active, sceptical citizen-consumer' against the 'provider power' of service organizations and workers. Despite criticisms of, and challenges to, the internal market in the NHS, Labour in office has kept most of the dispersed and competitive structures of service provision developed during the 1980s and 1990s. Across a whole range of services, Labour has maintained the basic organizational structures. It has also tended to add to or intensify the processes of fiscal discipline and scrutiny or evaluation to which service providers are subjected (Bochel and Bochel, 1998; Deakin and Parry, 1998). Similarly, it has continued to emphasize 'value for money' scrutiny, while stepping back from compulsory competitive tendering. In some respects, Labour may be advancing the reform of the state beyond the New Right's efforts, or may be trying to remedy design flaws in the Conservative reforms. In the latter case, there have been attempts to address some of the fragmenting effects of organizational changes, through conceptions of 'joined up government' and an enthusiasm for 'partnerships'. In other directions, proposals to reform the administration of benefits around an 'active' relationship with the service user/consumer carry forward many of the organizational design messages from the New Right; as does the commitment to 'continuous improvement' to be expected of local government and other public service providers. The overarching themes of a 'pragmatic' performance orientation ('what counts is what works') and the commitment to 'modernization' seem to share the tendencies that New Labour inherited from the New Right and advance them further (Newman, 1998; Finlayson, 1998). In this vein, Blair has sought to redefine 'radicalism':

We will be a radical government. But the definition of radicalism will not be that of doctrine, whether of left or right, but of achievement. New Labour is a party of ideas and ideals but not of outdated ideology. What counts is what works. (Blair, 1998b, quoted in Powell, 1998, p. 23)

4   The structure of the book

This book examines the intersection of welfare reconstruction and managerialism in relation to New Labour in a number of ways. We explore specific policy areas (health, housing, criminal justice, etc.) in order to see whether they reveal common trends and tendencies. Such an approach deepens our understanding of the reconstruction of the welfare state and New Labour's contribution to it by moving beyond the general political project into its articulation with specific policy issues, problems and practices. We also explore some of the cross-cutting themes that have been highlighted in New Labour's approach to the 'organizational settlement' and the problems of governance. Questions of performance management and evaluation, the anti-bureaucratic tide, governing through partnerships, and the project of modernization itself are significant New Labour themes. But we begin in Chapter 2 by considering the extent to which the rise of managerialism is a local or an international phenomenon. Both academic commentaries and political texts have claimed that global trends underpin or drive the necessity of reform – but to what extent are there shared conditions, processes and changes? Norman Flynn's analysis suggests that reformers in different countries may justify managerial change upon identical grounds. For example, it is commonly argued that managerial reforms are a prerequisite for national economic success in an increasingly competitive global environment. The superiority of the private over the public sector is another shared justificatory theme. However, Flynn draws on data from a variety of countries to show that managerialism does in fact take on a range of guises in different national contexts, and he points to significant divergences in the sources, scope, priorities and practices of managerial reform, and the constraints upon it.

Our attention then shifts from an examination of international trends to the particular case of the UK and, more specifically, to New Labour's agenda for the 'modernization' of welfare. We ask, to what extent do New Labour's plans for modernization build upon, undo or transform the work of re-imagining and reconstructing welfare that was begun by Conservative governments in the 1980s and 1990s? And is New Labour's modernization agenda essentially a managerializing agenda? As Janet Newman argues in Chapter 3, it is necessary to move beyond the superficial representation of modernization as a rational and common sense programme designed to eradicate anachronistic practices in the management of public services. Rather, modernization is better

understood as a discourse that seeks to harness the language and techniques of managerial reform to a new political agenda. As our discussion
of the politics of the Third Way in the previous section has indicated,
precisely what that political agenda entails has been hotly debated. But
Newman argues it is characterized by a somewhat uneasy combination
of expansive social goals (like combating social exclusion) and the economic goal of public expenditure reduction. In unpacking and subjecting
to critical scrutiny some of the key constitutive elements of the modernization agenda, Newman considers the relationship between the NPM of
the New Right and the 'modern management' of New Labour. She
argues that while there are significant continuities, notably the continued
emphasis on efficiency and performance, there are clear differences. For
example, unlike the New Right's managerialism, modern management
acknowledges the harm done by organizational fragmentation, and it
seeks to transcend the limitations of consumerist and client-based
models of participation by encouraging user participation.

The managerialization of welfare has political and ethical implications and it is these which are the focus of Chapter 4. For Paul du Gay, a
defining feature of managerialism, or what he refers to as entrepreneurial governance, is the desire to generalize the enterprise form to all forms
of conduct. Focusing on the reinvention and modernization of the British
Civil Service under New Right and New Labour governments, du Gay
suggests that advocates of entrepreneurial governance may overlook
some of the virtues of bureaucratic conduct and of the doctrine of
ministerial responsibility that they seek to displace. Whilst there may be
virtues and defects associated with both bureaucratic and entrepreneurial governance, du Gay argues that the virtues and defects of a risk-
averse yet reliable and fair bureaucratic administration may be prefer-
able to those associated with the creative, risky, innovative style of
entrepreneurial modes of engagement.

In constructing his critique of entrepreneurial governance, du Gay
suggests that the continuities between New Right and New Labour
approaches are of greater significance than any apparent discontinuities.
In particular, he takes issue with those who think that New Labour's
commitment to community, partnership, participation and stakeholding
indicates a break from the entrepreneurial ethos favoured by the
Conservatives. This raises the important issue of how we are to reconcile
New Labour's promotion of the apparently 'cuddly' notion of partnership with its attachment to the harder-edged entrepreneurial techniques
of cost-cutting, target-setting, performance monitoring and competition.
Are partnership and entrepreneurial governance essentially contradictory and conflicting strategies? Is the commitment to collaborative
modes of conduct primarily a political strategy designed to win support
from welfare professionals for what remains an essentially hard-nosed
economistic agenda? Or do partnership approaches represent a different
kind of managerialism – one that is primarily designed to rectify the

problems of organizational fragmentation and top-down decision making that were generated by what Newman describes in Chapter 3 as 'the "cut and thrust", "lean and mean" discourses of business turn-around and downsizing which pervaded public management in the 1980s'? Tom Ling's unpacking of the concept of partnership in Chapter 5 sheds some light on these questions. Whilst the idea of partnership is not new, its nature, purpose and significance have shifted over the last 30 years. Ling suggests that this has been in response to the changing modalities of the British state. When what Ling calls bureaucratic *government* dominated in the 1970s, the concept of partnership was generally used to denote the relationship between central and local government. In the 1980s the shift to what Ling refers to as *governance* was accompanied by an emphasis on public–private partnerships, which operated in the context of a marketized system of public service provision. The context that is now emerging, Ling suggests, is one of *governmentality*. Here partnerships are used to circumvent some of the problems created by governance, including the problem of legitimacy prompted by the exclusion of particular organizations and social groups from decision-making arenas. Governmentality is paradoxically author-itarian and inclusivist at the same time because it seeks to turn 'hard-to-reach groups', like voluntary bodies, user groups and 'unhealthy' indi-viduals, into 'compliant collaborators' in an effort to build a more 'inclusive' society. By examining two contemporary examples of part-nership in the health care arena – Health Improvement Programmes and the Private Finance Initiative – Ling demonstrates the broad nature of the partnership concept. He also explores the dubious political moti-vations that can underpin the use of partnership strategies, and some of the tensions, conflicts and practical limitations associated with them.

Lynn Poole's examination of the NHS reforms in Chapter 6, lends further weight to the view that New Labour's modernization agenda aims to resolve some of the design flaws of the New Right's managerial-ism. In particular, New Labour has been critical of the inequalities of access and the proliferation of red tape produced by the Conservatives' health reforms, and the fact that the reforms were imposed on, rather than negotiated with, the medical profession and other stakeholders. There is therefore a new emphasis on teamwork, co-operation and the involvement of the medical and nursing professions in an effort to mobilize the support and co-operation of health care professionals and the public. At the same time, Poole demonstrates New Labour's com-mitment to extending particular aspects of the New Right's managerialist policies. In particular, elements of competition between providers are to remain. There is a continued emphasis on managing the health service in order 'to get more for less'. And there is an enhanced emphasis on making individuals more responsible for their own health as part of a wider strategy to shift the burden of responsibility for health care from the state to individuals. Thus, rather than dismantling structural barriers to equality and good health, Poole argues, the reforms aim to establish a framework of support for individual effort. There is also an intensified commitment to improving performance through increased monitoring, surveillance and regulation of health care provision by the state.

In an effort to understand what is distinctive about New Labour's programme of welfare restructuring, Allan Cochrane's Chapter 7 takes a historical look at local government reform. His analysis usefully reminds us that the preoccupation of policy makers with modernization and management reform has a history that spans at least four decades. However, discourses of modernization and management have taken on different guises at different junctures within this period and they have been mobilized in various ways to support a range of contrasting strategies for welfare reform. From 1965 to 1975, the rhetoric of modernization was used to support a strategy that used big business as a model for reform. The reforms of this period were underpinned by a belief in the value of large scale organization, rational planning and technical expertise, and they were aimed at bolstering rather than dismantling the social democratic state. In contrast, the subsequent period of modernization, from 1976 to 1990, saw the logic of state welfarism challenged. This period was characterized by the establishment of controls on local government spending, the creation of alternatives to local authority provision, the abolition of the metropolitan councils and the Greater London Council, 'ratecapping' and the imposition of the community charge – reforms fuelled not only by a commitment to the reduction of public expenditure, but by a belief that markets represented a superior mode of social and economic engagement. During this period, local government was reconfigured as an 'enabler' of services. Cochrane calls the current period of reform 'modernization through managerialization'. This period began in the early 1990s with the Citizen's Charter initiative which established a quasi-contractual form of relationship between public service providers and 'consumer-citizens', and with the creation of unitary authorities, many of which enthusiastically embraced a managerialist agenda. Cochrane argues that the Blair government is extending the managerialization of local government and welfare more widely, through the establishment of new political structures, the pursuance of 'Best Value' with its emphasis on consultation, 'fair competition' and regulation, and through the promotion of 'joined-up working'. In a variety of ways these reforms, Cochrane writes, will undermine the traditional role of the local politician.

The following six chapters then focus on specific services which local government has a responsibility for providing – or increasingly 'enabling' – housing, social services, crime reduction, leisure and education. Roberta Woods's analysis of the implications of the Best Value regime for housing management reveals a number of continuities with Conservative housing policy. Perhaps the most significant of these is that, despite predictions that changes in the system of accounting introduced by New Labour would reverse the trend towards the de-municipalization of housing, New Labour appears to want to encourage the transfer of *more* housing stock to voluntary and private-sector providers. At the same time, the government would like housing policy to play a major role in the promotion of social inclusion. Woods does not view the direct management of housing by local government as a necessary condition for solving the problems experienced by some estates. However, there is a danger that a further de-municipalization of housing will contribute to the growth of exclusionary discourses rooted in a stigmatization of council tenancy. Woods questions how far it will be possible to counter the stigmatizing discourses of welfare dependency associated with council tenancy within a context where de-municipalization is the favoured option. The tension between policies of de-municipalization and the commitment to combating social exclusion is one of a number of contradictions that Woods identifies within New Labour's policy framework for housing. Local authorities are now expected to work in partnership with other agencies in order to deliver joined-up objectives and combat social exclusion. At the same time they must involve communities. And they have to do all of these things with limited powers, insufficient resources and within the context of having to meet increasingly detailed and prescriptive central government expectations. Woods's analysis raises the question of whether New Labour's programme of modernization for housing may in fact turn out to be unmanageable.

New Labour's reforms for the social services are legitimated by a discourse of failure, directed both at previous governments and the social services themselves. Amongst the accusations levelled at social care professionals are that they have failed to protect those in their care and that they are inflexible, inconsistent and inefficient. In Chapter 9, Mary Langan argues that, although New Labour's indictment of the social services and community care is highly contestable, its discourse of failure has been remarkably successful in contributing to a widespread perception that social services and community care have indeed failed. Ths 'failure' is to be remedied by a liberal dose of managerialism. For example, under the Best Value regime, local authorities have to establish performance measures and carry out 'fundamental performance reviews'. These are meant to inform 'local performance plans' which set out targets for improvement in the context of a 'user-centred' approach. Having identified the major elements of New Labour's modernization project for the social services, Langan explores its limitations. She rehearses some of the arguments against the application of business practices to social services that were made in response to Conservative reforms, and she discusses what she views as New Labour's limited conception of user involvement. Finally, Langan argues that the techniques of quality control being put in place by New Labour may further erode what she calls 'community spirit' – the 'local and moral economy that still prevails and, arguably, still sustains the best social work practice'.

McLaughlin and Muncie's examination of New Labour's modernization agenda for the criminal justice system in Chapter 10 alerts us to the crucial role that party political competition plays in the development of policy. The analysis presented in this chapter suggests that contemporary social and criminal justice policies need to be understood in the context of the Labour Party's ambition to convert itself into the natural party of government. McLaughlin and Muncie argue that Labour's tough stance on crime in the early to mid-1990s played a key role in the party's ideological reincarnation as New Labour and its subsequent landslide victory in the 1997 election. They also contend that, in office, New Labour policies have continued to be 'more designed to fulfil [the government's] electoral contract with "Middle England" than to promote social inclusion'. However, the government's claim to be tough on the *causes* of crime, has won support for its modernization project from some who believe that New Labour policies mark a shift towards an inclusionary restorative version of justice and towards a recognition of the need to focus on the social and economic conditions within which crime occurs. Through a specific focus on youth justice, this chapter explores some of the tensions and contradictions in New Labour's 'tough on crime and tough on the causes of crime' project, a project which draws on a somewhat uneasy combination of managerialist, communitarian and authoritarian populist discourses.

Urban parks and other open spaces are not usually thought of as coming under the remit of social or welfare policy. However, as Alan Clarke argues in Chapter 11, there is a long history of parks, and the provision of public leisure facilities more generally, being viewed as contributing to 'recreational welfare'. The discourse of recreational welfare has its roots in the municipal politics of the 1890s, but is currently in the process of being reinvented. At its heart is the belief that, if managed in the correct way, leisure can lead to self-improvement for the individual and greater social cohesion. In his analysis of the managerialization of leisure policy over the last 20 years, Clarke begins by identifying some key limitations of the Conservative policy of compulsory competitive tendering (CCT). He then goes on to examine some of the problems and possibilities associated with CCT's New Labour successor, Best Value. Best Value has been presented as enabling local authorities to escape from the narrow economistic interpretations of efficiency and effectiveness promoted by CCT. However, Clarke suggests that much of the writing on Best Value has been informed by a technicist agenda that is in danger of failing to recognize and value cultural diversity in the use of parks and the countryside and of restricting opportunities for authentic public debate about alternative ways of imagining the use of public open spaces. This is despite the fact that within New Labour discourses of modernization and the Third Way more generally there is a strong rhetorical emphasis on revivifying local democracy and valuing diverse cultural identities.

This tension between New Labour's preference for technicist, managerial solutions to the problems of welfare governance, and its apparent commitment to a variety of social goals, including democratic renewal, the creation of a more inclusive society and the equalization of opportunity, is particularly visible in relation to education policy. In Chapter 12, Ross Fergusson uses the case of education to ask whether managerialism's 'inherent propensities to favour what can be measured, monitored, and encapsulated in pithy expressions of mission and priority' is as capable of fulfilling social democratic objectives as it is of delivering neo-liberal ones. Fergusson suggests that there is an apparent disjuncture between the managerial means and the social ends of New Labour's modernization agenda, since managerialism is generally associated with its antipathy to democratic decision making and with a propensity for top-down structures of control. But he also points out that 'there is nothing inherently collegial, collectivist or democratic about the management methods historically associated with social democracy, however central these values may have been to its political project.' Fergusson goes on to conclude that some elements of managerialism may be positively embraced by teachers and lecturers committed to social democratic ends, where they are directed at raising the attainment of disadvantaged students. However, professional compliance has its limits, and the uneasy combination of managerial methods and social democratic ends is vulnerable to disruption, especially if conflicts over the coercive nature of the new performance regime in education and the link between pay and performance intensify.

Jenny Ozga's account in Chapter 13 of the attempted modernization of the teaching profession draws particular attention to New Labour's heavy preoccupation with the economic goals of education. Ozga suggests that, by giving primacy to waged work as the passport to social inclusion, the government is able to subsume the social purposes of education within the economic goal of preparing young people for the 'modern dynamic economy' that New Labour wants to build (Blair, 1998a). In this way, the government is able to reduce the need for separate consideration of the social and cultural work that education performs, and this, she argues, leads to a neglect of the role that education can play in developing 'essential capacities for social interaction and for political practice'. This 'economizing' of education is evident too in the installation of more entrepreneurial styles of governance into educational institutions. Performance related pay (PRP), for example, can be viewed as an attempt to reconstruct teachers as 'entrepreneurs of the self'. Ozga also draws attention to the pragmatic concerns that appear to be driving reform, in particular the problems of teacher recruitment and retention. However, her historical account of state policies for the management of teachers' work suggests that a heavier dose of managerialism may not be the solution to these problems. She goes on to argue that managerial reform may be particularly inappropriate in the Scottish context, where there are few problems of recruitment and retention, high levels of parental support and where teachers have relatively high status and considerable autonomy.

Whilst the arrangements for PRP are perhaps most ambitious in education, New Labour is committed to extending PRP to other welfare sectors. For example, the establishment of a performance management framework is one of the tasks required of local government under the Best Value regime. Under John Major's leadership, the Conservatives had been committed to the introduction of PRP into the public services. It was viewed as a tool by which to gear the activities of workers more tightly to government objectives and was part of the government's broader project to make the public sector more emulative of the private sector. But, by the end of Major's term of office in 1997, only limited progress in the introduction of PRP had been made. The New Labour government appears to have taken up the PRP policy with greater vigour than their Conservative predecessors. However, as Barbara Waine argues in Chapter 14, New Labour has sought to distance its performance management strategy from that of the Conservatives by pursuing a more holistic and sophisticated set of measures with a greater emphasis on quality than the narrow efficiency indicators used by the Conservatives. Waine considers some of the practical difficulties associated with trying to develop a sophisticated approach to PRP. In particular, she looks at the problems of arriving at measures that can be defined consistently, the susceptibility of performance management systems to manipulation, and the difficulties involved in finding universal measures that are appropriate for organizations operating in different social and economic circumstances, and that are fair and acceptable to all of the diverse groups whose work is being measured.

What has emerged from all of the chapters in this book is the enhanced role the New Labour government is according to practices designed to monitor, assess and regulate the performance of those organizations that deliver public services. Whilst auditing has historically been associated with practices of financial regulation, its role has been extended in recent years to encompass a broader evaluative and normative remit. In the final chapter of the book John Clarke, Sharon Gewirtz, Gordon Hughes and Jill Humphrey consider the emergence and consequences of the new conceptions of audit and inspection which have come to dominate contemporary discourses of public sector reform. It is argued that the groundwork for an extended conception of audit was laid by the Conservative governments of the 1980s and 1990s. The New Right had derided professionals and bureaucrats as self-interested and untrustworthy and so some mechanism was needed to restore public trust in public services. Audit emerged to fill this role and to resolve the thorny issue of how to control disparate public service agencies within the context of a complex, competitive, devolved and dispersed system of provision. The requirement to make themselves auditable generates dilemmas for and conflicts within organizations – over defining objectives, choosing indicators, the attribution of causality and how to make comparisons. Audit practices also have unexpected outcomes and perverse effects and, because they focus on individual units of organization, they may threaten the success of joined-up government. In addition, the rise of audit has consequences for the evaluative agencies themselves. They have a dual role as both central government agents responsible for overseeing the activities of dispersed provider organizations and as the supposed representatives of the public interest. Moreover, the public itself is variously understood – both by government and the evaluative agencies themselves – as sometimes consisting of taxpayers, sometimes of consumers or, increasingly, as consisting of differentiated and diverse 'communities'. The latter conception of the public raises particular difficulties for processes of evaluation. More specifically, how can a recognition of the significance of difference and diversity be reconciled with, or accommodated to, the unitary assumptions of the audit paradigm? Thus, whilst the new practices of audit and inspection may have emerged out of the need to resolve the problems created by devolved and dispersed forms of public services organization, the rise of evaluative agencies and processes itself generates new difficulties, tensions and conflicts which will need to be managed.

By now it will have become clear that the evaluations offered in this book are necessarily provisional. The book was completed in the Spring of 2000 and reflects on the politics and policy of New Labour up to that point. Exploring the intersection of welfare reconstruction, managerialism and the political programme of New Labour is a challenging process, not least because these three elements represent both established trends and unstable trajectories. And, as Newman points out in Chapter 3, we cannot read off from the language of modernization what the changes will mean in practice. Modernization is an unstable discourse, one that is emergent, beset with tensions and the focus of conflict and contestation, and it is therefore impossible to predict with any certainty what the outcomes of New Labour's modernization agenda will be. This is a theme that is reiterated throughout the book.

The chapters contained here try to map both where we are and how we got here and they also reflect on the tensions, instabilities, difficulties and possibilities that might influence the direction of future changes.

References

Anderson, P. and Mann, N. (1997) *Safety First: The Making of New Labour*, London, Granta Books.
Andrews, G. (1999) 'New Left and New Labour: modernization or a new modernity?' *Soundings*, 13, pp. 14–24.

Bartlett, W., Roberts, J. and Le Grand, J. (eds) (1998) *A Revolution in Social Policy: Quasi-market Reforms in the 1990s*, Bristol, The Policy Press.

Blair, T. (1998a) *The Third Way*, London, Fabian Society.

Blair, T. (1998b) 'Europe's left of centre parties have discovered the "third way"', *The Independent*, 7 April, p. 14.

Bochel, C. and Bochel, H. (1998) 'The governance of social policy', in Brunsdon, E., Dean, H. and Woods, R. (eds) *Social Policy Review 10*, London, Social Policy Association.

Brivati, B. and Bale, T. (eds) (1997) *New Labour in Power: Precedents and Prospects*, London, Routledge.

Butcher, T. (1995) *Delivering Welfare: The Governance of the Social Services in the 1990s*, Buckingham, Open University Press.

Butcher, T. (1998) 'Managing the welfare state', in Jones, H. and MacGregor, S. (eds) *Social Issues and Party Politics*, London, Routledge.

Clarke, J. (1991) *New Times and Old Enemies*, London, HarperCollins.

Clarke, J. (forthcoming) 'Making a difference? Markets and the reform of public services in the UK', in Schröter, E. and Wollmann, H. (eds) *Modernizing Public Services in Germany and the UK*, Basingstoke, Macmillan.

Clarke, J. and Newman, J. (1993) 'The right to manage: a second managerial revolution?' *Cultural Studies*, 7 (3), pp. 427–41.

Clarke, J. and Newman, J. (1997) *The Managerial State*, London, Sage.

Clarke, J. and Newman, J. (1998) 'A modern British people? New Labour and welfare reform', paper presented to the Discourse Analysis and Social Research Conference, Denmark, September.

Clarke, J., Cochrane, A. and McLaughlin, E. (eds) (1994) *Managing Social Policy*, London, Sage.

Corrigan, P. and Joyce, P. (1999) 'The third way and local government', paper presented to ESRC seminar on 'The Third Way in Public Services', London, April.

Cutler, T. and Waine, B. (1998) *Managing the Welfare State*, 2nd edition, Oxford, Berg.

Deakin, N. and Parry, R. (1998) 'The Treasury and New Labour's social policies', in Brunsdon, E., Dean, H. and Woods, R. (eds) *Social Policy Review 10*, London, Social Policy Association.

Department of Social Security (2000) *The Changing Welfare State: Social Security Expenditure*, London, DSS.

Driver, S. and Martell, L. (1997) 'New Labour's communitarians', *Critical Social Policy*, 17 (3), pp. 27–46.

Driver, S. and Martell, L. (1998) *New Labour: Politics after Thatcherism*, Cambridge, Polity Press.

Dunleavy, P. and Hood, C. (1994) 'From old public administration to new public management', *Public Money and Management*, 14 (3), pp. 9–16.

Dwyer, P. (1998) 'Conditional citizens? Welfare rights and responsibilities in the late 1990s', *Critical Social Policy*, 18 (4), pp. 493–518.

Farnham, D. and Horton, S. (eds) (1996) *Managing the New Public Services*, Basingstoke, Macmillan.

Ferlie, E., Ashburner, L., Fitzgerald, L. and Pettigrew, A. (1996) *The New Public Management in Action*, Oxford, Oxford University Press.

Finlayson, A. (1998) 'Tony Blair and the jargon of modernization', *Soundings*, 10, pp. 11–27.

Fitzpatrick, T. (1998) 'The rise of market collectivism', in Brunsdon, E., Dean, H. and Woods, R. (eds) *Social Policy Review 10*, London, Social Policy Association.

Flinders, M. and Smith, M. (eds) (1999) *Quangos, Accountability and Reform*, Basingstoke, Macmillan.

Flynn, N. (1997) *Public Sector Management*, Hemel Hempstead, Prentice-Hall/Harvester Wheatsheaf.

Flynn, N. and Strehl, F. (eds) (1996) *Public Sector Management in Europe*, Hemel Hempstead, Harvester Wheatsheaf.

Gamble, A. (1988) *Free Economy, Strong State*, London, Lawrence and Wishart.

Giddens, A. (1994) *Beyond Left and Right*, Cambridge, Polity Press.

Giddens, A. (1998) *The Third Way: The Renewal of Social Democracy*, Cambridge: Polity Press.

Gould, P. (1998) *The Unfinished Revolution: How the Modernizers Saved the Labour Party*, London, Little, Brown and Company.

Hall, S. (1988) *The Hard Road to Renewal*, London, Verso.

Hay, C. (1996) *Restating Social and Political Change*, London, Sage.

Hoggett, P. (1996) 'New modes of control in the public service', *Public Administration*, 74, pp. 9–32.

Hood, C. (1991) 'A public management for all seasons?' *Public Administration*, 69 (1), pp. 3–19.

Hughes, G. (ed.) (1998) *Imagining Welfare Futures*, London, Routledge/Open University.

Hughes, G. and Lewis, G. (eds) (1998) *Unsettling Welfare*, London, Routledge/Open University.

Jaques, M. (1998) 'Wrong', *Marxism Today* Special Issue, November–December.

Johnson, N. (ed.) (1995) *Private Markets in Health and Welfare*, Oxford, Berg.

Jones, C. and Novak, T. (1999) *Poverty, Welfare and the Disciplinary State*, London, Routledge.

Jones, H. and MacGregor, S. (eds) (1998) *Social Issues and Party Politics*, London, Routledge.

Katz, M.B. (1995) *Improving Poor People*, Princeton, Princeton University Press.

King, D. and Wickham-Jones, M. (1999) 'Bridging the Atlantic: the Democratic (Party) origins of Welfare to Work', in Powell, M. (ed.) *New Labour, New Welfare State?* Bristol, The Policy Press.

Lavalette, M. and Mooney, G. (1999) 'New Labour, new moralism: the welfare politics and ideology of New Labour under Blair', *International Socialism*, no. 85, pp. 27–48.

Lister, R. (1999) 'From CORA to RIO', paper presented to ESRC seminar on 'The Third Way in Public Services', London, April.

Mackintosh, M. (1998) 'Social markets', in Trigg, A., Himmelweit, S., Costello, N., Dawson, G., Mackintosh, M., Simonetti, R. and Wells, J. *Understanding Economic Behaviour, Markets*, Milton Keynes, Open University.

Mandelson, P. and Liddle, R. (1996) *The Blair Revolution: Can New Labour Deliver?* London, Faber.

Marquand, D. (1998) 'The Blair paradox', *Prospect*, 30 (May), pp. 19–24.

Mink, G. (1998) *Welfare's End*, Ithaca, NY, Cornell University Press.

Mouffe, C. (1998) 'The radical centre: a politics without adversary', *Soundings*, 9, pp. 11–23.

Newman, J. (1998) 'Managerialism and social welfare', in Hughes, G. and Lewis, G. (eds) *Unsettling Welfare*, London, Routledge/Open University.

Organization for Economic Cooperation and Development (1995) *Governance in Transition: Public Management Reform in OECD Countries*, Paris, OECD.

Pollitt, C. (1993) *Managerialism and Public Services*, Oxford, Basil Blackwell.

Pollitt, C. and Bouckaert, G. (2000) *Public Management Reform: a Comparative Analysis*, Oxford, Oxford University Press.

Powell, M. (ed.) (1998) *New Labour, New Welfare State?* Bristol, The Policy Press.

Rao, N. (1996) *Towards Welfare Pluralism*, Aldershot, Dartmouth.

Secretary of State for Social Security and Minister for Welfare Reform (1998) *New Ambitions for Our Country: A New Contract for Welfare*, Cm 3805, London, The Stationery Office.

Skelcher, C. (1998) *The Appointed State*, Buckingham, Open University Press.

Stoker, G. (ed.) (1999) *The New Management of British Local Governance*, Basingstoke, Macmillan.

2

Managerialism and Public Services: Some International Trends

Norman Flynn

This chapter asks the question: is there a world-wide tendency towards a unified way of managing public services? The stark answer is that if there is such a tendency it still has a long way to go before there is uniformity. The difference in experience between trying to register a birth in Jamaica and getting permission to invest in Singapore could not be greater and illustrates the importance of power, culture and the nature of the task in determining how public services work. But, while there are obviously differences among professional cultures and national or regional ways of managing, perhaps there are some pressures on governments that transcend these differences and may lead to similar solutions to the problem of managing state activities.

At an ideological level, it may be important that the collapse of Communism in eastern Europe and the search for market solutions in China leaves residual command economies only in places such as Burma, North Korea and Cuba. Along with the victory of the market solution may come the death of the hierarchical bureaucracy, sheltered from competitive pressures and hidden from public view. The choice between market and hierarchy is a convenient simplification of the many choices of modes of governance available.

Within the market, some general tendencies may also have relevance. From the start of mass production, bureaucracy was not confined to state activities but was the mode of management and control in the big corporations in Europe and the US. Increasing global competition is supposed to have exposed the rigidity of this way of managing: product and investment cycle times have got shorter, competitors can finance unexpected entry into markets and companies have to make decisions faster and better than ever. This new environment requires new ways of working and new sorts of organization. If companies transform them-selves, can public bureaucracies stay unchanged?

These abstract notions have practical ways of transforming themselves into reasons for governments to change the way that public organizations are run. Two sets of people have an interest in the changes: the electorate in their various groupings and alliances, and business. What we have seen in the past two decades or so is a variety of reasons why governments have turned their attention both to the question of what governments should do (and what should be done by the private sector, by individuals or by civil society) and how what governments should do should be managed (through new ways of organizing existing institutions, abolishing them or creating new forms).

Governments in many parts of the world have seen the efficiency of government organizations as an important element in creating national competitiveness in an increasingly competitive world. Red tape and over-regulation and a civil service that is unfriendly to business are seen as disincentives for inward investment and a competitive disadvantage for home-based businesses. Reform of public organizations is often seen as a part of a national effort to improve efficiency and competitiveness in places as diverse as France, Malaysia, New Zealand and Britain. Palan and Abbott (1996) have described this process as the 'competition state'. They argue that while competition creates anxiety among governments it does not necessarily produce the same solutions in every case. Others, such as the OECD Public Management Group, have argued that there is a single best way of running state functions, including various lists of features that emulate the operation of companies in a competitive market. These include the use of competition as a way of reducing costs, a more flexible workforce, more charging for services at the point of delivery, performance related pay, short term contracts and so on. Where feasible, this sort of approach is made a condition of getting financial help from international institutions, such as the Inter-American Development Bank, the International Monetary Fund and the Asian Development Bank. Even where financial help is not being sought, there are institutions such as the OECD and management consultants that encourage such management methods and assume that there is a single set of problems looking for a unique set of solutions. Cynics would say the consultants have a set of solutions looking for problems. The reason that this debate about whether there is a single way forward is important is that if it is correct, the bargaining position of those who have different ideas is weakened. If those advocating change are able to demonstrate that everybody else is doing this, and it works, then counter-proposals are less likely to get a hearing.

There is also a strong argument that pressures have produced different results in different countries. By 1995, Hood – who is credited with coining the expression 'New Public Management' – expressed doubts about whether there was indeed a new paradigm, and noticed national and regional differences. Similarly, Pollitt (1995) noticed that while many countries had developed new approaches whose characteristics he listed, the lists were not identical and indeed overlapped only in part. By 1996, Lawrence Lynn (paper published 1997) expressed scepticism about the whole project, arguing that one of the central tenets of reducing direct state involvement and 'steering not rowing' had not been vigorously pursued even in the US where the approach had been most forcefully propagated. Rather than a new paradigm, Lynn argued that there might only be a new 'meta-language' used by management consultants and national and supra-national agencies. As a UN report put it in 1998, there has been 'a remarkable commonality of nomenclatures and formal organizations among countries, even though the underlying national realities remain extremely divergent' (p. 17). Guy Peters (1996) identified four strands of reform efforts: market mechanisms, deregulation, participation and flexibility, operating with different emphases in different countries. Indeed, Peters argues that there are four 'models', each based on one of these four features. While useful heuristically, each element in this classification may be apparent in a single country, although with different emphases. The changes could be classified as being concerned with three issues: a concern to reduce spending because of fiscal problems; a concern by governments or political parties to create or sustain support because of some threat to their legitimacy; the struggle for power in governments in which reform efforts may be used as a way of gaining or retaining power.

1 Managerial changes and their causes

1.1 Costs

At different times in the 1980s, many countries had fiscal crises. In some cases they were caused by economic downturn, as government revenues failed to keep pace with government spending. In other cases spending grew in response to various demands but it was politically difficult to

Table 2.1 *General government total outlays as a percentage of nominal GDP*

	1970	1975	1980	1985	1990	1995	1997	1999*	2000*
Australia	–	31.4	31.4	36.5	34.8	36.2	35.0	33.6	33.3
Austria	37.6	44.3	47.1	50.4	48.6	52.5	49.8	49.4	49.2
Belgium	41.5	50.8	57.0	60.7	53.6	53.6	51.7	50.5	49.9
Canada	34.1	39.2	39.6	46.0	46.7	46.5	42.6	41.8	41.2
Czech Republic	–	–	–	–	–	44.8	45.3	46.1	46.1
Denmark	–	47.1	55.0	58.0	56.0	58.8	56.4	53.8	52.5
Finland	30.0	37.6	38.1	43.8	45.4	57.9	54.1	49.0	48.6
France	38.5	43.4	46.1	52.1	49.8	54.3	54.2	53.9	53.5
Germany	38.3	48.4	47.9	47.0	45.1	49.8	47.9	46.9	46.3
Greece	–	27.9	30.4	42.9	48.2	48.3	42.9	41.7	41.1
Hungary	–	–	–	–	–	49.2	45.0	40.7	40.9
Iceland	–	–	32.5	35.7	39.3	39.0	36.7	35.9	35.5
Ireland	–	–	48.2	51.0	39.0	37.6	34.7	32.8	32.1
Italy	32.8	41.1	41.9	50.9	53.6	52.7	50.6	49.4	48.8
Japan	19.0	26.8	32.0	31.6	31.3	35.6	35.2	38.4	39.1
Korea	–	17.1	19.3	17.6	18.0	20.5	21.9	25.7	25.7
Luxembourg	–	–	–	–	13.4	13.2	13.2	12.8	12.7
Mexico	–	–	–	–	17.2	17.7	15.5	13.9	13.5
Netherlands	41.3	50.2	55.8	57.1	54.1	51.3	48.7	47.5	47.3
New Zealand	–	–	–	–	48.8	38.8	38.5	41.4	40.4
Norway	34.9	39.8	43.9	41.5	49.7	47.6	44.3	47.2	47.5
Poland	–	–	–	–	60.8	49.3	46.8	44.7	43.7
Portugal	19.5	28.0	23.2	40.2	40.6	44.6	43.9	43.7	44.1
Spain	21.6	24.4	32.2	40.2	42.5	45.5	42.2	40.8	40.3
Sweden	42.8	48.4	60.1	63.3	59.1	65.6	62.3	59.6	58.1
Switzerland	–	–	–	–	41.0	47.5	48.8	49.2	49.3
Turkey	–	–	–	–	27.9	26.5	24.3	23.9	25.2
United Kingdom	37.2	44.8	43.4	44.4	41.8	44.4	41.0	40.3	40.6
United States	30.0	32.8	31.4	32.9	32.8	32.8	31.6	31.2	31.1

* Estimates and projections. *Source*: OECD, *Economic Outlook* 64, December 1998

Source: Analytical Databank, OECD

increase taxation to match the rise in spending. If permanent deficits are
not to be tolerated there is an obvious and small set of solutions that can
be used in varying combinations: increase taxes, cut services, increase
efficiency. If the first two of these solutions are chosen, the third
becomes essential: while it raises taxes or cuts services any government
must try or be seen to try to increase efficiency. Similarly, to cut services
is difficult electorally and may require public persuasion.

Table 2.1 shows that government spending as a percentage of GDP
was rising in most OECD countries during the 1970s and 1980s. It
also shows that the pressure was lifted in most places by 1995 as the
public spending figures peaked (the exceptions are Japan, Korea and
Switzerland). While the spending was rising, especially where spending
was over 50 per cent, you might expect governments to try to take
measures to improve efficiency. What is most interesting is that there
were less vocal and visible attempts at big changes in Denmark, where

spending peaked at nearly 60 per cent and Germany where it peaked at around 50 per cent than in the US where spending never rose to 33 per cent of GDP.

Improving efficiency or changing the way in which services are managed was never likely to solve fiscal crises. In a rational world this might be thought to undermine one of the key rationales for managerialism. Claims were made during the 1980s in countries such as the US, UK and New Zealand that contracting out services produced a step reduction in costs of up to 20 per cent of previous costs (Walsh, 1991; Domberger et al., 1986) but such savings were never spread over a very wide range of services nor were they big enough to be reflected in overall spending figures. The search for efficiency savings applied only to the running costs of services, rather than, for example, the level of subsidies for farmers or welfare benefits.

The efficiency effects of new ways of managing were exaggerated, naturally. For example, in the UK all reductions in running costs for the period 1991–96 could be attributed to the transfer of functions or to reduced services, especially defence (Flynn, 1997, p. 207). In any case, the fiscal crises were attributable less to inefficiency than to an accretion of functions and spending programmes. However, there can be no doubt that fiscal problems make politicians look for savings, not least for symbolic purposes. These are twofold: electors and taxpayers need to be assured that their money is being used efficiently; and employers and workers in industries facing competitive pressure need assurance that their anxiety is shared by the government and public sector workers.

One of the main concerns of governments entering reform programmes has been to reduce costs without cutting the volume of services. Barzelay (1992) pointed out that this was probably the main error of public services trying to imitate management in the manufacturing sector: if there was no measure of outputs, independent of cost, the search for improved efficiency was chimerical. So the search for efficiency improvements produced a need for a definition of outputs that could be compared with costs. Such definitions and measures are a necessary condition for evaluating management changes: without a measure of the cost of a unit of output, assessing the success of any management change is a matter of guesswork.

This is true whatever the nature of the structural and other changes being made. A system in which there are contracts between government and either internal or external service providers (as has been established in Sweden, New Zealand and the UK) requires some units of output to be specified in the contract. The alternative is to contract for results, an approach adopted in the US for contracts for drug rehabilitation work and training for re-employment schemes, for example. Where it is not possible to specify results or outcomes clearly enough to make a contract work, governments are forced to measure units of work or output. Unfortunately such efforts have not been successful enough to cure the error that Barzelay spotted. Even in Sweden, which has had a budget system based on outputs and contracts for a decade, there are still technical difficulties in measurement (Blondal, 1998). Since 1998 the British government has further turned its attention to outcome targets, especially in the proposals contained in the White Paper 'Modernising government' (Flynn 1999a).

Despite the problems of definition and measurement, many efforts have been made to improve efficiency. In some countries, governments have introduced competition: public sector organizations are made to compete with alternative providers in an attempt to reduce the cost of service provision. This has involved two main processes: the definition of services and costs so that a competitive bidding process can be introduced; and efforts to reduce costs to make prices competitive. Other efforts involved simply cutting budgets and/or staffing levels while attempting to maintain service levels.

Still others were concerned with changing the way in which work is done and supervised. Changes in work processes have been of two contradictory types: one set of changes involves mechanizing and making routine activities that were previously under the workers' control, such as nursing and teaching; the other changes involve taking activities that were previously routine and mechanized and applying techniques of quality improvement and self-management so that workers have to make a bigger contribution to the design of work processes.

In addition to increasing efficiency, governments have made efforts to reduce public expenditure. Some of these involve reducing the public services provided in one of three ways: simply cutting budgets; transferring responsibility to individuals, to the 'third sector' or to the market; and transferring responsibility to local governments.

Some governments have changed accounting practices to make public accounts balance. One device has been to change the way in which capital expenditure is counted. A move from counting spending when it is made, to counting it as the assets are used up can reduce any single year's spending. This was the main reason for the New Zealand accounting changes to 'accruals' accounting and such a device has also been used in, for example, the UK and Norway. Incidentally this is a major part of the explanation for New Zealand's dramatic fall in spending as a percentage of GDP from 1990 to 1995 in Table 2.1.

A prerequisite of the search for efficiency improvements is an accounting system that exposes costs. Even if simple budget cuts are to be made, politicians like to know the likely impact of the reductions. Traditionally, government accounts were concerned with the allocation of expenditures to functions or departments. A concern with efficiency requires a measurement of cost. In turn this requires that workers and managers count their activities and allocate their costs to activities. In many sectors this requires a change in attitude by which professionals think about the cost of what they do, as well as the professional standards by which they do it. The movement from expenditure to cost accounting has been very widespread, occurring for example in the US, northern Europe, Singapore, Hong Kong, New Zealand and Australia.

1.2   Legitimacy

The second set of problems that governments tried to solve in part by management changes was concerned with legitimacy. This occurred in different ways in different countries. In Japan in the early 1990s the legitimacy of the Civil Service was challenged as the recession lengthened and civil servants could no longer claim credit for economic growth. In northern Europe there was some political dissatisfaction with the standards of services provided by social democratic regimes from the mid-1980s and parties tried to regain credibility by engaging in various consultation and service redesign measures. In the US, pressure came less from voters than from business, which blamed 'red tape' for inefficiency and frustration. The challenges were both to the ruling parties and to the institutions of the state, including the bureaucracies. Politicians could distance themselves from blame by diagnosing failure of the bureaucracy rather than the party. This was much more common in the US and the UK, where governing parties presented themselves as the champions of the people against the bureaucracy. In such circumstances, radical action was necessary: champions cannot gain support through minor measures. The 'reinventing laboratories' in the US and the very public campaigns about standards of service through the charters in the UK were part of this crusade. Service standards were defined in other countries, such as through charters in France, but with much less publicity.

There were other pressures on governments from business. As international competition increased in the 1980s, especially with new, smart and efficient entrants into the US markets from Japan and then other Asian countries, governments were increasingly held responsible by business for 'national competitiveness'. If the Japanese government could act in the interest of 'Japan Inc.', why, then, could not the US government do the same for US Inc., or the British, or much later the German and Malaysian governments? This pressure did not imply that the governments should all behave in the same way, rather that they should accept some responsibility for their nation's competitiveness. This came to have serious implications both for policy and for management, as a new form of corporatism brought together government and business, but less frequently labour, to deal with issues of national competitiveness. What this form of corporatism implies is that the government does not act as arbitrator between employers and employees but represents the interest of business as being the same as the national interest.

To generate support from business, governments have several options. The most immediate is to create opportunities for business, or sections of business, to make money. Privatization is the main way this can be done: the buyers of privatized industries and the banks and advisers involved in the process are the main beneficiaries of the privatization process. Similarly, contracting services out offers a chance to make money. While the producers of military hardware are the most obvious beneficiaries of government contracts, there are many others, traditionally in civil engineering but now increasingly in the computer hardware and software industries. Examples include the US insurance industry's influence on the Clinton government's attempts to design a universal health care system or the aerospace industry's profits from military supply. Almost everywhere state monopolies on tele-communications have given way to profitable market opportunities. Less obvious, perhaps, is the way in which water supply and manage-ment contracts are devised to enable the large French water companies to manage water supply in various parts of the world. Private provision or publicly funded but privately delivered services are not put in place just because of the potential efficiency gains but also because they provide an opportunity for profit.

In some cases, the response to business is to deregulate or reduce the amount of control the governments have over businesses. A main thrust of reforms in the US has been the effort to reduce 'red tape' or 'bureaucracy'. Similarly, the Malaysian government has been presenting itself as more friendly to business (Sarji, 1996). A further connection between governments and business is the 'demonstration effect' of changes in the ways in which businesses are managed. The term 'demonstration effect' refers to processes through which one organiza-tion promotes its own practices which are then taken up by another organization. There is a view that the hierarchical bureaucracies were a product of a period of economic and political development during which mechanized mass production made large bureaucracies, repetitive tasks, standardized products and strict rules of behaviour the norm in business as well as in government. Such an approach is sometimes referred to as Fordism, after the social and technical characteristics of Ford car plants. Relaxation of those conditions, both social and technical, has been referred to as 'post-Fordist' (see Burrows and Loader, 1994, for this analysis in relation to the welfare state). This argument applies to the nature of the products or services, which can be customized in some way to meet individual requirements and the nature of the production process, in which the division of labour is relaxed and jobs become more flexible. The implication of this development for management is that new forms of control are required: direct supervision of people carrying out routine tasks is replaced by methods that develop self-management. The argument can be exaggerated: in practice the large public sector employers, dealing with tax collection, benefits and pensions payments, still have standardized products and management processes that are designed to make sure that the calculations are done correctly. In other areas, it could be argued that recent tendencies to define and measure services as part of the process of management or contracting make services more standardized rather than less, and require a management style concerned with direct supervision. Nevertheless, there is no doubt that politicians and managers learn from the trends occurring in the private sector, whether in the use of technology or methods of managing people. Legitimacy may also be enhanced by implementing current ideas about management, or at least by using current managerial language.

When governments are faced with opposition or doubts from citizens or business they have taken various steps to justify their actions or generate or create support. One strand is the improvement of accountability through which governments try to demonstrate how well they are doing. While progress has been slow at a high level, accounting for the effectiveness of government policies and programmes, at a lower level, accountability for the efficient use of funds has made a lot of progress.

A second strand is to generate support from the electorate through processes of consultation and participation. A main thrust of management reform in northern Europe has been about generating support through involvement. The main theme of the 'new steering model' that has been adopted in many municipalities in Germany and the Netherlands has been involvement of the public in planning and designing public services. While these efforts have also involved decentralized budgets and the definition and costing of services, the main purpose has not been cutting costs. In recent years these approaches have spread to the canton level in Switzerland.

Improvement of customer service and service quality is another way that governments try to make public services more popular. Access to services through single access points (called the 'one stop shop' in the UK) has been tried in many European countries, including Italy. In other places there have been campaigns, such as the Japanese 'Polite and Considerate Public Service Campaign' or the PS21 (Public Services for the 21st Century) campaign in Singapore.

These processes are quite separate from those that help businesses become more competitive. They are concerned with maintaining support for the institutions of the state and the level of taxation being levied. The form that they take depends on the local circumstances. Public involvement in choosing what services to provide and how is very different from a managerial approach to service design and customer orientation. One view is that the two approaches represent different political cultures. Kickert (1995) argues that the customer-service approach to managerialism is essentially Anglo-American, while the approach in the Netherlands and elsewhere in Europe is more concerned with democracy.

1.3   Power struggles

Managerial reforms have been used as a way of contesting for power within government. The most obvious example of this is in New Zealand, where radical reforms tried to take power away from the professionals, especially in health and education sectors, and put the politicians in control (Boston et al., 1996). While expenditure cuts may have been the underlying motive, the form that the reforms took, establishing a way of choosing the required outputs from public institutions, was designed to make decisions very explicit and to allow the politicians to make them.

One of the motivations for the UK reforms under the Thatcher and Major governments was to enable central government to gain control over institutions inimical to their political purposes, such as local authorities, health authorities and parts of the central government apparatus (Jenkins, 1995). In Japan, factions of the ruling Liberal Democratic Party gained control of parts of the apparatus of government and used them to promote their own interests. However, it is not always politicians who launch managerial changes. In some countries (for example, the Netherlands, Finland and Sweden) public management reform has been shaped and fuelled largely by mandarins rather than by ministers. In others the pendulum has swung this way and then that. In Denmark, for example, agencies were put at arm's length during the 1980s and then brought back into ministries during the 1990s, partly because of fears of loss of political control.

Reforms that downgrade or promote particular departments or commissions are also part of the factional power struggles. Particular departments, such as ministries of finance or ministries of personnel, promote reforms in their own interests in many countries. What this suggests is that the form of management changes and restructuring is likely to be influenced by the existing power relationships and the resources available to change them.

2   Local conditions and institutional constraints on changes

The balance of these influences on governments varies across the world. First, fiscal conditions differ. Switzerland and Hong Kong are two examples of countries that have tried quite radical reform in the way in which services are managed, during periods of healthy finances. There is also, in Japan, an example of very little real change in management style in the Civil Service despite the world's biggest fiscal deficit. Nor does fiscal crisis automatically generate the same solution everywhere. One solution for national governments' fiscal problems is to transfer responsibility for services from central to sub-national governments, together with fiscal responsibility, as was done in the Netherlands and Japan in the mid-1980s. However, this was by no means a universal solution.

Similarly, problems of legitimacy vary. The concerns of US business with 'big government' and obstructive public officials are not necessarily shared in Europe where, in general, reform efforts are designed to improve services for the public rather than streamlining procedures for businesses. These changes do not necessarily imply that there was a legitimacy problem, but if there was, it was not the same as that of the US Federal government.

Pressures from 'globalization' or national competitiveness have also produced different responses from governments. Perhaps Singapore has the most investment-friendly government procedures, whereby officials steer investors individually through any legal and fiscal processes. Other governments have made attempts to reduce 'red tape' for investors but the principal influence of 'globalization' is at the level of rhetoric, with much talk of modernization and national competitiveness, and in the sphere of social policy and what is sometimes called the 'social wage'. Competitiveness is used as a reason for cutting or not increasing the 'burden on business' of taxes or social contributions.

When we look at the impact of the desire of businesses to make money from tax-funded services we also see a variety of patterns. It is perhaps ironic that the term 'steering not rowing' (Osborne and Gaebler, 1992) was one of the slogans associated with public sector reforms in the US and yet there has been virtually no transfer of functions from directly employed state workers to contractors: the pattern of employment and contracting has not changed in the way in which it did in the UK, for example (Lynn, 1997). Patterns of opportunity for contracting vary somewhat from country by country. Until the privatization of water supply in the UK only France had major water contracts, dating from the nineteenth century. The US has the only major private prisons provision in the world. In most parts of the 'first world' school education is mainly a state function, as is some form of basic medical care. There have been transfers of functions and direct provision from the state to private companies, but this has mainly occurred in developing countries where privatization has been made a condition of loans or aid funds. In the richer countries of North America, Europe and Asia, the pattern of division between direct state provision and contracting is relatively stable even though it varies between countries.

The demonstration effect of management changes in business also has different impacts in different countries. It is possible to choose what to copy from a wide range of business experiences. Some trends, such as the casualization of employment and the lengthening of working hours, are difficult to implement in some environments where there are strong trade unions or long-standing agreements. De-layering, the removal of tiers of management to cut costs and shorten lines of communication, has been attempted by some governments but not as widely as in businesses. The removal of whole layers of middle management that has happened in manufacturing and service businesses has not happened to the same extent in government organizations.

While governments have many reasons to change how public services are run, they also face a series of difficulties in implementing change. In some countries 'reform' of civil service systems is almost constant. Japan, for example, has had public service 'reform' processes since the establishment in 1962 of the 'First Provisional Commission for Administrative Reform' to improve public sector productivity. That these efforts persist may imply that there is continuous improvement or that continuous effort is required to achieve change.

Three sets of constraints face governments trying to introduce management changes. First, there are the alliances that any reform effort faces. Just as many reforms are designed to change political power, so those holding power can use their positions to resist change if their power is challenged. Secondly, there are beliefs and habits of working that may be hard to change. At a superficial level these might simply be familiar ways of working that are hard to shift, while at a deeper level they may involve deeply held beliefs that change management programmes cannot reach. The third set of constraints is technical. If change involves abandoning traditional, hierarchical supervision, there may be problems since certain processes in public services are simply easier to organize that way. Conversely, if change involves increasing measurement and control, certain services, especially those that involve high degrees of discretion, may be adversely affected by the imposition of managerial controls.

2.1   Existing alliances

If management reforms threaten interests without compensation, people may organize to resist the changes. The most obvious organizations, the trade unions, have not been the source of significant constraint on changes. More important have been the connections among people involved in the changes. Examples include the network of people in the UK educated in a small number of schools and universities who occupied senior positions in central departments of government and were little affected by the managerial changes that affected the service delivery agencies. Other examples include the classmates from the Tokyo Law School who have tended to dominate the Japanese Civil Service and have proved resilient to changes, and the networks of party cadres who have slowed down the reform process in the People's Republic of China (PRC). As well as these connections, there are professional networks, especially in fields such as medicine and engineering, that look after their members. One good example is that of the civil engineering profession in France, which has managed to survive most reform efforts. Once professions have captured a ministry or other organization they are difficult to dislodge or reform.

In some countries there are powerful ministries that are able either to resist changes that affect them or to shape changes to their own advantages. A commonly powerful ministry is the Ministry of Finance, which is strong in the UK, Japan and France, for example. Other strong departments include the diplomatic service or the armed forces. Sometimes there are alliances among ministries, professionals and politicians, especially factions of parties or whole parties. In Japan, factions of the ruling LDP are connected with particular ministries and commissions whose fortunes are tied to those of the faction. Reform of a powerful faction's areas is unlikely (Flynn, 1999b).

Constitutional protection of public institutions is also a source of inertia. In federal government in Germany and Austria, for example, the fact that civil servants have a constitutional immunity from interference by politicians (an arrangement put in place to prevent a resurgence of Fascist control over state institutions) means that changes in employment and management practices are difficult to bring about (Flynn and Strehl, 1996). If this is combined with a high degree of public support, it is almost impossible for politicians to bring about changes. The obvious strategy to adopt in these circumstances is to take action to reduce public support for particular occupations or professions.

These sources of power and inertia mean that 'reform' efforts have an uneven impact. Management changes that involve a reduction in status, power or autonomy are resisted by those affected by them. The outcome depends on the balance of power and the participants' ability to mobilize it as the reforms are implemented.

2.2 Culture and beliefs

Underlying the power of professionals and other groups involved in public service delivery is often a widespread set of beliefs about how things should be organized. For example, in some countries there is support and respect for the Civil Service as an institution and for civil servants as carriers of certain beliefs and values. Sometimes, as in Germany, the protection that this respect creates is backed by the constitution. This may be connected with attitudes to the role of the state and the level of taxation. In Scandinavia, efforts by Conservative parties in the late 1980s and early 1990s to reduce the role of the state and cut the very high levels of taxation were short-lived as political views swung back to more traditional values. The opposite may also be the case. Especially in societies that have a colonial history, the Civil Service is sometimes regarded as corrupt and self-seeking. Lack of trust in institutions and a belief in individual and family self-reliance do not generate support for public servants.

Table 2.2 Some examples of 'reform' efforts and institutional constraints

	New Zealand	Sweden	France	Japan	PRC	Malaysia	Singapore
Main reasons for change	Fiscal deficits Political struggle	Fiscal deficits	Part of 'modernization' campaign	Loss of public confidence Deficit	Cost and impact on economy	Impact on economy	Legitimacy?
Structure change	Autonomous agencies	No change	Decentralization	Reduce number of ministries from 22 to 13	Reduce number of ministries from 40 to 29		Not recently
Control	Control by contract	Changed relationships Ministries and agencies	More autonomous 'centres'	More political control over ministries 'Executive agencies'	State-owned enterprises to be independent of ministries		
Scale reduction	Budget cuts	Budget cuts	Budget cuts	4 per cent over 4 years	25 per cent?	Freeze	Cash limits No control on numbers of staff
Privatization	Enterprises	No	Some	Railway, other sectors proposed	Education, health, state-owned enterprises	State industries	No
HR change	Performance and short contracts	Some flexibility	Pay changes	(Some) promotion on merit	More open recruitment Promotion on merit	New appraisal scheme 'New Remuneration System'	Performance bonuses Outside recruitment at senior level

Deregulation	Yes	Yes	Attempted		Free state-owned enterprises' managers from regulation	
Accountability	Performance targets (outputs)	Performance contracts as part of budget	Charters	Access to information	State-owned enterprises' performance	Clients' Charter
Anti-corruption campaign	No	No	No	Yes	Yes	Yes — Big pay rises in 1989 as disincentive to corruption
Customer service improvements	Competition			'Polite and Considerate Public Service' campaign		'Manuals' approach to quality — Work Improvement teams — PS21
Institutional constraints	Motivation and recruitment	Problem of measuring output and outcome	Power of ministries and of professions	Political factions and network connections	Cadres networks	Power of civil servants — Nothing serious

Sources: Flynn, 1999b; Kaneko, 1997; Lam and Chan, 1996; Flynn and Strehl, 1996; Sarji, 1996; O'Uchi, 1995; Boston et al., 1996

Within the public services there may also be beliefs that are hard to change. Respect for seniority, for example, may inhibit the implementation of ideas about promotion on merit. In the United Kingdom there has been quite strong resistance to the idea of performance related pay, which is seen by some as an unworthy substitute for a sense of public duty and pride in the job. Tony Blair, the British Prime Minister made speeches during 1999 expressing exasperation at the unwillingness of public servants to change their working habits and saying that they have the attitude that old ways of working are the best. While this impression may not be recognized by some who worked through the Conservative years of reorganization and reform, the frustration expressed indicates that attitudes and beliefs among public servants are seen by one politician at least as a constraint on management changes.

2.3   Technical

There are some occupations to which it is difficult to apply managerial reforms of any type, whether the move is towards or away from mechanization. In general, those occupations that require a high degree of discretion and judgement in day-to-day work are difficult to manage in a mechanistic way. Conversely, those occupations that are routine and mechanized are hard to manage through self-management. When the mode of management includes some reliance on paying for performance these differences become more obvious. The debate about the best ways to manage types of work is not unique to the public sector: the argument about management control and worker motivation has been carried on since the Luddites opposed the separation of family life and work life and the subjection of work to managerial control. What is special about certain public sector occupations is that managerial control through measurement and specification either of outputs (the volume of work done) or outcomes (the results) in the absence of a measure of value, raises arguments about what should be measured and how that becomes part of the debate about who should control the work. Where the value of output can be measured (however imperfectly) by market price, the struggle for control can be focused on the management–worker relationship.

3   A variety of experience

Table 2.2 shows a summary of recent managerial changes in a variety of countries. It starts with the main driving force for change, then summarizes some of the main changes and lists the institutional constraints on changes. While such short summary phrases cannot capture the complexity and subtlety of the changes in each case, the table is sufficient to show that there are different pressures and different priorities in different local circumstances. The most common element among the countries is the fact that there are budget cuts everywhere except Singapore (the table refers to events before the Asian economic crisis of 1997–98). The other elements vary: privatization is most apparent in the People's Republic of China; drastic restructuring of ministries is happening in both Japan and the PRC, but not elsewhere; 'management of people' changes vary from the use of performance contracts to changing recruitment processes. The explanation for the variety of experience lies both in the different reasons for the changes and in the institutional framework within which they take place. Extension of such a description to more countries would confirm the variety of forces for change, and in the main ideas in the change programmes and the constraints on the successes of governments in their efforts. There is no single form of 'managerialism' that suits all circumstances although many national governments and supra-governmental organizations contain believers in market-style ways of managing.

Claims of homogenization through globalization are exaggerated. Those proposing managerial changes in public services may use three devices: the appeal to national competitiveness in a globalizing world market; the hegemony of market-type ideas as opposed to any other form of governance; and an appeal to the superiority of 'the private sector'. The Howard government used all three in its recent reforms of the Australian Public Service. All three are simplifications given credibility by their appeal to a unified language of managerial terms, often in English.

Local political and institutional circumstances mean that there is still a big difference in public services, not just between places like Jamaica and Singapore, but between schools and tax offices, welfare departments and engineering offices.

Managerial type reforms of customer service concern the relationships between workers and their supervisors and between workers and the users of their services. Democratic type reforms concern the relationship between citizens and government. Both sets of changes involve a struggle for control, in one case over work and in the other over the distribution and use of public funds and other resources. Both take place within the context of the power of the participants, including fractions of political parties, different sectors of business, the variety of professional and other occupational groups involved in public service and organized and disorganized groups of citizens.

References

Barzelay, M. (1992) *Breaking through Bureaucracy: A New Vision for Managing in Government*, Berkeley, University of California Press.

Blondal, J. (1998) *Budgeting in Sweden*, OECD Working Papers Vol. VI, 47, Paris.

Boston, J., Martin, J., Pallot, J. and Walsh, P. (1996) *Public Management: The New Zealand Model*, Auckland, Oxford University Press.

Burrows, R. and Loader, B. (eds) (1994) *Towards a Post-Fordist Welfare State?* London, Routledge.

Domberger, S., Meadowcroft, S.A. and Thompson, D.J. (1986) 'Competitive tendering and efficiency', *Fiscal Studies*, 7 (11).

Flynn, N. (1997) *Public Sector Management*, London, Prentice-Hall/Harvester Wheatsheaf.

Flynn, N. (1999a) 'Modernising government in Britain', *Parliamentary Affairs*, October, pp. 582–97.

Flynn, N. (1999b) *Miracle to Meltdown in Asia: Business, Government and Society*, Oxford, Oxford University Press.

Flynn, N. and Strehl, F. (eds) (1996) *Public Sector Management in Europe*, London, Prentice-Hall/Harvester Wheatsheaf.

Hood, C. (1995) 'Contemporary public management: a new global paradigm?' *Public Policy and Administration*, 10 (2).

Jenkins, S. (1995) *Accountable to None: The Tory Nationalisation of Britain*, London, Hamish Hamilton.

Kaneko, Y. (1997) 'Administrative reform efforts in the government of Japan: her experiences and current progress', *IIAS Round Table*, Quebec City, 14–17 July.

Kickert, W.J.M. (1995) 'Public governance in the Netherlands: an alternative to Anglo-American managerialism', *Administration and Society*, 28 (1).

Lam Tao-chiu and Chan Hon, S. (1996) 'China's new civil service: what the Emperor is wearing and why', *Public Administration Review*, 56 (5).

Lynn, L.E. (1997) 'The new public management as an international phenomenon: a skeptical view', *Advances in International Comparative Management*, Supplement 3.

Osborne, D. and Gaebler, T. (1992) *Reinventing Government*, Reading, MA, Addison-Wesley.

O'Uchi, M. (1995) 'A sensible analysis of administrative reform', in Masujima, T. and O'Uchi, M. (eds) *The Management and Reform of the Japanese Government*, Tokyo, Institute of Administrative Management.

Palan, R. and Abbott, J. (1996) *State Strategies in the Global Political Economy*, London, Pinter.

Peters, B.G. (1996) *The Future of Governing: Four Emerging Models*, University of Kansas Press.

Pollitt, C. (1995) 'Justification by works or by faith?', *Evaluation*, 1 (2).

Sarji, A. (1996) *Civil Service Reforms: Towards Malaysia's Vision 2020*, Selangor, Darul Ehsan, Pelanduk Publications.

United Nations (1998) *Rethinking Public Administration, An Overview*, New York, Division of Public Administration and Development Management.

Walsh, K. (1991) *The Impact of Competitive Tendering*, London, Department of Environment.

3

Beyond the New Public Management?
Modernizing Public Services

Janet Newman

Contents		

In the 1980s and early 1990s social welfare was transformed through an articulation between the new managerialism and the political ideology of the New Right (Clarke and Newman, 1997). The 'New Public Management' (NPM) was a term used to describe a series of reforms which reshaped the relationships between public and private sectors, professionals and managers, and central and local government. Citizens and clients were recast as consumers, and public service organizations were recast in the image of the business world (Newman, 1998). The election of a Labour government in 1997 signalled a shift in the political terrain. The early years of the Labour administration saw a raft of new policy proposals and a programme of reform for social services, the criminal justice system, the NHS, local government and other sectors. Both the emerging policy agenda and the programme of institutional reform were underpinned by a *discourse of modernization*. This chapter attempts to unravel this discourse, and its interaction with the New Public Management, through studying a range of policy documents, White and Green papers and ministerial pronouncements.

Studying discourse through documentary analysis is an imperfect technique for at least two reasons. First, it can isolate the study of language from the study of practice. Language in this type of document is used as much to legitimize change as it is to set out what the changes will mean in practice, and the underpinning ideological structures can easily be misread. Secondly, my focus on drawing out themes within the discourse of modernization may mean that insufficient attention is paid to differences between documents concerned with different sectors and to the subtle shifts of emphasis over time as key ministers come and go and political compromises are made. Nevertheless studying discourse provides important clues about the interaction of continuity and change in the development of the new government's approach, and suggests significant implications for the management of public services.

1   Modernization as discourse

At first sight modernization presents itself as a rational and common-sense project to update public service management:

> We believe in active government and we believe in public service, but if government is going to be effective at delivering services in the way people want them for today, it has to be modernised, it has to be updated and that's what this White Paper is all about. (Prime Minister, cited in Cabinet Office, 1999a, p. 2)

Modernization is presented as a necessary process of updating services to match the expectations of modern consumers (who, for example, expect services to be organized for the convenience of those using them) and to meet the business requirements of the 'modern' world (for example, by drawing on developments in IT). At this level modernization can be viewed as continuing the process of reform begun under previous administrations, aiming to open up those parts of the public sector that had failed to be transformed by the market mechanisms and consumer ethos of the Thatcher and Major years. It continues the attack on the 'producer dominance' associated with monopoly forms of provision, and seeks to sharpen accountability to users and other stakeholders. There is a continued focus on the containment of welfare expenditure, on organizational efficiency and performance, and on the search for business solutions to social and policy problems. However, the Labour government has also sought to distance itself from the outright assault on public services which took place under Conservative administrations. The emerging discourses of best value, partnership, public consultation and democratic renewal appear to offer an expanded concept of 'managing for public purpose', going beyond the narrow confines of efficiency-seeking organizational restructuring, 'downsizing', contracting and quasi-markets. Modernization also offers a more dynamic image of the process of management itself. The passive language and internal focus of earlier policy documents is replaced by an active, outward-looking discourse: for example, the front cover of the leaflet *Modernising Government* displays a series of images of public service action surrounded by text which reads: 'developing . . . involving . . . delivering . . . listening . . . supporting . . . helping . . . engaging' (Cabinet Office, 1999b, cover).

To understand this shift it is necessary to unpack the modernization discourse, looking beneath the surface imagery of change as a rational process of getting rid of old-fashioned practices. Modernization is a discourse which sets out an agenda for change across different sectors (health, education, criminal justice, local government, the Civil Service). It also denotes a wider political transformation, involving the reform of key relationships in the economy, state and civil society. It offers a particular conception of citizen (empowered as active, participating subjects); of work (as the source of opportunity for the 'socially excluded'); of community (non-antagonistic and homogeneous); and of nation (setting out Britain's place in the changing global economy). It links a search for a distinctive political project – the elusive 'Third Way' – with a process of public sector reform. Viewed in this context, the *modern* public management takes on a different inflection: it is a fundamentally political project, to which the rhetorics, narratives and strategies of managerialism are harnessed.

Despite significant areas of continuity in the focus on performance and efficiency, the discourse of 'modern management' suggests some subtle shifts from that of the 'new public management'. First, modern management presents itself as being not just about short-term efficiency but about longer-term effectiveness. For example, the reform of financial arrangements and the introduction of the three-year comprehensive spending review have introduced a longer planning cycle for public service organizations, linked to longer-term goals and targets. Secondly, while the NPM was predominantly concerned with institutional reform (introducing competitive tendering, quasi-markets and purchaser/ provider splits) modern management is presented as a set of tools and techniques which can be used to help achieve the policy outcomes on education, social exclusion and welfare reform at the heart of Labour's political agenda. Thirdly, while NPM was focused on the benefits of competition, modern management appears to place more emphasis on collaboration. The political goal of 'joined-up government' is matched by the managerial techniques of building partnerships and strategic alliances. The concepts of stakeholding, relational contracts, trust, risk sharing, and collaborative advantage offer an image of leading edge business practice which appears radically different from the 'cut and thrust', 'lean and mean' discourses of business turnaround and down-sizing which pervaded public management in the 1980s.

The articulations between managerialism and modernization are fundamental to the political project of the Labour government. They operate around a number of different themes explored in the following sections. The themes must be understood as emergent and unstable: each is the focus of continued social and political agency that aims to reshape – and hold – a new settlement following the change of government.

2   Innovation and the politics of restructuring

Modernization is based on a set of narratives that construct the imperative for public services to change. The requirements of globalization, enterprise and flexibility are set against the problems of parochialism and bureaucratic inertia of unreformed welfare institutions.

> Reform is a vital part of rediscovering a true national purpose, part of a bigger picture in which our country is a model of a 21st century developed nation: with sound, stable economic management; dynamism and enterprise in business; the best educated and creative nation in the world; and a welfare state that promotes our aims and achievements. But we should not forget why reform is right, and why, whatever the concerns over individual benefits, most people know it is right. Above all, the system must change because the world has changed, beyond the recognition of Beveridge's generation. . . . We need a system designed not for yesterday, but for today. (Blair, 1998, pp. iii–iv)

Narratives of change which link the global to the local to the personal constitute a set of cascading imperatives to change (Clarke and Newman, 1997, Ch. 3). 'Innovation' is a key theme around which this narrative of modernization has been constructed. A White Paper, *Our Competitive Future: Building the Knowledge Driven Economy*, spells out the role of innovation in modernizing the UK:

> The modern world is swept by change. New technologies emerge constantly, new markets are opening up. There are new competitors but also great new opportunities. . . . This world challenges business to be innovative and creative, to improve performance continuously, to build new alliances and ventures. . . . In Government, in business, in our universities and throughout society we must do much more to foster a new entrepreneurial spirit: equipping ourselves for the long-term, prepared to seize opportunities, committed to constant innovation and improved performance. (Blair, foreword, DTI, 1998, p. 5)

In policy documents relating to public services the discourse of innovation relates a narrative of past failure and future possibility. For example, in the introduction to the White Paper on modernizing local government, John Prescott argues that:

> councils need to break free from old fashioned practices and attitudes. There is no future in the old model of councils trying to plan and run most services.

Equally there is no future for councils which are inward looking – more concerned to maintain their structures and protect their vested interests than listening to their local people and leading their local communities. (Department of the Environment, Transport and the Regions, 1998, p. 4)

This normative discourse carries injunctions for public service organizations to change. First, it sets out a view of how services are to be delivered, linked to the discourses of quality management, customer services and user involvement, all of which require constant incremental improvements. Secondly, it is linked to the need to break traditional models of service provision. An innovative organization is viewed as one which is prepared to challenge old and 'outdated' assumptions. This means, among other things, breaking the traditional pattern of who should deliver services, and the pattern of what those services should comprise (i.e. universal or standard provision as against services targeted to areas of 'greatest need'). As well as denoting specific aspects of reform, the discourse of innovation also carries normative injunctions for the public sector to become more like the private: 'We say to business that it must be innovative. That we are entering a knowledge driven economy. The same applies to government. Too often there is a fear of risk and change and experiment' (Prime Minister, 'Modernising Central Government' conference, October 1998, quoted in DTI, 1998, p. 60).

Tony Blair personally endorsed a book which argued that the public sector lagged behind the private in its capacity to meet the challenges of globalization and the rise of the knowledge-driven economy: 'The space for innovation is minimal, the incentives are feeble, the personal rewards uncertain and the pay-off from success comes only in the long term' (Leadbeater, 1999, p. 208). Blair picked up these themes in a much publicized speech to the British Venture Capitalist Association in July 1999, berating the public sector for its unwillingness to innovate and calling for it to become more entrepreneurial.

Innovation as a concept thus links managerial and political agendas; it articulates the ideas of business entrepreneurialism and dynamism with a willingness to challenge and transform the shape and role of the public sector. However, this articulation is not seamless. Innovation in public services is a more difficult concept because the requirements of control and accountability place constraints on risk taking and entrepreneurial action. These tensions derive from the unfinished settlement of the New Public Management: the institutional requirements for accountability and control meant that elements of bureaucracy remained a necessary requirement, despite the rhetoric that they were an evil to be eradicated. There are also disparities between the potency of the discourse and the actual freedoms – legal, financial, political – which would enable organizations to become innovative. Many of the new policy proposals are designed to encourage innovation through pilot schemes or action zones in which the usual controls are relaxed in order to foster new forms of practice. But the elements of modernization which imply the need for decentralization, flexibility and local autonomy are often subordinated to other priorities by a government anxious to exert strong control from the centre to ensure that its political project is carried through.

Innovation as a discourse has a tendency to become detached from its object: it is an 'empty signifier' in that innovation is deemed to be good whatever the content or substance of the innovation itself. Rather than taking innovation as a universal good, it is important to ask whose innovation is being pursued and whose interests it will serve. It is clear that professionally driven forms of innovation (in the forms of service that are available) or user-driven innovation (in how needs and aspirations are to be met) are subordinated to managerial forms (innovation in how services are to be provided and to whom they should be targeted). There may be significant tensions between the form of innovation which is designed to produce efficiency (often through the use of IT) and the form of innovation designed to secure user-led change. There may also be tensions between the idea of innovation as a process of continuous development and change, as in the DTI document and the business literature, and the more prescriptive lists of particular changes set out in the various White Papers on public sector modernization. Rather than signalling a continuing process of evolution and adaptation, modernization can denote an end state based on specific forms of structure or practice. What counts as innovation today may become tomorrow's blueprint, underpinned by a centrally driven and prescriptive process of reform. At the same time, alternative conceptions of change are closed off by the particular conception of modernization being presented as necessary and inevitable.

3   Performance and the politics of decentralization

While the discourse of innovation underpins the drive for change, the focus on performance provides the most significant line of continuity with the New Public Management. There are, however, some shifts of emphasis. While the New Right viewed competition and the use of market mechanisms as the key driver of performance improvements, the Labour government appears to be taking a more pragmatic approach to the use of the market (Hughes and Newman, 1999; Newman, forthcoming). Compulsory competitive tendering and market testing is being replaced by a 'best value' regime applying to local authorities, the police, housing associations and other bodies, while the setting up of Primary Care Groups in the NHS blurs the distinction between the purchasers and providers of health care. These reforms suggest a softening of the approach to contracting, with more emphasis on quality as well as cost, and more discussion of 'relational' contracts between purchaser and provider. Both reflect elements of what are perceived to be modern commercial practice.

Underpinning these shifts is a move away from competition as a politically imposed strategy to the presumption that competition is one of the *managerial* tools through which performance can be improved. It is linked to a decentralized approach in which there is scope for managers to make purchasing and contracting decisions according to the requirements of their business, albeit within a set of political expectations that competition will 'normally' provide the best solution. But offsetting the apparent enlargement of managerial discretion is a strengthening of central controls. For example, the tightening of the performance regime is the main thrust of the White Paper, *Modernising Social Services*:

> One big trouble social services have suffered from is that up to now no Government has spelled out exactly what people can expect or what the staff are expected to do. Nor have any clear standards of performance been laid down. This government is to change all that. (Foreword by the Secretary of State, Department of Health, 1998, p. 2)

Different strategies are used, including the setting of rigorous standards and the publication of information on individual councils' performance against them; the establishment of a new Commission for Care Standards in each region to regulate domiciliary and residential care; and the setting up of a new body to regulate professional performance and oversee social work training. These strategies can be viewed as attempts to exert tighter controls over activities previously the province of professional judgement, forming a clear line of continuity with NPM. Similar shifts are evident in the changes in the management of the Probation Service. Even the strongest bulwarks of professional power – medicine and surgery – are becoming subject to tighter regulation and the standardization of performance norms (following highly publicized examples of surgeon error at Bristol Royal Infirmary). Threats of direct intervention for organizations not achieving the desired performance improvements is a common theme across all sectors: 'If you are unwilling or unable to work to the modern agenda, then the government will have to look to other partners to take on your role' (Blair, 1998, p. 22).

The division of local authorities, schools and other services into heroes (or 'beacons' for others to follow) or villains ('failing' services) lays the foundation for the exercise of additional powers for Secretaries of State to intervene where the agenda for change is not delivered. These powers are accompanied by additional incentives for schools, hospitals, local authorities and other agencies to change in order to secure access to additional funds or powers.

The increasing imperative for agencies to meet centrally determined standards of performance is likely to invoke a neo-Taylorist form of managerialism in which work is co-ordinated by the standardization of work processes rather than professional judgement (Pollitt, 1993). This performance focus stands in stark contrast to the language of decentralization, flexibility and innovation. The interplay of these different discourses of managerialism informs the different inflections of modernization in the reform programmes for different sectors.

4 'Joined-up' government and the politics of partnership

The government's programme of reform involves the idea of 'joined-up' government at the level of both policy and management. Policy making, it was argued, needs to be more joined-up and strategic, meaning that different policies which contribute to a particular issue are made in a holistic way. Management must focus on integrating the delivery of related services by pooling budgets and other resources and by working in partnership across organizational boundaries. The White Paper, *Modernising Government*, presents an account of why this focus is needed, acknowledging that it is in part a product of earlier managerial reforms:

> This emphasis on management reform has brought improved productivity, better value for money and in many cases better quality services – all of which we are determined to build on. On the other hand, little attention was paid to the policy process and the way it affects government's ability to meet the needs of the people . . . in general too little effort has gone into making sure that policies are devised and delivered in a consistent and effective way across institutional boundaries – for example between different government departments, and between central and local government. Issues like crime and social exclusion cannot be tackled on a departmental basis. An increasing separation between policy and delivery has acted as a barrier to involving in policy making those people who are responsible for delivering on the front line. . . . Too often the work of Departments, their Agencies and other bodies has been fragmented and the focus of scrutiny has been on their individual achievements rather than on their contribution to the government's overall strategic purpose. (Cabinet Office, 1999a, Ch. 2, paras 4 and 5)

This quotation contains a number of key ideas which contribute to the narrative of change. First, the previous focus on managerial reforms at the expense of policy issues is criticized. Secondly, the fragmenting effects of managerialism are viewed as having negative consequences in that organizations are judged according to their individual achievements rather than on their contribution to an overall 'strategic purpose'. Thirdly, the opening up of sharper lines of separation between policy and management is viewed as limiting the input of managers to the policy process, and the White Paper calls for more 'inclusion' of frontline workers in the shaping of policy. This final theme is reflected in other key documents. For example, the replacement of the Citizen's Charter programme by *Service First* was introduced as follows:

> in the past too many initiatives were imposed from the top down, and not locally owned by staff and users. We must now take the Charter programme forward. We want a programme that is driven by the needs of users, and whose aims are shared by all staff, particularly those on the front line. A programme based on true partnership, both between users and providers, and between different parts of government. (Cabinet Office, 1998, p. 1)

The language of change centred on user focus, shared aims, owner- ship and partnership strongly evokes the culture change discourse of managerialism used by Tom Peters and others, and is used to contrast the present approach to that of the previous government. The idea of joined-up government is central to a narrative of past failure and future reform. For example, the Social Exclusion Unit (SEU) summarizes the failure of past initiatives aimed at tackling the problems of 'poor neighbourhoods' as follows:

> There are many reasons for this failure. They include the absence of effective national policies to deal with the structural cause of decline; a tendency to parachute solutions in, rather than engaging local communities; and too much emphasis on physical renewal instead of better opportunities for local people. Above all, a joined up problem has never been addressed in a joined up way. Problems have fallen through the cracks between Whitehall Departments, or between central and local government. And at the neighbourhood level, there has been *no one in charge* of pulling together all the things that need to go right at the same time. (SEU, 1998, p. 9, emphasis added)

This notion of joined-up-ness intertwines policy and management agendas in a way that conflates the traditional distinctions between them. The issues of health, the environment, education, regeneration, community safety, social exclusion and others have been termed 'wicked issues', suggesting that it is difficult to reach agreement on the nature and cause of the problem. They are, at the same time, issues on which collaboration is required to develop the desired policy outcomes. This paradox lies at the heart of the rhetoric of finding 'joined-up solutions to joined-up problems'. The policy areas most closely linked to the political project of New Labour – crime and disorder, social exclu- sion, regeneration – are precisely those which cut across existing insti- tutional boundaries. The SEU quotation implies that a different kind of policy agenda requires a new kind of management: one concerned with the design and management of interacting systems; with developing partnerships; and oriented towards strong leadership. The ethos of partnership is a key theme:

The government will take its drive for more joined up and responsive services further by actively encouraging initiatives to establish partnership delivery by all parts of government in ways that fit local circumstances; and establishing common targets, financial frameworks, IT links and so on that support such arrangements. (Cabinet Office, 1999a, Ch. 3, para. 22)

This is an important shift. The managerialism of the Thatcher and Major years was primarily concerned with achieving efficiency savings in order to address the key political goal of that period: reducing public expenditure. While this theme continues, the modern managerialism evoked in the discourse of New Labour appears to be harnessed to delivering outcomes in key areas of social and public policy that cut across traditional boundaries.

The expansionary promise of this shift may, however, be limited by two political constraints. The first lies in the intractable politics of inter- and intra-organizational collaboration. While the discourse of partnership signifies equality of power, shared values and the establishment of common agendas and goals, the reality tends to be very different. Indeed the discourse itself serves to create an illusory unity which masks the need to engage with the gritty political realities of divergent interests and conflicting goals. The focus on collaboration and inclusive processes tends to direct attention away from proper analysis of the barriers created by inequalities of power and resources. Research with public and voluntary sector managers engaged in partnership activity highlights the problems arising from differences in organizational purpose, procedures and structures, professional languages, account- abilities and power (Huxham, 1996; Huxham and Vangen, 1996).

The second constraint lies in the tensions between the requirement that different organizations continue to produce year-on-year efficiencies and the requirement that they collaborate to deliver broad political outcomes. The economic policies of New Labour aim to satisfy business and a middle-class electorate that the government can be trusted to manage the economy. The goal is to be viewed as a prudent guardian of the economic achievements of the Thatcher years; expenditure on wel- fare services is to be contained at least as much as under previous administrations. This means that the capacity of organizations to colla- borate to achieve policy outcomes will be severely constrained. While there have been some attempts to develop 'cross-cutting' performance indicators, the predominant focus of the external reviews of perform- ance discussed in the previous section is based on the efficiency of an organization in delivering whatever happens to be its core business (managing housing stocks, catching criminals or educating young people). Few have the resources, even working in partnership, to address the real causes of ill health or social exclusion, even if they could agree on what the causes were. As a result, new policies – however broad in concept – often result in a series of relatively small scale projects based in different agencies. While each has value in its own terms, they tend to suffer from a lack of integration (each partner shapes initiatives in a way that matches its own agenda) and a lack of continuity (projects are often based on short-term funding arrangements).

More effective management is unlikely to resolve the tensions between the economic and social goals of New Labour. Indeed Mackintosh argues that the NPM itself contributes to problems of co-ordinating and integrating services at a local level, and that this in turn has implications for patterns of social exclusion and inclusion. She suggests that collaboration between providers around client needs in social care is not compatible with a new public management structure which 'stresses competition for contracts based on price, arm's length working relationships and output based performance indicators' (1998, p. 89). Furthermore, front-line workers are marginalized by the same management processes. This, Mackintosh argues, involves both a widening of class divisions within the public sector, excluding lower-level professionals from the management of need, and a delegitimation of advocacy, which works to the detriment of the most vulnerable users. It is also evident that 'best value', like compulsory competitive tendering (CCT) before it, embodies a more conscious assessment of labour as a cost – a cost which has to be driven down in order to enable a service to compete effectively. The primary effect will be a further squeeze on the wages of the most vulnerable groups of staff (those in services regarded as peripheral, and therefore most likely to be subject to market testing or outsourcing). Driving down labour costs will transfer costs to other state agencies (those administering social security, family credit, etc.). It may also exacerbate the very social problems (ill health, family failure, social exclusion) that the government wishes to overcome.

'Joined-up government', then, is likely to remain an aspiration rather than become an established institutional feature of the modernization agenda. This does not however detract from its power as a discourse – a discourse which creates a new inflection for managerialism as a tool for delivering social outcomes through partnership and collaboration, and a welcome release from the narrow and internal focus of the NPM. This is already producing important shifts in the languages and practices of public management and is likely to have significant implications for the reshaping of notions of leadership, strategy and organizational culture on which it draws.

5   Participation and the politics of representation

A repeated theme in the policy documents on modernization is an emphasis on the need for more public participation in decision making. Public participation is central to the image of a modern European

nation-state: an image of a state which engages citizens in the development of civil society and which fosters democratic decision-making
processes. Participation is also viewed as a source of enhanced policy
and management decision making. As the SEU quotation in the previous
section suggests, solutions to local problems which 'engage local communities' are more likely to be effective than those which are 'para-
chuted in'.

The emphasis on participation in the modernization agenda has led
to a huge growth in technologies of participation drawn from marketing
and consumer research in public services. But while the consumerist
emphasis of the Thatcher and Major years centred on the idea of public
services becoming more accountable to users, the modernization agenda
extends the focus to citizens and communities through citizens' juries,
citizens' panels, and community-based participation exercises. New
managerial technologies are being deployed to strengthen the legitimacy
of political decisions in local government, health and education, especially where such decisions concern the rationing of scarce resources.
This has given greater legitimacy to existing groups of staff working
with service users and communities to involve them more closely in
decision making. The relationship between the increasing use of such
managerial technologies and traditional forms of representative
democracy is, however, deeply ambiguous. Participation raises concerns
about who is to participate, at what level of decision making, and on
whose terms. The discourse of representative democracy sits uneasily
with the discourse of direct public involvement. What is the notion of
the public that is to be encouraged to participate? What is the conception
of the citizen, the community or the user that is interpellated in the
discourse of participation? Such conceptions tend to be delimited by an
uneasy conjunction of managerialist views of consumerism (individualized and defined through the transaction) and professional views of
users (as the ongoing recipients of welfare services, defined through the
assessment of their needs).

Attempts to move beyond consumerist and client-based models of
participation raise difficult political questions. Participation has traditionally been via the electoral process, through which citizens have
selected individuals to 'represent' their interests. The sphere of electoral
control has been eroded in recent years as functions have been removed
from local government and as new forms of governance have emerged
based on appointed, rather than elected, bodies (Skelcher, 1998). At the
same time interest has developed in new forms of 'dialogic' democracy
through which citizens are engaged in various kinds of deliberative
forums. Such techniques present potential challenges to the traditional
patriarchal and paternalistic relationships between public services, users
and citizens. They open up new spaces that can be captured by user
groups, voluntary organizations and community bodies seeking to claim
a stronger role in decision making. As a consequence they have often

elicited deep resistance on the part of professionals, managers and local authority councillors, many of whom have rediscovered the tenets of liberalism in order to question the 'representativeness' of new voices. But it is important to question what is meant by the term 'representative' in this context. What is at stake is an uneasy configuration of political notions of representation, based on liberal democracy, and managerial concepts of ensuring representative sampling in the new technologies of participation.

Neither of these models of representation deals adequately with the politics of diversity. Public participation has the potential to give greater voice to groups traditionally excluded from policy-making processes: the elderly, people with disabilities, young people, people from different minority ethnic groups and so on. But including a representative number of, for example, women in a sample of those to be consulted does not mean that women's interests will be surfaced in the responses. As Nancy Fraser argues, the public realm cannot easily be viewed as a single discursive terrain:

> members of subordinated social groups – women, workers, people of colour, gays and lesbians – have repeatedly found it advantageous to constitute alternative publics. I propose to call these *subaltern counterpublics* in order to signal that they are parallel discursive arenas where members of subordinated social groups invent and circulate counter discourses, which in turn permit them to form oppositional interpretations of their identities, interests and needs. (Fraser, 1997, p. 81, author's emphasis)

Notions of public discourse that are drawn from formal models of representative democracy are unlikely to acknowledge the validity of such counter-publics, and may seek to marginalize any 'oppositional interpretations' which they attempt to raise. The models of public dialogue and community involvement that are emerging in public management typically rest on ungendered and unracialized conceptions of 'the public' and non-antagonistic images of 'community' (Hughes and Mooney, 1998). Differences of interest, of identity and of social or economic position are dissolved in a general orientation towards inclusiveness. The cross-cutting of multiple lines of interest and identity, and of overlapping and competing 'publics' is rendered invisible precisely by the attempt to constitute the public realm as a realm of equal subjects.

Where inequality is acknowledged, notions of participation tend to be subordinated to other discursive interpellations. Many of the cross-cutting issues referred to in the previous section focus on the needs of particular groups – the old, the young unemployed, the socially excluded, lone mothers. Such groups are constituted as 'outside' mainstream society, represented as modern, affluent, active and, above all, employed citizens. Concerns around social exclusion sharpen perceived links between youth, ethnicity and criminality. The focus on lone mothers raises important links between gender, poverty and employment, while threatening an authoritarian set of conditions for accessing state benefits. Each of these groups is constituted as the object, rather than the subject, of social action, and tends to lie outside the body of active, responsible citizens to whom exercises in public participation are addressed. This theme in the modernization agenda, then, raises questions about how far participation and new forms of democratic practice can resolve tensions in the unstable social settlement (Clarke and Newman 1997; Hughes and Lewis 1998). It also opens up key issues concerned with the politics of representation and the politics of diversity. Such political questions cannot be resolved in the managerial domain, however sophisticated the new technologies of participation that are developed.

6   Conclusion

The themes I have selected for this chapter represent only part of the modernization agenda. They have been chosen to illustrate a mode of analysis rather than to describe a particular process of reform. Nevertheless, they suggests ways in which managerialism is being harnessed to a new political agenda. Managerialism is a discourse which sets out the necessity of change; a set of tools to drive up performance; and a means through which an organization can transform itself to deliver a modernized notion of public purpose to a modern conception of 'the people'. But, like NPM, it continues to challenge the autonomy of welfare professionals and it seeks to address the 'failure' of traditional welfare agencies.

It is important not to 'over-read' the changes. New discourses may be little more than the froth on social action: a new vocabulary through which politicians, managers or professionals legitimize their actions. Organizations seek to secure legitimacy by adopting institutional features of their environment – the paraphernalia of participation, the ritual of efficiency plans, the celebration of partnership and so on can all be adopted as ceremonial forms of action which remain loosely coupled to the realities of organizational action and the delivery of services (Meyer and Rowan, 1991). But this does not detract from the power of modernization as discourse. Its conceptual underpinnings render it more acceptable to staff, policy shapers, professionals and managers than the earlier focus on privatization and the outright rejection of the value of a public sector.

So does modernization represent a new form of managerialism which takes us beyond the reform programmes of the New Public Management and its ideological roots in the New Right? The era of the Thatcher and Major governments installed managerialism as the basis of a new organizational settlement, and it is this settlement that now forms the basis for delivering the New Labour government's agenda. The economic goals of New Labour mean that there is unlikely to be substantial change in the focus on efficiency and performance. Indeed this focus has been sharpened and deepened to the extent that it may prevent the other discursive themes being fully elaborated. However, changes are evident at three levels. First, the boundary between policy and management that was drawn very distinctly in the NPM is being challenged, and the negative consequences of organizational fragmentation are being recognized in the discourse of 'joined-up government'. Secondly, the technologies of managerialism have shifted, partly in line with conceptions of 'modern' business practices which emphasize the idea of collaboration between strategic partners, less adversarial and longer-term models of contracting, and the need to build relationships with multiple stakeholders. Thirdly, managerialism has become subject to a new set of discourses of citizen and user participation. This presents an apparent challenge to the 'logics of decision making' on which managerialism is based. In one NPM model, managers were free to take decisions within the legislative and policy frameworks set by politicians. Relations with consumers were governed through limited feedback mechanisms such as market research and complaints procedures, and relations with the public channelled through the traditional mechanisms of representative democracy. The discourse of modernization suggests that users are not only to be given choice through the mechanisms of markets and quasi-markets (however limited such choice turns out to be in practice) but given voice through their active participation in decisions on service design and planning. Relations with the public are viewed as more direct: the discourse positions the public as stakeholders whose views are to be sought through various forms of participative and dialogic democracy. This third set of shifts presents a possible challenge to the role and power base of managers by subjecting them to more direct forms of influence and control by citizens and users.

However, there are limits to how far the new agenda may become embedded. New forms of practice present challenges to traditional institutions and the relations of power on which they are based. The issue is how far there is a will – by politicians and managers – to inscribe them into the way in which organizations are governed. The possibilities of the new agenda are also constrained by the interplay of tensions within it. This chapter has suggested several lines of tension. The requirement of managerialism for devolution and flexibility (required to enable organizations to be innovative and entrepreneurial) is in tension with the requirements of central control to ensure that standards and performance targets are met. The focus on 'joined-up' government and inter-organizational collaboration requires new styles of leadership and management which sit uneasily with existing models. The capacity of managers to deliver business success for their organizations while also collaborating to achieve the more diffuse goals and outcomes involved in tackling 'cross-cutting' issues may be limited. The focus on achieving long-term outcomes required by the new policy agenda goes against the grain of delivering short-term efficiencies. The new agenda offers many points of engagement – even excitement – for managers who felt themselves to be constrained by the goals of previous regimes. But it is already clear that in reorganizing services to tackle the new policy agendas, the 'old' agenda of meeting short-term targets and efficiency savings cannot be ignored – indeed it is still paramount. The government's emphasis on change masks important continuities with the Thatcher and Major approach to public sector reform. The social goals of the Blair government evident in policies of health, education, regeneration, social exclusion and so on, sit uneasily alongside its economic goals, which require a continued squeeze on public expenditure and an extension of the traditional NPM agenda.

The discourse of modernization is still emergent and unstable: it is the focus of continued social and political agency in the struggle to shape a new settlement. The form in which it is realized will depend on the relative success or failure of different tiers and spheres of governance as they struggle to win legitimacy (Cooper, 1998). For example, 'performance' is likely to be the focus of conflict between different tiers of government as the strong drive to centralize clashes with the rhetoric of local control and flexibility. The outcomes of the reform agenda will depend on the working through of such contradictions and the shaping of new alliances between established political formations – trade unions, anti-racist and women's movements, 'old' Labourites and so on – with those seeking to shape a new political agenda. These processes create spaces in which the discourse of modernization can be reshaped and attached to counter-discourses. It may yet be possible for user, citizen or 'community' groups to appropriate the discourses of innovation, participation and accountability and to use them to challenge the managerial form in which they are embedded.

The outcomes are also likely to depend on the interaction of the social and economic goals of the Labour government. These tensions between political goals are, however, partially masked by the deployment of managerial discourse: managerialism apparently neutralizes and displaces the conflicts between different agendas (social, political, economic) and between the requirements of different stakeholders (government, citizens, users, 'communities'). A modern public service, then, is likely to be one in which a series of conflicts must be managed, contradictory imperatives balanced, and new and old agendas reconciled. Whether the tools and technologies of managerialism are capable of enabling public service organizations to fulfil these roles is another question.

References

Blair, T. (1998) *Leading the Way: A New Vision for Local Government*, London, Institute for Public Policy Research.

Cabinet Office (1998) *Service First – the New Charter Programme*, London, The Stationery Office.
Cabinet Office (1999a) *Modernising Government*, Cm 4310, London, The Stationery Office.
Cabinet Office (1999b) *Modernising Government* (Leaflet), London, The Stationery Office.
Clarke, J. and Newman, J. (1997) *The Managerial State*, London, Sage.
Cooper, D. (1998) *Governing Out of Order: Space, Time and the Politics of Belonging*, London, Rivers Oram Press.
Department of the Environment, Transport and the Regions (1998) *Modern Local Government – in Touch with the People*, Cm 4014, London, The Stationery Office.
Department of Health (1998) *Modernising Social Services: Promoting Independence, Improving Protection, Raising Standards*, Cm 4169, London, The Stationery Office.
Department of Trade and Industry (1998) *Our Competitive Future: Building the Knowledge Driven Economy*, Cm 4176, London, The Stationery Office.
Fraser, N. (1997) *Justice Interruptus: Critical Reflections on the 'Postsocialist' Condition*, London, Routledge.
Hughes, G. and Lewis, G. (eds) (1998) *Unsettling Welfare: The Reconstruction of Social Policy*, London, Routledge.
Hughes, G. and Mooney, G. (1998) 'Community', in Hughes, G. (ed.) *Imagining Welfare Futures*, London, Routledge.
Hughes, M. and Newman, J. (1999) 'From New Public Management to New Labour: from "new" to "modern"', paper presented to the Third International Symposium on Public Management, University of Aston, March.
Huxham, C. (ed.) (1996) *Creating Collaborative Advantage*, London, Sage.
Huxham, C. and Vangen, S. (1996) 'Working together: key themes in the management of relationships between public and non profit organizations', *International Journal of Public Sector Management*, 9, 5–17.
Leadbeater, C. (1999) *Living on Thin Air: The New Economy*, London, Viking.
Mackintosh, M. (1998) 'Public management for social inclusion', in Minogue, M., Polidano, C. and Hulme, D. (eds) *Beyond the New Public Management: Changing Ideas and Practices in Governance*, Cheltenham, Edward Elgar.
Meyer, J. and Rowan, B. (1991) 'Institutional organizations: formal structure as myth and ceremony', in Powell, W. and diMaggio, P.J. (eds) *The New Institutionalism in Organizational Analysis*, Chicago, University of Chicago Press.
Newman, J. (1998) 'Managerialism and social welfare', in Hughes, G. and Lewis, G. (eds) *Unsettling Welfare: The Reconstruction of Social Policy*, London, Routledge.
Newman, J. (forthcoming) 'What counts is what works? Constructing evaluations of market mechanisms', in *Public Administration*.
Pollitt, C. (1993) *Managerialism and Public Services*, Oxford, Blackwell.
SEU (1998) *Bringing Britain Together: A National Strategy for Neighbourhood Renewal*, Cm 4045, London, Social Exclusion Unit.
Skelcher, C. (1998) *The Appointed State*, Buckingham, Open University Press.

4

Entrepreneurial Governance and Public Management: The Anti-Bureaucrats

Paul du Gay

Anti-bureaucratic sentiment has been a pervasive element of political discourse for over a century. Pervasive but not uniform. Different political discourses have problematized state bureaux in very specific and non-transferable ways. Marxist problematizations of capitalist state bureaux as instruments of ruling class power, for example, have been informed by a very different set of political assumptions and objectives from those informing certain radical feminist problematizations of bureaucracy as constitutively masculinist.

Throughout the 1980s and 1990s successive Conservative administrations in Britain conducted a range of radical reforms of the public sector that were underpinned by yet another distinctive variant of bureau-problematization. This latter version derived from two particular discursive locales – public choice theory, on the one hand, and contemporary managerialism, on the other. There were, and are, obvious differences between the two – with public choice casting the problem of bureaucracy as one of 'control' and seeking measures through which elected representatives might tame its autonomy by making it more responsive to their wishes, and managerialists problematizing the defects of the public bureau in terms of its failure to work more like a commercial enterprise. However, they can nonetheless be seen to work together to constitute a particular discursive formation. For example, public choice theorists have advocated many managerialist measures to achieve tighter political control of public bureaux, while managerialists have frequently cited public choice axioms concerning the budget-maximizing propensities of bureaucrats who are not subject to the disciplines of the market in making the case for public bureaux being structured more like private sector businesses (Campbell, 1993, p. 123).

Over time, these problematizations of public bureaux and the practical interventions associated with them have come to be known collectively as the New Public Management (NPM) or 'entrepreneurial governance'. According to the authors commonly charged with formulating the latter term, 'entrepreneurial governance' consists of ten 'essential principles' which link together to 'reinvent' public sector organizations.

> Entrepreneurial governments promote *competition* between service providers. They *empower* citizens by pushing control out of the bureaucracy, into the community. They measure the performance of their agencies, focusing not on inputs but on *outcomes*. They are driven by their goals – their *missions* – not by their rules and regulations. They redefine their clients as *customers* and offer them choices – between schools, between training programs, between housing options. They *prevent* problems before they emerge, rather than simply offering services afterward. They put their energies into *earning* money, not simply spending it. They *decentralize* authority, embracing participatory management. They prefer *market* mechanisms to bureaucratic mechanisms. And they focus not simply on providing public services but on *catalysing* all sectors – public, private and voluntary – into action to solve their community's problems. (Osborne and Gaebler, 1992, pp. 19–20)

These ten elements or principles have comprised something like an interacting set or 'system' for governments seeking to 'enterprise up' state bureaux. So, for example, the separation of purchasing from providing was a prerequisite for the introduction of market-type mechanisms, which were, in turn, a crucial means of disaggregating 'traditional bureaucracies'. Similarly, the setting of performance targets was a useful precursor to moving the terms of employment for bureaucrats towards fixed-term contracts and performance related payment schemes (Pollitt, 1995).

In this chapter I am concerned with unpacking the constitutive elements of this mentality of 'entrepreneurial governance', with exploring some of its ethico-political consequences for the practice of bureaucratic administration within the British public services and with assessing the extent to which New Labour's discourse of governmental modernization extends or challenges the 'entrepreneurial ideal'.

1 Entrepreneurial governance and the problematization of bureaucracy

If 'entrepreneurial governance' has one overarching target – that which it most explicitly defines itself in opposition to – then it is the impersonal, procedural, hierarchical and technical organization of the classic Weberian public bureaucracy. The case against bureaucracy begins with what are represented as the unchallengeable diktats of 'the external environment'. Among the latter are included a crisis in governmental authority resulting from an 'unsustainable' growth in public expenditure, the dislocatory effects consequent upon an explosion in the deployment of new information and communication technologies and those associated with the competitive pressures resulting from 'global' systems of trade, finance and production. While different authors privilege different combinations of phenomena, they all agree that the result of these developments is an environment characterized by massive uncertainty in which 'predictability is a thing of the past' and where only those organizations able rapidly and continuously to change their conduct and become more enterprising will survive. Because 'bureaucracy' is held to constitute a 'mechanistic' system of organization best suited to conditions of relative stability and predictability it becomes the first casualty of 'a world turned upside down' (Peters, 1994; Champy, 1995).

> In this environment, bureaucratic institutions . . . public and private . . . increasingly fail us. Today's environment demands institutions that are extremely flexible and adaptable. It demands institutions that deliver high-quality goods and services, squeezing ever more bang out of every buck. It demands institutions that are responsive to the needs of their customers, offering choices of non-standardized services; that lead by persuasion and incentives rather than commands; that give their employees a sense of meaning and control, even ownership. It demands institutions that empower citizens rather than simply serving them. (Osborne and Gaebler, 1992, p. 15)

Quite obviously, one key feature of 'entrepreneurial governance' is the crucial role it allocates to 'the commercial enterprise' as the preferred model for any form of institutional organization of goods and services. However, of equal importance is the way in which the term refers to habits of action that display or express 'enterprising qualities on the part of those concerned', whether they be individuals or institutions. Here, 'enterprise' refers to a plethora of characteristics such as responsiveness to users' desires and needs, self-reliance, and the ability to accept greater responsibility for oneself and one's actions (du Gay, 1991; Keat, 1990).

Thus, as Graham Burchell (1993, p. 275) has suggested, a defining feature of 'entrepreneurial governance' is its generalization of an 'enterprise form' to all forms of conduct – 'to the conduct of organizations hitherto seen as being non-economic, to the conduct of government, and to the conduct of individuals themselves'. While the concrete ways in which this entrepreneurial rationality has been operationalized have varied quite considerably within the UK, for example, the forms of action they have made possible for different institutions and persons – schools, general practitioners, prisons and so forth – do seem to share a general consistency and style.

One characteristic feature of this style of governance is the crucial role it accords to 'contract' in redefining organizational and personal relations. The changes affecting hospitals, government departments and so forth in the UK over the last two decades have often involved the recasting of institutional roles in terms of contracts strictly defined, and even more frequently have involved a contract-like way of representing relationships between institutions and between individuals and institutions (Freedland, 1994, p. 88). An example of the former, for instance, occurred when fund-holding medical practices contracted with hospital trusts for the provision of health care to particular patients where previously that provision was made directly by the National Health Service. Examples of the latter included the relationships between central government departments and the new executive or Next Steps agencies – where no technical contract existed as such, but where the relationship is governed by a contract-like 'Framework Document' which defines the functions and goals of the agency, and the procedures whereby the department will set and monitor the performance targets for the agency.

Thus, 'contractualization' typically consists of assigning the performance of a function or an activity to a distinct unit of management – individual or collective – which is regarded as being accountable for the efficient (i.e. 'economic') performance of that function or conduct of that activity. By assuming responsibility for these activities and functions – both for carrying them out and for their outcomes – these units of management are in effect affirming a certain kind of identity or personality. This identity or personality is basically entrepreneurial in character. In other words, contractualization requires these units of management to adopt a certain entrepreneurial form of relationship to themselves 'as a condition of their effectiveness' and of the effectiveness of this form of governance (Burchell, 1993, p. 276). To put it another way, contractualization makes these units of management function like little businesses or 'enterprise forms'.

As Colin Gordon (1991, p. 43), for example, has argued, entrepreneurial forms of governance involve the reimagination of previously distinct domains of existence as forms of the economic. 'This operation works', he argues, 'by the progressive enlargement of the territory of economic theory by a series of re-definitions of its object.'

One crucial dimension of this process is the reconceptualization of the individual producer/consumer as an economic agent perpetually responsive to modifications in its environment. As Gordon (1991, p. 43) points out, 'economic government here joins hands with behaviourism'. In other words, entrepreneurial governance doesn't simply make up people as 'enterprise forms' but rather as 'entrepreneurs of themselves'.

This conception of the individual as an 'entrepreneur of the self' is firmly established at the heart of contemporary programmes of organizational reform in the public sector. In keeping with the entrepreneurial imbrication of economics and behaviourism, contemporary programmes of organizational reform characterize employment not as a painful obligation imposed upon individuals, nor as an activity undertaken to meet purely instrumental needs, but rather as a means to self-development and individual empowerment. Organizational success is therefore premised upon an engagement by the organization of the self-optimizing impulses of all its members no matter what their formal role. This ambition is to be made practicable through a variety of techniques such as the decentralization of management authority within public agencies and through shifting the basis of employment from permanency and standard national pay and conditions towards fixed-term contracts, local determination of pay and conditions and performance related pay.

Performance management and related techniques, for example, involve a characteristically 'contractual' relationship between individual employees and the organization for which they work. This involves 'offering' individuals involvement in activities – such as managing budgets, training staff, delivering services – previously held to be the responsibility of other agents – such as supervisors, personnel departments and so forth. However, the price of this involvement is that individuals themselves must assume responsibility for carrying out those activities and for their outcomes. In keeping with the rationality of entrepreneurial governance, performance management and related techniques function as forms of 'responsibilization' which are held to be both economically desirable and personally 'empowering'. This requirement that individuals become more personally exposed to the risks and costs of engaging in a particular activity is represented as a means to their empowerment because it is held to encourage them to build resources in themselves rather than simply to rely on others to take risks and endure uncertainties on their behalf. As such, and as Colin Gordon (1991, p. 48) again indicates, entrepreneurial governance makes its own rationality intimately their affair.

Entrepreneurial governance therefore involves the reconstruction of a wide range of institutions and activities along market lines. At the same time, guaranteeing that the optimal benefits accrue from 'marketization' necessitates the production of particular forms of conduct by all members of an organization. In this sense, governing organizational life in an enterprising manner involves 'making up' new ways for people to be; it refers to the importance of individuals acquiring and exhibiting specific 'entrepreneurial' capacities and dispositions.

Refracted through the gaze of enterprise, 'bureaucratic culture' appears inimical to the development of these entrepreneurial capacities and dispositions. The bureaucratic commitment to norms of impersonality, adherence to procedure, the acceptance of hierarchical sub- and superordination, an ethos of responsibility and so forth is seen as antithetical to the cultivation of those entrepreneurial skills and sensibilities which alone can guarantee a 'manageable' and hence sustainable future.

Because advocates of entrepreneurial governance presuppose that no organizational context is immune to what they see as the effects of a rapidly changing, increasingly complex economic and social environment, they assume that ostensibly different organizations – hospitals, charities, banks, government departments – will have to develop similar norms and techniques of conduct, for without so doing they will lack the capacity to pursue their preferred projects. The urgency with which such claims are deployed gives the very definite impression that 'There Is No Alternative'. As the management guru Rosabeth Kanter (1990, p. 356) forcefully declares, 'organizations must either move away from bureaucratic guarantees to (post) entrepreneurial flexibility or stagnate, thereby cancelling by default any commitments they have made'.

While such insistent singularity has obvious attractions – for one thing it offers the sort of easily graspable and communicable slogan that can act as a catalyst for change – it neglects the fact that the generalization of entrepreneurial 'principles' to all forms of organizational conduct may of itself serve to incapacitate an organization's ability to pursue its preferred projects by redefining its identity and hence what the nature of its project actually is.

While there are obvious similarities between forms of managerial and other non-manual work in public bureaux and private enterprises, there are also significant differences – mainly imposed by the constitutional and political environment within which that work is conducted – which suggest that it might be unwise for public bureaucrats to model their conduct too closely on entrepreneurial lines. For example, it sometimes appears as if advocates of entrepreneurial governance believe that it is possible and desirable to keep politics and public services entirely separate (Barzelay, 1992; Osborne and Gaebler, 1992). Because public sector management is conceptualized in terms of the managerially efficient (i.e. 'economic') delivery of services to customers, crucial dimensions of the context within which such management processes occur – the political context of representative democracy, for example, in which managers must think not only about their immediate customers, but about their accountability to citizens, and to citizens' representatives (i.e. elected legislators) – can fall below the horizon of visibility.

As advocates of entrepreneurial governance often appear incapable of conceptualizing public bureaux in anything other than negative terms, they cannot imagine what sort of positive role those bureaux might be performing. Texts such as those by Osborne and Gaebler (1992) tell their readers very little about the technical, political or ethical organization of any actually existing public bureau. Instead their main role appears to be to frame the difference between the vocational ethics of the bureaucrat and those of the entrepreneur from the perspective of entrepreneurial principles. In other words, rather than describing and analysing the ethos of bureaucratic office in any given political context, the entrepreneurial critique seeks to assess the public bureaucracy in terms of its failure to achieve objectives which enterprise alone has set for it.

If one followed the line adopted by Osborne and Gaebler and others one would have to assume that the processes that evolved in traditional civil service systems did so in a perverse insistence that money be wasted rather than from a recognition that too much flexibility in allocating money opened the door to corruption. Similarly, the rules, regulations, detailed record keeping and general 'snaggishness' of the bureau against which Osborne and Gaebler rail were hardly developed with the sole purpose of inhibiting entrepreneurial activity but were seen as a price worth paying to ensure probity and reliability in the treatment of cases (du Gay, 1994; Jordan, 1994). The idea, continually propounded by successive Conservative administrations in Britain during the 1980s and 1990s, that the enormous and comparatively sudden changes in administrative culture that they presided over had improved efficiency, effectiveness, economy and accountability with few if any adverse consequences of any kind simply beggars belief (see, for example, Waldegrave, 1993).

Is it really feasible to assume, for example, that honesty and integrity in public management will take care of itself while the structures and practices that are generally believed to have helped constitute it – common patterns of recruitment, rules of procedure, permanence of tenure, restraints on the power of line management – have been reduced, diluted or removed? Administrative culture is simultaneously a malleable and yet fragile entity and is affected by many things: changes in institutions or structures, changes in personnel, and changes in codes of behaviour. As far as Whitehall is concerned, there have been dramatic changes in all these areas. 'A tradition might survive change in one but hardly in all of them simultaneously' (Greenaway, 1995, p. 372).

Rather than assuming the innate superiority of new managerial arrangements, it might be more productive to admit that both bureaucratic and entrepreneurial forms of conduct exhibit their own particular 'defects' and 'virtues'. The question is whether, in a political environment such as that characteristic of Westminster-style democracies, the virtues and defects associated with an ordered, cautious, reliable bureaucratic administration are more acceptable than those associated with a more entrepreneurial style. That such a question is still worth posing despite the scope and speed of the changes that have taken place can be gauged from a brief examination of some of the ethico-political and constitutional issues that have arisen in the UK as a result of ongoing radical reforms of the Civil Service.

2 Reinventing government: the 'long march' through Whitehall

While there were a number of well publicized changes in central government administration in Britain during the years of Conservative rule, by far and away the most important resulted from the Next Steps programme initiated by the so-called Ibbs Report – entitled *Improving Management in Government* (Efficiency Unit, 1988). This report recommended that many services traditionally provided by government departments directly controlled by ministers should be semi-devolved to executive agencies headed by chief executives linked to the main departments through a contract-like 'Framework Document' which would set out their tasks and responsibilities and their overall performance targets.

The Framework Document would also specify the financial and personnel freedoms judged necessary to meet the agency's performance targets. Thus agencies would be structured to concentrate on what the government conceived to be the crucial feature of public service, 'value for money', i.e. issues of costs, staffing and quality of service.

The Conservative government's acceptance of the report's recommendations heralded a change in the identity of the Civil Service of quite enormous significance. Following what was conceived to be best current private sector practice the unitary (bureaucratic) structure of the British Civil Service was substituted for a quasi-autonomous multi-divisional structure, where operational responsibilities were separated off from strategic and monitoring responsibilities (Corby, 1993, 1998).

In addition to this commitment to 'contractualization' – in the form of a policy/administration dichotomy – the government's programme for restructuring simultaneously involved a parallel commitment to corporatization – to constituting the service providers as essentially corporate managerial entities capable of being separately accountable for their own budgets (Freedland, 1994, 1996). To this end, the Government Trading Act, 1990, made it easier for executive agencies to be assigned and to operate with distinct funding (not all of it granted from parliamentary monies), while the Civil Service (Management Functions) Act, 1992, made it possible for the management of employment within executive agencies to be delegated from central departments to the agencies.

Overall, the government did almost everything possible to foster a sense of corporate responsibility and corporate identity on the part of executive agencies. For example, agencies were encouraged to devise their own corporate plan and mission statement and to elaborate their own organizational arrangements for the pursuit of their particular set of aims and objectives. In order to increase individual civil servants' 'sense of ownership and personal identification' with their own product, performance related pay was introduced throughout agencies while amongst senior staff and an increasing range of other managerial personnel personalized, fixed-term contracts became the norm. Open competition for agency posts, whereby people from outside the Civil Service can be brought into key positions and bring to bear their own particular managerial competencies upon public business, has also played its part in creating this sense of corporate identity – over one third of current agency chief executives are appointed from outside the service.

As a result of these and other changes it is quite obvious that the new executive agencies are affirming a specific type of identity or personality, one that we can instantly recognize as 'entrepreneurial' in orientation, and one that is, it must be said, very different from that traditionally associated with the British Civil Service – where common systems of recruitment, remuneration and organization as well as common standards of conduct contributed to a powerful *esprit de corps* (Chapman, 1991).

So in what ways then might the Next Steps initiative be said to have undermined the bureaucratic ethos in the British Civil Service? I want to focus on just one aspect of the Next Steps initiative – though I believe there are many more that could be chosen – which has had a significant effect on the traditional conduct of bureaucratic office: the dichotomy it engenders between responsibility for 'policy', on the one hand, and 'operations', on the other, and the problems of democratic political accountability that have arisen as a result.

2.1   The policy/operations dichotomy and the ethos of bureaucracy

The doctrine of individual ministerial responsibility to Parliament 'has always been the working convention that governs the relationship between ministers and their civil servants' (O'Toole and Chapman, 1994, p. 119). This doctrine means that it is the minister and the minister alone who is responsible to Parliament for everything that takes place in her department and for everything that her officials either do or fail to do. It therefore facilitates both party political impartiality and the anonymity of officials that is a central feature of the British Civil Service. Together these elements of the doctrine give protection to the advice civil servants can give to ministers, allowing it to be free, frank and open, and give to the minister the confidence that she has the loyalty of her officials (O'Toole and Chapman, 1994, p. 119).

Naturally, it is impossible to believe that ministers can personally know or control everything that happens in their departments. Only the most politically important issues end up on the minister's desk. This has always been the case and recognized to be the case by constitutional and political commentators. All other decisions are handled by civil servants, who have no constitutional personality of their own and who always act in their minister's name. After all, it is up to officials to know what the minister's policy is and it is up to ministers to make known that policy to them. They can then act according to that policy. If the policy leads to political problems then clearly that is a matter for the minister. If the civil servants make a mistake they are subject to internal disciplinary procedures. 'In all circumstances, however, external accountability is to Parliament' (O'Toole and Chapman, 1994, p. 121).

This is not to say that there have been no problems with the doctrine of ministerial responsibility. Events such as the Westland Affair, the Ponting Affair, the Lewis case and the Arms for Iraq scandal have indicated that, when it suits them, ministers can use constitutional conventions for ambiguous ends and are only too happy to hide behind their officials (O'Toole, 1997, 1998). By and large, though, despite doubts about the way ministers have discharged their duties to Parliament, it is true to say that the doctrine of ministerial responsibility was kept intact, that is, until the onset of the Next Steps initiative. As O'Toole and Chapman have argued:

> even the introduction of the relatively influential departmental select committee system of the House of Commons did not undermine the doctrine that it was ministers who answered to parliament and it was ministers who were the public manifestations of their departments, civil servants remained largely anonymous, ministers took both the credit and the blame for the actions of those civil servants and citizens knew where the buck stopped. Next Steps has made all of this less clear. (O'Toole and Chapman, 1994, p. 119)

According to its authors, one of the crucial aims of the Next Steps programme was to separate the spheres of influence and tasks of politicians and bureaucrats, with the latter becoming defined primarily as managers. This means at central government level excluding ministers from the day-to-day management of services, allowing them to concentrate on the development of sound policy and thus enabling the bureaucrats to get on with what they should have been doing all along: that is managing. In other words, once the goals and objectives have been set it's just a matter of 'staying close to the customer' as in any other business context. Service delivery is thus 'depoliticized', as it should be. The quasi-contractual relationships between ministers and the agencies which their departments sponsor allow the ministers to monitor those agencies to ensure that they are operating within the limits set. Ministers are still formally accountable to Parliament for the policies and the

frameworks within which the policies are carried out but not for operational matters, which are the responsibility of the agencies. Such a
dichotomy it is argued adds 'transparency' to the accountability process
(Goldsworthy, 1991; Butler, 1994).

This sounds all very sensible, but a nagging question remains. Where
does policy end and administration begin and who decides? One thing
is worth noting from the outset. The convention of ministerial responsibility never required that ministers should be the policy makers and
officials merely the advisers and administrators. This is because policy
making and administration are not, in practice, separable types of
activity. There is, for example, considerable historical evidence that
throughout the life of the Westminster conventions – i.e. those conventions derived from the British parliamentary system – civil servants,
particularly senior ones, have been called upon to make policy decisions
sometimes because their minister was otherwise engaged but also partly
by virtue of their unchallengeable experience and judgement. However,
there are policy implications in the work of civil servants throughout the
organizational chain (Baker, 1971; Chapman, 1988).

As Parker (1993, p. 70), for example, has argued, 'what we have in
legislation are statements of greater or lesser generality, which become
meaningful only in application to particular cases'. As only a small
portion of such applications can be directly handled by responsible
representatives the rest have to be handled by officials. The imprecision
of the original statements of purpose inevitably leave some margin for
discretion to ministers and officials – a margin which may permeate to
very low levels of the administrative hierarchy. Anyone with discretion
helps to determine policy. Furthermore there is the reverse process,
equally inevitable, and even more completely beyond the scope of such
a simple dichotomy, whereby officials, in the course of their duties, play
a part in the deliberate formulation of new purposes, in so far as
experience in administering a 'policy' suggests or leads to new ways of
improving or modifying it (Parker, 1993: 70–1).

If the policy/administration dichotomy can be seen to be a discredited way of conceptualizing the relationship between the work of
ministers and that of civil servants under Westminster conventions,
what does its concerted operationalization through the agency system
mean for the doctrine of ministerial responsibility and the constitutional
role of civil servants?

Put somewhat cynically, it means that Next Steps agencies are the
ideal organizational innovation for ministers. Because ministers still
retain formal accountability to Parliament for the conduct of policy and
yet are simultaneously able to decide what is and what is not a policy
issue, they are now in a position 'both to have their cake and eat it'
(O'Toole and Chapman, 1994: 120). This makes the task of parliamentary
scrutiny that much harder, as ministers are able to side-step criticism on
the floor of the house by redirecting questions to agency chief executives

as they see fit. As the well-publicized cases involving the Child Support Agency and the Prison Service have indicated, ministers have played a major role in both the strategic and the operational management of agencies, yet they have had more or less *carte blanche* to refuse to answer parliamentary questions about the work of those agencies if they see fit. There can be no doubt that the policy/administration dichotomy has increased the power of ministers but at the expense of weakened parliamentary accountability (O'Toole and Chapman, 1994; Bogdanor, 1996).

The role of civil servants has also been altered by the introduction of the policy/administration dichotomy. Despite no formal constitutional change in their position, civil servants have found themselves increasingly taking on the role of politician as well as that of manager as ministers refuse to answer questions on issues they define as 'operational' while still interfering in the day-to-day running of agencies (Lewis, 1997). Because policy and administration are not easily separated it has often fallen to civil servants to defend the work of their agencies in public when ministers will not, and this has had implications for public perceptions of their role. More pressingly perhaps, as a number of examples have indicated, civil servants have been positioned as political scapegoats by ministers who have been unwilling to take responsibility when matters have gone amiss and who have been able to define the problem in question as an 'operational' issue (Lewis, 1997; O'Toole, 1998).

To sum up: unlike previous exercises in internal restructuring and agency separation, the Next Steps programme was, in essence, designed to set up agencies which would be separately accountable in a *financial* rather than a *political* sense. The targets and criteria of assessment for the agencies were intended to be, and have been, financial ones; the emphasis has been on 'efficiency' and 'value for money'; the implicit comparison has been with the 'efficiency' of the management of private sector organizations (Freedland, 1996). Considerable importance has been invested in the appointment of the agency chief executive as Accounting Officer of the agency in question. The 'empowerment' of the agency chief executive is, both philosophically and practically, the creation of the position of managing director of a distinct quasi-commercial or business enterprise which operates as a dependency (or wholly-owned subsidiary) of a government department. What this clearly indicates is that the 'culture' and 'conduct' which the Next Steps programme is designed to inculcate in executive agencies is one of financial or commercial accountability and 'entrepreneurial' rationality (Doig and Wilson, 1998).

As we have seen, one of the main effects of the Next Steps programme is to undermine the doctrine of political ministerial responsibility for departmental decision making through transmuting and fragmenting it into two distinct accountabilities each of which is primarily a financial accountability. On the one hand, executive agencies have a primary decision-making role and responsibility for the decisions they make. But this responsibility in the sense of answerability 'is conceived of and expressed in terms primarily of financial accountability, that is to say in terms of a liability to show that there has been efficient financial management and adherence to targets and budgets' (Freedland, 1996, p. 28). On the other hand, the parent department retains a kind of responsibility for the decision making which occurs at agency level. But the separation of the agency as a distinct centre of decision making means that the departmental responsibility has been turned into a secondary and essentially supervisory one. The parent department has become in effect accountable for its supervision of the agency.

> Moreover, that departmental accountability is, in a way which mirrors that of the agency, increasingly conceived of in financial terms – the primary role of the parent department tends to become that of accounting to the Cabinet and Parliament for the efficiency and good financial management of the departmental operation as conducted through the subsidiary agencies. As if by a conjuring trick, the spell of financial accountability has enabled ministerial responsibility not only to be sawn in half but actually to be spirited off the stage. (Freedland, 1996, p. 28)

The enthusiastic promulgation of narrowly financial criteria of accountability and efficiency thus creates a situation in which, if the relationship between the agency and the parent department is working in the way it is intended to work, the decision makers and decision making at agency level cannot be seen as part of an integrated (bureaucratic) departmental structure, a departmental unity, such as the constitutional doctrine of political ministerial responsibility essentially demands.

3   From 'reinventing' to 'modernizing' government

One key organizing presupposition linking programmes and strategies for the reformulation of social governance under the Thatcher and Major administrations with those currently being developed and espoused by the Blair administration is a widespread scepticism concerning the powers of government to know, plan, calculate and steer from the centre. The state is no longer to be required to answer all of society's needs for health, security, order or productivity. Individuals, firms, organizations, 'communities', schools, parents and housing estates must themselves take on – as 'partners' – a greater proportion of the responsibility for resolving these issues. This involves a double movement of responsibilization and autonomization. Organizations and other actants that were once enmeshed in what are represented as the 'bureaucratic' lines of force of the 'social' state are to be made more responsible for securing their own future survival and well-being. Yet, at one and the same time, they are to be steered politically from the centre 'at a distance' through the invention and deployment of a host of governmental techniques which can shape their actions while simultaneously attesting to their independence – techniques such as audits, devolved budgets, relational contracts and performance related pay (Rose, 1999).

Embedded in these contemporary programmes and strategies for the reformulation of social governance is a particular ethic of personhood – a view of what persons are and what they should be allowed to be. Thus a certain 'ethic of self' which stresses autonomy, responsibility and the freedom/obligation of individuals to actively make choices for themselves can be seen to infuse New Labour's attempts to 'modernize' the British Civil Service as much as it permeated successive Conservative attempts to 'reinvent' that same institution (Cabinet Office, 1999). Indeed, the similarities are perhaps even more striking than that. As Tony Blair put it, New Labour's 'modernizing government' programme is fundamentally concerned with 'stimulating more entrepreneurship' within the British Civil Service (*Guardian*, 7 July 1999, p. 2) through, for instance, making civil servants more individually responsible for achieving specific policy outcomes. Such a shift would be accomplished, it was further observed, only by instilling more of a 'private sector work culture' (*Observer*, 1 August 1999, p. 2) within Whitehall. The political stripe of the government may have changed but the 'mentality of governance' appears to exhibit considerable continuity. So, while commentators frequently point to New Labour's preoccupation with 'community', 'partnership', 'participation' and 'stakeholding' in order to highlight the present government's distinction from the Conservative's entrepreneurial ethos of public sector reform, they often do so without indicating the ways in which key elements of that latter ethos – the modes of authority and subjectification they idealize, for example – are held in place within New Labour's project of modernization.

3.1   New Labour and the 'entrepreneurial ideal'

As far back as 1991, John Smith, then Shadow Chancellor of the Exchequer, made it quite clear that the Labour Party was entirely behind the Next Steps programme of reform initiated by the then Conservative regime. 'Any government will want a Civil Service which is as effective and efficient as possible,' he argued. 'Next Steps provides the flexibility to enable the Civil Service to respond both to changes in what a Government wants and to changes in Government' (quoted in House of Commons Treasury and Civil Service Committee, 1991, p. ix). While this line was somewhat modified as a result of the fiascos in the Child Support and Prison Service agencies – with Labour spokespersons frequently arguing for clearer hierarchical lines of authority in keeping with the doctrine of ministerial responsibility – it is evident that integrated (bureaucratic) departmental structures, such as the doctrine of ministerial responsibility essentially requires, are anathema to New Labour's project of root and branch 'governmental modernization'. This is in large part because 'bureaucracy' is identified with the sorts of capacities and dispositions that 'modernization' is precisely designed to break with – the traditional, the inefficient, the risk-averse, the self-serving, the unresponsive.

So while the White Paper *Modernising Government* is at pains to point out that this government, unlike successive Conservative administrations, 'will value the public service, not denigrate it' (Cabinet Office, 1999, p. 6), that does not mean 'an unchanging public service, a public service at any price' (p. 55). Rather, it means a public service that must 'operate in a competitive and challenging environment. Public services and public servants must strive to be the best, and must make the best better still' (p. 55). Although the public services are expected to imitate the 'best, wherever that is found' (p. 56), the first place they will be expected to look is a familiar one.

As the Minister for the Cabinet Office puts it, 'we need to make sure that government services are brought forward using the best and most modern techniques, to match the best of the private sector' (p. 5). These techniques – which include (yet again) performance related pay, cutting red tape, delayering, resource accounting and so forth – are deemed by the government to be crucial vehicles in moving 'away from the risk-averse culture inherent in government' (p. 55) and in stimulating the qualities of innovation, responsibility, responsiveness, creativity and enterprise on the part of both individual public servants and public service organizations which it regards as necessary 'to meet the challenges of the twenty-first century' (p. 61).

These 'entrepreneurial' dispositions and capacities are positively contrasted with current practices and forms of conduct which, as we have seen, are represented – bizarrely given the constant 'reinventions' of the last two decades – as 'deeply resistant to change', 'unnecessarily bureaucratic' and hence as preventing 'public servants from experimenting, innovating and delivering a better product' (p. 55). Consequently, in order to ensure that the sorts of capacities and dispositions the government regards as essential to 'modernization' flourish, 'there has to be a change of culture. This needs to be led from the top and driven throughout the organization' (p. 60). It will involve revising 'the core competencies for staff and appraisal systems to reflect the qualities we seek' (p. 56). Overall, everything possible will be done to 'encourage the public sector to test new ways of working by suspending rules that stifle innovation. It will encourage public servants to take risks, which, if successful, will make a difference' (p. 61).

While the White Paper continually draws implicit distinctions between pro-private sector, anti-public service, market-mad Tories and the more public service oriented, 'what matters is what works' New Labour 'vision', one could nonetheless be forgiven for thinking that many of the tropes of 'modernization' sound remarkably familiar. Consider the example of what the White Paper refers to as 'risk aversion'. The White Paper says that 'the cultures of Parliament, Ministers and the civil service create a situation in which the rewards for success are limited and penalties for failure can be severe. The system is too often risk averse. As a result, Ministers and public servants can be slow to take advantage of new opportunities' (p. 11). The government therefore proposes removing 'unnecessary bureaucracy' in order to encourage public servants to 'experiment with new ways of working' so that they might become 'as innovative and entrepreneurial as anyone outside government' (p. 11).

You may feel you have heard these sentiments somewhere before. You would not be wrong. One place is the Next Steps report (Efficiency Unit, 1988) which paved the way for 'agencification'. For example, the Next Steps report said there was in government 'a lack of clear and accountable management responsibility' (para. 14); and that senior managers must be prepared 'to show real qualities of leadership and to take and defend unpopular decisions' (para. 35). When the Next Steps report was published, questions were asked about what exactly these sentiments meant and about their degree of fit with existing consti-tutional practice – with the convention of ministerial responsibility, for example (Chapman, 1988; Bogdanor, 1996). In the event, these serious questions received no convincing answers but they acted as markers for what, as we saw earlier, became real problems associated with agenci-fication. Some enthusiasts, not only from the major political parties but also amongst civil servants themselves, seemed somewhat muted or changed their views when the main difficulty that emerged from the creation of the Next Steps agencies was precisely this point about risk and accountability in the context of British constitutional 'regime values' (Chapman, 1999, p. 15).

Like the Conservatives before them, and in the manner commended by Osborne and Gaebler, New Labour wants 'to foster a new entre-preneurial spirit' (Tony Blair, foreword, DTI, 1998, p. 5) amongst public servants. It is, by its own admission, in the game of encouraging 'public servants to take risks, which if successful, will make a difference' (Cabinet Office, 1999, p. 61). But what if they fail? As Jordan puts it:

> Were the Crown Agents 'entrepreneurial'? Was the BCCI money borrowing/ relending scheme of the Western Isles Council not a perfect example of risk-taking? What of the creative accounting of local authorities such as Hammersmith that ended up in the courts when losses were made? Wasn't the taking of the student games to Sheffield a commendable piece of innovation and enterprise? (Jordan, 1994, p. 274)

One only has to mention these very few cases to appreciate that extreme care should be taken in 'modernizing' in this particular direction.

The *Modernising Government* White Paper (Cabinet Office, 1999) says that 'through bureaucracy and an attachment to existing practices for their own sake', public servants have had their creativity, initiative and enterprise stifled (p. 57). The assumption is that 'red tape and established procedure' should be suspended and public servants given the opportunity to experiment to see what works best (p. 11). The sentiments expressed here echo Osborne and Gaebler's (1992) *cri de coeur* for a legitimate 'permission to fail' on the part of 'entrepreneurial' public sector employees. They quote approvingly Florida's *State Management Guide*: 'If a department or program does not have the opportunity to do things wrong, authority is lacking to do them right'(p. 136). This seems politically incredible, even suicidal. Could a politician with any hope of re-election realistically expect to maintain voter confidence in the light of some policy disaster or the other by pleading 'experiment'? Moreover, how does such permission to fail or right to experiment sit with New Labour's obsession with performance measurement and accountability? Less than a page after stating that public servants should be less 'risk-averse' and more experimental the *Modernising Government* White Paper is demanding the linking of job tenure to performance and the achievement of specified objectives (Cabinet Office, 1999, pp. 61–2).

As Jordan (1994, p. 274) points out, 'the argument here is not that when bureaucratic government fails we should label it "entrepreneurial"', but that the disadvantages of cautious, predictable, ordered bureaucratic administration may ultimately be more *politically* acceptable than the disadvantages of a more entrepreneurial, experimental, creative and risky style.

4   Concluding comments

New Labour's discourse of 'modernization' places the 'entrepreneurial ideal' at the centre of its proposed reforms of the public services in much the same way as its Conservative predecessors placed it at the centre of theirs. A crucial feature of this ideal is an assumption that no organizational context is immune to the uncertainties of unrelenting 'change' and that as a result, all organizations – public, private and voluntary – need to develop similar norms and techniques of conduct, for without so doing they will not survive (du Gay, 1996). As the Prime Minister put it,

> the modern world is swept by change. . . . In Government, in business, in our universities and throughout society we must do much more to foster a new entrepreneurial spirit: equipping ourselves for the long term, prepared to seize opportunities, committed to constant innovation and improved performance. (Foreword, DTI, 1998, p. 5)

While such insistent singularity has obvious attractions – offering as it does an easily graspable narrative that can act as a catalyst of transformation – it does tend towards an approach to management that has proven, historically, at best questionable. For even if one accepts that there may be some generic management principles that are 'universally' applicable (and that is a cosmic 'if') they are always applied in a specific context, including a value context. The nature of the management task, and the appropriateness of the management method deployed, can be defined only in relation to the objectives of the organization being managed, the values to be upheld by its managers as determined by its governors and the status of its relationships with its users, whether citizens, clients, consumers or customers. In this sense, as Rohr (1988, p. 167) indicates, management is best understood as a 'function of regime and not as a universal science'.

As I argued earlier, while there are undoubted similarities between forms of managerial and other non-manual work in public bureaux and commercial enterprises, there are also significant differences in regime values – mainly imposed by the constitutional and political environment within which public governmental work is conducted – which may make it highly undesirable for public officials to model their conduct too closely on that of their private sector counterparts – no matter how 'hybridized' a form such imitation may take. For while state bureaucrats bear a real responsibility for the efficient and effective use of resources at their disposal and to this end should be ready and able to use such methods of management as will offer the best prospect of optimal performance, their function cannot be exhaustively defined in such terms. Because a system of representative government requires officials to act as custodians of the constitutional values it embodies, it cannot frame the role of bureaucrats solely in terms of efficient management, performance, responsiveness and securing results. The pursuit of better management in government, no matter how important it might be in and of itself, has to recognize the constitutional and political limits to which it is subject.

Simply representing the public bureaucracy as an inefficient, unresponsive, outmoded or conservative form of organization fails to take account of the crucial ethical and political role the bureaucracy may play. If bureaucracy is to be reduced and an entrepreneurial style of management adopted, then it must be recognized that while performance indicators may be achieved and achieved quickly and 'economic efficiency' might be improved, in the short term at least, the longer-term costs associated with this apparent 'securing of results' may well include antipathy to corruption, fairness, probity and reliability in the treatment of cases and other forms of conduct that were taken somewhat for granted under traditional arrangements. As Chapman has argued:

> When attention is focused on public sector management as distinct from management in other contexts, a distinctively bureaucratic type of organization, with accountability both hierarchically and to elected representatives,

may mean that far from being inefficient it is in fact the most suitable type of organization. . . . Consequently, regarding bureaucracy as an inefficient type of organization may reflect a superficial understanding of bureaucracy and, perhaps, a blinkered appreciation of public sector management. Bureaucracy may be more expensive than other types of organization but that is not surprising when democracy is not necessarily the cheapest form of government. (Chapman, 1991, p. 17)

We are in no danger of forgetting the disasters to which bureaucracies are prone if we remind ourselves every now and again of the threats – including those posed by overly enthusiastic proposals for 'modernization' – against which they offer protection. After all, as Dunleavy and Hood (1994, p. 16) have argued, what's at stake in these reforms are not just 'bread and butter issues of operations, costs and short-term response. Ultimately, the issues involved are constitutional, in that they affect the foundations of political life and capacity.'

References

Baker, R. (1971) 'Organization theory and the public sector', in Chapman, R.A. and Dunsire, A. (eds) *Style in Administration*, London, Allen and Unwin.

Barzelay, M. (1992) *Breaking through Bureaucracy*, Berkeley, University of California Press.

Bogdanor, V. (1996) 'A threat to democracy?' in Barberis, P. (ed.) *The Whitehall Reader*, Milton Keynes, Open University Press, pp. 195–7.

Burchell, G. (1993) 'Liberal government and techniques of the self', *Economy and Society*, 22 (3), pp. 266–82.

Butler, R. (1994) 'Reinventing British government', *Public Administration*, 72, pp. 263–70.

Cabinet Office (1999) *Modernising Government*, Cm 4310, London, HMSO.

Campbell, C. (1993) 'Public service and democratic accountability', in Chapman, R.A. (ed.) *Ethics in Public Service*, Edinburgh, Edinburgh University Press.

Champy, G. (1995) *Reengineering Management*, London, HarperCollins.

Chapman, R.A. (1988) 'The art of darkness', inaugural lecture, University of Durham, Durham.

Chapman, R.A. (1991) 'Concepts and issues in public sector reform: the experience of the United Kingdom in the 1980s', *Public Policy and Administration*, 6 (2), pp. 1–19.

Chapman, R.A. (1999) 'The importance of *Modernising Government*', *Teaching Public Administration*, 19 (1), pp. 1–18.

Corby, S. (1993) 'How big a step is Next Steps? Industrial relations developments in the Civil Service executive agencies', *Human Resource Management Journal*, 4 (2), pp. 52–69.

Corby, S. (1998) 'Industrial relations in Civil Service agencies: transition or transformation?' *Industrial Relations Journal*, 29 (3), pp. 194–206.

Department of Trade and Industry (1998) *Our Competitive Future: Building the Knowledge Driven Economy*, Cm 4176, London, Stationery Office.

Doig, A. and Wilson, J. (1998) 'What price new public management?' *Political Quarterly*, 69 (3), pp. 267–76.

du Gay, P. (1991) 'Enterprise culture and the ideology of excellence', *New Formations*, 13, pp. 45–61.

du Gay, P. (1994) 'Making up managers: bureaucracy, enterprise and the liberal art of separation', *British Journal of Sociology*, 45 (4), pp. 655–74.

du Gay, P. (1996) *Consumption and Identity at Work*, London, Sage.

Dunleavy, P. and Hood, C. (1994) 'From old public administration to new public management', *Public Money and Management*, 14 (3), pp. 9–16.

Efficiency Unit (1988) *Improving Management in Government: The Next Steps*, London, HMSO.

Freedland, M. (1994) 'Government by contract and public law', *Public Law*, Spring, pp. 86–104.

Freedland, M. (1996) 'The rule against delegation and the Carltona doctrine in an agency context', *Public Law*, Summer, pp. 19–30.

Goldsworthy, D. (1991) *Setting up Next Steps*, London, HMSO.

Gordon, C. (1991) 'Governmental rationality: an introduction', in Burchell, G. and Miller, P. (eds) *The Foucault Effect*, Brighton, Harvester Wheatsheaf, pp. 1–51.

Greenaway, J. (1995) 'Having the bun and the halfpenny: can old public service survive in the new Whitehall?' *Public Administration*, 73, pp. 357–74.

House of Commons Treasury and Civil Service Committee (1991) *The Next Steps Initiative: Seventh Report [from the] Treasury and Civil Service Committee, Session 1990–91*, HC 1990–91.496, London, HMSO.

Jordan, G. (1994) 'Re-inventing government: but will it work?' *Public Administration*, 72, pp. 21–35.

Kanter, R. (1990) *When Giants Learn to Dance*, London, Unwin Hyman.

Keat, R. (1990) 'Introduction', in Keat, R. and Abercrombie, N. (eds) *Enterprise Culture*, London, Routledge.

Lewis, D. (1997) *Hidden Agendas: Politics Law and Disorder*, London, Hamish Hamilton.

Osborne, D. and Gaebler, T. (1992) *Reinventing Government*, Reading, MA, Addison-Wesley.

O'Toole, B. (1997) 'Ethics in government', in Thompson, B. and Ridley, F. (eds) *Under The Scott-Light: British Government Seen through the Scott Report*, Oxford, Oxford University Press, pp. 130–42.

O'Toole, B. (1998) '"We walk by faith not by sight": the ethic of public service', in Hunt, M. and O'Toole, B. (eds) *Reform, Ethics and Leadership in Public Service*, Aldershot, Ashgate.

O'Toole, B. and Chapman, R.A. (1994) 'Parliamentary accountability', in O'Toole, B. and Jordan, G. (eds) *Next Steps: Improving Management in Government*, Aldershot, Dartmouth.

Parker, R. (1993) *The Administrative Vocation*, Sydney, Hale and Iremonger.

Peters, T. (1987) *Thriving on Chaos*, Basingstoke, Macmillan.

Peters, T. (1994) *The Pursuit of Wow! Every Person's Guide to Topsy-Turvy Times*, New York, Random House.

Pollitt, C. (1995) 'Justification by works or by faith? Evaluating the New Public Management', *Evaluation: the International Journal of Theory, Research and Practice*, 1 (2), pp. 133–54.

Rohr, J. (1988) 'Bureaucratic morality in the United States', *International Political Science Review*, 9 (3), pp. 167–78.

Rose, N. (1999) 'Inventiveness in politics', *Economy and Society*, 28 (3), pp. 467–96.

Waldegrave, W. (1993) 'The reality of reform and accountability in today's public service', Public Finance Foundation/BDO Consulting Inaugural Lecture, 5 July, London, CIPFA.

5

Unpacking Partnership: The Case of Health Care

Tom Ling

The idea of 'partnership' has emerged as a central part of policy arenas as different as youth policy, biotechnology and urban regeneration. It is a core idea in recent approaches to managing the public sector. It is seen, generally, as 'a good thing' although very little empirical work has been done to justify either the claim that policies in the past failed because of a lack of partnership or that new partnership arrangements have demonstrably improved outcomes. Commentaries about partnerships exist from a variety of academic and non-academic sources. Collectively this literature amounts to methodological anarchy and definitional chaos.

This chapter first establishes the range and variety of partnerships using a typology. It then places the emergence of partnership arrangements in health care within the wider context of the recent evolution of the British state. In doing so it draws upon discussions about government, governance and governmentality and applies these to the question

Figure 5.1 *A typology of partnerships*

Partnership members	Links between partners

• Individuals
• Parts of organizations
• Whole organizations
   public
   private
   voluntary
	• Formal/informal/contractual
	• High or low trust
	• Equal or hierarchical
	• Focused or broad-sweep
	• Co-evolution, coupling and convergence

Scale and boundaries	**Context of partnership**
• National/local/global • Number of partners • Boundaries (where are they drawn) • Boundaries (tight or loose) • Boundaries (own mandate or given)	• 'Fit' with existing institutional architecture • Maturity of relationships • Legitimate or illegitimate • Resource dependency • Impact/steerage capacity

of partnerships in health care. Finally, the chapter compares and contrasts the Health Improvement Programme and the Private Finance Initiative as two different examples of partnership in the health field before drawing together some conclusions.

1   A typology of partnerships

Typologies are always in danger of forcing a complex and unwilling world into arbitrary categories. At best, however, they open up a field of inquiry to systematic and ordered study so that we understand complexity, rather than are overwhelmed by it. In Table 5.1 I suggest four dimensions through which partnerships might be compared and contrasted. These concern the membership of the partnerships, how these members are linked together in the partnership, the scale and boundaries of the partnership, and the wider context within which the partnership operates. These dimensions should be used to order the investigation of partnerships and should not be thought of as an argument in themselves.

2   Partnership members

My first question concerns the membership of the partnership. The White Paper, *Saving Lives. Our Healthier Nation* (Department of Health, 1999, p. 119) states: 'The goals of this health strategy will be achieved only by a joint effort. That means individuals taking steps to improve their own health, and . . . new more effective partnerships formed at local community level between the NHS, local authorities and other agencies.'

There is, then, an effort to recruit both individuals and organizations to partnerships. This is formally and clearly expressed in the Health

Improvement Programmes (HImP) which we discuss below. In the Private Finance Initiative (PFI), which I also discuss in this chapter, the partners are obviously very different. Where, for example, an NHS Trust enters into PFI funding for building a new hospital, it creates a contractually based partnership for at least thirty years in which the partners take responsibility for designing, building, financing and operating the hospital. We can see from these brief examples that partners may be individuals or organizations, and organizations might be public, private or voluntary.

3   Links between partners

The term 'partnership' is used to describe a bewildering range of links between partners. The definition of partnership in *Partnership in Action* (Department of Health, 1998) seems to include joint commissioning, the removal of the internal market and its replacement by partnership within the NHS, joint investment plans (NHS with social services), improved co-ordination between different public agencies in the delivery of services, and pooled budgets. These potential partners have 'a duty of partnership' which is formalized in a way very different from the informal 'partnership' between the NHS and the individual proposed in *Saving Lives: Our Healthier Nation* (Department of Health, 1999).

We can see, therefore, that partnerships may be more or less formal and more or less contractual. They may be based on very trusting relationships, a sense of generosity of spirit, long-term reciprocity and a delight in the success of other partners. But equally, they may be based on cautious, short-term alliances which will be broken as soon as narrow sectional interests are compromised. Often there will be a lead agency (as with many health partnerships such as Health Action Zones and HImPs) and relationships may be hierarchical with some partners obviously exercising more power than others. The purpose of the partnership may be tightly or loosely defined.

There is also a question about whether a partnership creates a convergence between the partners (in other words, the structure and behaviour of the partners become increasingly similar) or whether the partners co-evolve such that each shapes the development of the others but in ways which maintain or reinforce the distinctiveness of each partner. In either case, the nature of the coupling of agencies needs to be investigated. The voluntary sector, for example, has frequently voiced the concern that partnerships in health policy require a form of coupling which forces them to change the very fabric of voluntary agencies; the chief executive of the National Council for Voluntary Organizations was concerned that 'The voluntary sector and other agencies are offered money to deliver the results but the way in which they do so is heavily dictated by the centre' (Etherington, 1999, p. 16).

4   Scale and boundaries

In partnerships size really does matter. We will be looking at more locally defined partnerships in Health Improvement Programmes but in areas such as research and development in new medical technologies the scale of such partnerships might be European or global. Similarly, part of the rationale of the Private Finance Initiative is that with the globalization of financial markets there are now niche players with a great deal of expertise in assessing and managing very specific forms of financial risk. PFI, it is argued, allows these particular skills to be exploited.

The number of partners is also significant since the mechanisms for aligning a large number of agencies within a partnership might be different. Where there are more than, say, five members with very different constituencies then aligning the partnership towards the mutual interests of all partners will be more complex. In this case the boundaries of the partnership, in terms of members drifting in and out of the partnership and in terms of the focus and purpose of the partnership, may become fluid and shifting. Some might see partnerships of such a scale as networks. It is also significant whether the boundaries of the partnership are given by one partner or whether the partnership is able to establish its own mandate through agreement.

5   The context of partnerships

Partnerships do not exist in a vacuum. They emerge from an existing institutional architecture. Some may reinforce and strengthen this architecture while others may undermine and challenge it. Most probably it will be a complex mixture of the two. An organization such as a local authority has its own constituency, culture and formal obligations. When it enters a partnership in a Health Action Zone, for example, the partnership will require it to do some things differently, or in addition, or even instead of its existing activities. How does the partnership 'fit' with these pre-existing structures?

The partnership is unlikely to bring together partners who have no prior knowledge of each other. The maturity of these relationships, and the history of past encounters, will colour the development of the partnership. The partnership might also have more or less legitimacy. For example, senior officers in the partner organizations might be enthusiastic but the project might lack legitimacy among the wider constituencies of the organizations. Similarly, resources for the partnership may come from a variety of sources. It might be funded from central government, from one of the public sector partners or from the private sector. In addition to financial resources are the knowledge, local linkages and trust which organizations can bring. Some might have a powerful and well-organized lobby behind them (users of a particular health service, for example) while others might have strong connections to individuals in positions of power.

Partnerships also introduce either implicit or explicit values when they seek to align the activities of partners. These come from the wider value system of society but they do so in a very particular way. Both the Health Improvement Programme and the Private Finance Initiative are, in part, attempts to change the values of the partners and we should interrogate these values if we are to understand partnerships adequately. 'Government by partnership' is often supported by those who believe that government by bureaucracy is ineffective and riddled with unintended outcomes. Yet, as we see below, the advocates of such a style of government have so far failed to provide persuasive evidence that this brand of government is demonstrably more effective.

Finally, we need to assess the impact that a partnership might have. Does it have the capacity to steer its environment towards a particular outcome? Is it, in practice, simply overwhelmed by powerful forces or can it redirect these? It could be argued that neither the HImP nor the PFI has the capacity to deliver its declared objectives and this will lead to acrimony and disintegration rather than common purpose and joined-up government.

6 Government, governance and governmentality

The assumptions about the state which 'grin through' this chapter draw upon Jessop (1990) as developed in Ling (1998). They are that the continued expansion of capitalism and the maintenance of an ordered society require many and varied tasks of the public sector. These tasks are not always compatible. Indeed the management of the social and economic systems is inherently fragile and requires constant attention. The public sector is therefore inevitably a site where multiple strategies are played out and these cannot be simply reduced to a small number of causal forces.

For agencies in and around the state, therefore, there is a sense of fluidity and uncertainty as different strategies come and go, different values are advocated and rejected, and different partners become incorporated and excluded. The action of state agencies depends upon their being informed about the shifting wider context, having a framework within which to order this information, and creating reflexive agencies to co-ordinate the work of the public sector. Associated with this fluidity are persistent problems facing decision takers in the modern state. These include:

- How do state officials know what is happening in the wider world?
- How do state officials order their priorities and determine their strategies?

- How can the work of the public sector be co-ordinated in response to these wider changes?
- How can independent government strategies be pursued in the face of widespread inequalities in power?

We have seen above that there is a variety of partnerships, which vary significantly along the four dimensions outlined. Now I want to suggest that these are shifting in a systematic way. In order to explore this I consider the argument that the changing nature of health partnerships reflects a wider change in the British state over the past thirty years. This could be described as a shift from government to governance and then from governance to governmentality.

In 'government' there are political leaders and public officials who are charged with delivering policies through ordered (often bureaucratic) rules. In relation to our four persistent problems listed above, government is characterized by the following.

- Information about the wider world is aggregated and centralized using a variety of statistical and interpretative techniques.
- Priorities and strategies are determined by clearly defined accountable and responsible bodies and posts.
- The public sector should either impose its values on the wider world (as with the welfare state) or it should leave the wider world to evolve in its own way (as with economic activity).
- State strategies should involve either incorporating powerful forces into the decision-making process, or working 'with the grain' of these forces. On rare occasions they might also involve challenging particular powerful actors.

This is a world described by Max Weber; it is rationalized, purposive and bureaucratic. In it 'partnership' has a more constrained role as a supplement to public provision. There is a clear separation between the decisions to be taken by legitimate authorities and those taken in a private or voluntary context. Much state building is concerned with creating and managing such bureaucratic structures.

In the post-war period, the 'government' model peaked in the run-up to the IMF loan in 1976. Then the state in Britain owned and directly controlled the provision of gas, electricity, water, coal and 90 per cent of health care. It was a producer of cars, a provider of airlines, and the owner of oil companies. One third of housing was controlled by local authorities and local government directly managed all its services. However, this model was already weakening. The capacity of the state to deliver on its commitments, its ability to avoid perverse outcomes, its problems with managing its own bureaucrats and professionals, all began to limit the state's capacity to respond to a growing crisis of profitability and rising unemployment. Rising costs and declining capacities combined with downward pressure on the tax base to force policy makers into a search for alternative approaches.

At this time the term 'partnership' itself was mainly used in official documents to describe a changing relationship between central and local government (see, for example, the White Paper *Policy for Inner Cities*, Department of the Environment, 1977). It was a partnership between the national representatives of the people and the local representatives. But it was a partnership to which 'the people' were rarely invited. However, important changes were beginning. Governance arose because of an accumulation of responses to the growing dilemmas of government. Government was at its weakest where it depended most upon the activities of non-state agencies over which it had limited leverage. For example, government could deliver a programme of slum clearance but the regeneration of urban economic and cultural life might require governance. Rhodes described this as being characterized by self-organizing networks (1991, 1992). One of the classic texts celebrating the governance world view is provided by Osborne and Gaebler (1992) who saw the emergence of governance as part of an inevitable and global shift away from public sectors which 'row', towards public sectors which 'steer'. Drawing on our four persistent problems, governance is where:

- It is accepted that state officials cannot collect and process sufficient information to allow public policies to be successfully pursued. Consequently, it is necessary to solicit the support of organizations which have such information.
- Because state officials and politicians are now dependent upon external organizations, they must develop their strategies and priorities through complex negotiations with non-state bodies.
- The co-ordination of policies becomes difficult because of a reliance upon mutuality, trust and a certain 'generosity of spirit'.
- Powerful interests become lodged within dense networks which privilege some voices, muffle others, and are only capable of delivering certain outcomes.

In governance, then, partnership enjoys a higher status than in government. Because there is a resource dependency in which state agencies want access to the capacities of other organizations, the relationship becomes less asymmetrical. Furthermore, partnerships may be a means of pursuing core objectives of public policy; they are not merely a way of providing a few additional services around the edges of the welfare state.

In the British case, a strategy of governance was introduced in a way that privileged a new public–private partnership. The intention was to liberate entrepreneurship in urban renewal, training, the running of utilities and other industries, transport and so on. Patterns of govern-ance in the 1980s were therefore shaped by a peculiar obsession with using markets or market-like mechanisms to provide co-ordination and reflexivity. This was also true in health care. The partial exhaustion of governance was caused by the unsurprising inability of private partners to sacrifice their interests in pursuit of public virtues. The steerage capacity of the state was therefore not uniformly enhanced. Instead, state strategies could only be pursued where these could be aligned with the interests of agencies which were themselves driven by market calculations. This was part of the context of the new managerialism discussed in the edited collection, *Managing Social Policy* (Clarke et al., 1994). What has been happening more recently is not merely an application of managerialism with a different spin, but the application of new managerialism in a different context.

The new context is one of an emerging governmentality. 'Governmentality' includes Rhodes's (1997, p. 57) concept of governance 'as self-organizing interorganizational networks' but it goes beyond this in key respects. A brief consideration of how governance addresses the four persistent problems suggests that it brings with it very real dilemmas. These include questions about how policy is to be co-ordinated, how powerful vested interests are to be overcome, and how logjams and inertia are to be avoided. In practice, governance was about limiting the rational-bureaucratic aspect of government while establishing a new partnership with the private sector. It was also about the exclusion and control of those who resisted this strategy (and, perversely, achieving this frequently involved rolling out new forms of government over the poor and the disaffected). This both failed to deliver on the state's own objectives (for example in urban renewal or training) and precipitated a growing democratic deficit which eroded the legitimacy of the regime.

Governmentality is a response to these dilemmas. The term derives from the work of Foucault and it was a theme he returned to persistently from the end of the 1970s until his death in 1984 (see Burchell et al., 1991). In the sense that it is used here it concerns the colonization of identity through which an obedient population and civil society is secured. The key to understanding it in this context is that it is concerned with making the voluntary sector, user groups and others fit to be partners within a new strategic arena. No longer will such groups be excluded. But prior to their participation in the partnership they must demonstrate their capacity to be good partners. Voluntary bodies or user groups, for example, must be able to demonstrate measurable outcomes from their work, they must have performance indicators, a vision, a mission statement, a business plan and so on. They can apply for funding to help them develop a marketing strategy or to stabilize their core business; there is no need to remain outside the partnership for ever. When they have developed the skills necessary to participate in the new partnership they will, of course, have transformed themselves into a different type of organization. Governmentality is concerned to reach the 'hard to reach groups' because it seeks to transform them into compliant collaborators in creating a more inclusive society. Neither idleness nor cultural difference should protect anyone from the opportunity to participate. This, in the sense used here, is how governmentality works. The 'self-organizing' aspect noted by Rhodes is eased and facilitated by the adoption of a common discourse amongst the members of the network and the pursuit of common funding streams. As expressed here it is a double-edged phenomenon with both an inclusive dimension and a more worrying authoritarianism.

In terms of our four persistent problems, governmentality is where:

- State officials trust their partners in non-state agencies to generate trustworthy information and to communicate through arrangements varying from funding applications to informal gatherings. State officials accept that they cannot generate all of the information they need 'in house'.
- Unlike governance, responsibility for determining key strategic objectives and for ordering priorities is hauled back towards the central government.
- The responsibility for co-ordinating the work of government is pushed back down to more local levels by two key devices. First 'joined-up government' requires agencies to focus on co-ordination in new ways. Secondly, the rules governing the membership of the partnerships are shaped by a variety of arrangements which ensure that the participants have become fit to be partners.
- Power politics, in governmentality, owes more to diplomacy, persuasion and the routinization of new identities than to confrontation and conflict. Awkward and incompatible voices have no say in the transformed debates and (at least in the British case) they can be quickly marginalized as out-dated and out of touch with the new realities.

7   Creating fit partners

Although governmentality today is being afforded a more central role, it has a long history. Looking first at the voluntary sector, it is worth noting that Beveridge never mentioned the idea of a voluntary sector (although he was interested in it as a principle of social action). Interest in it as a sector, and as an object of policy, coincides with growing concerns about the capacity of the welfare state to deliver. In 1974 the Volunteer Centre UK secured independence from the National Council of Social Service and set up a network of volunteer bureaux. Amidst a growing debate about the virtues and vices of the sector, the Wolfenden Report was published in 1978. This established the 'voluntary sector' as an object of policy and in subsequent years we see the National Council for Voluntary Organizations establish a Management Development Unit in 1980; tax reforms in 1986 to facilitate donations to the voluntary sector; Charles Handy's publication of *Understanding Voluntary Organizations* in 1988 (Handy, 1988); the Left becoming more interested in communitarianism and civil society in the early 1990s; and the Deakin Report (NCVO, 1996) celebrating the virtues of a managerialized but independent and legally privileged voluntary sector.

In this history we can see a double movement. The first is the self-organized creation of a network of organizations which come to describe themselves as a sector, which claims to have a unique role, and which seeks to become professional, well managed, and properly focused. The second movement takes place in the state, which gives the voluntary sector a privileged legal, political and cultural status and actively solicits its participation in addressing a growing range of issues.

Partnership is also about a new relationship with the private sector. The idea that the private sector should be charged with any responsibility other than the pursuit of its own self-interest has a complex history but it has taken root with more force in recent years. The schools-industry movement in the 1970s identified a wider role for the private sector in influencing factors close to the firm, such as training and education (see Finn, 1987). During the 1990s, however, private companies came to identify themselves with even wider goals with the concept of the ethical company and the good neighbour (for example, see the RSA's 1997 report *Tomorrow's Company*). In the wake of Brent Spar and Shell's perceived support for an unacceptable regime in Nigeria, the company has sought to embrace social responsibility. Similarly, BP has produced its first 'Social Report' and announced its intention of working towards a new, auditable standard on social accountability. Whether this is the same private sector which mis-sold £4 billion-worth of pensions in the 1980s is debatable but what is clear is that the task of meeting the 'public good' is increasingly seen as part of the responsibility of the corporate sector.

If the boundaries between state and society have become blurred in relation to the voluntary and private sectors, much the same could be said for the relationship between the individual and the state. Consider the public health White Paper *Saving Lives: Our Healthier Nation* (Department of Health, 1999). In it, the Chief Medical Officer of Britain offers us 'Ten Tips for Better Health' (p. xiv):

- Don't smoke. If you can, stop. If you can't, cut down.
- Follow a balanced diet with plenty of fruit and vegetables.
- Keep physically active.
- Manage stress by, for example, talking things through and making time to relax.
- If you drink alcohol, do so in moderation.
- Cover up in the sun and protect children from sunburn.
- Practise safer sex.

- Take up cancer screening opportunities.
- Be safe on the roads: follow the Highway Code.
- Learn the First Aid ABC – airways, breathing, circulation.

There are at least two points worth making about this. The first is that White Papers in the age of government were dry documents laying out a proposed course of action with some accompanying justification. They were addressed to the key decision takers in society. Now they are an opportunity to offer us all homely advice on 'talking things through' – perhaps after safer sex or on the way home from the First Aid lesson. This is the consequence of 'governing by culture' and the style is entirely appropriate to a health White Paper that reflects the growing importance of governmentality. The second point is that this is an individualized approach stressing the responsibilities of each person as a partner with the government. Indeed, the White Paper asserts that part of what is different about the New Labour government's approach to health policy is its use of local partnerships for health with people and organizations (Department of Health, 1999, p. 119). This need for partnership with patients and local people is emphasized as far back as the 1992 document *Local Voices* (NHSME, 1992) and restated often up to and including the *Our Healthier Nation* White Paper (see Whitehead and Ray, 1999). The individualized meaning of these partnerships becomes clear if we consider a response to the Chief Medical Officer's ten tips from Dave Gordon of the Townsend Centre for International Poverty Research at the University of Bristol. In a widely circulated e-mail he proposes an alternative top ten tips:

- Don't be poor. If you can, stop. If you can't, try not to be poor for long.
- Don't have poor parents.
- Own a car.
- Don't work in a stressful, low paid manual job.
- Don't live in damp, low quality housing.
- Be able to afford to go on a foreign holiday and sunbathe.
- Practise not losing your job and don't become unemployed.
- Take up all benefits you are entitled to, if you are unemployed, retired or sick or disabled.
- Don't live next to a busy major road or near a polluting factory.
- Learn how to fill in the complex housing benefit/asylum application forms before you become homeless and destitute.

The point is well made. The example also reminds us that governmentality may be an attempt to reshape the self-organization of individuals and organizations but there are no guarantees that it will succeed. Within the architecture of social, economic and cultural life there are many and varied limits to governmentality. Just as government

and governance can be seen as strategies which contain their own limitations, so too can governmentality. The voluntary sector, for example,
has indeed been fundamentally changed by becoming an object of policy
but it remains a source of opposition as well as a vehicle for delivering
the 'Third Way'. And the past fifteen years are littered with failed
'health promotion' campaigns which failed significantly to change individual behaviour. Equally, companies face many pressures apart from
the desire to be ethical.

So what we have seen is a broad shift in the past thirty years from an
approach which emphasized government to one which included governance and, more recently still, an approach which emphasizes governmentality. However, it is important to note that all three are at work at
any one time in contemporary Britain and it is not certain how the
balance between these will change in the future.

7.1   Two examples: the Health Improvement Programme and the Private Finance Initiative

There is now a statutory duty on health authorities to work with other
NHS bodies and local authorities to produce health improvement
programmes (HImPs). This is reinforced by a 'duty of partnership' on all
NHS bodies and local authorities to work together. Mandatory partnerships of this sort are also to be found in crime and disorder, youth
offending teams, education action zones, and early years development
plans. There are new requirements and opportunities to share resources
and work collaboratively. Simultaneously, the 1998 White Paper *Modernising Social Services* announced a raft of changes some of which were
designed to reconfigure relationships between the providers of social
care and health care. National Priorities Guidelines also enforce a
framework that gives health and social services shared national priorities. In eleven parts of the country the partnership concept was taken
further to include the voluntary and private sectors more fully, in the
health action zones launched in March 1998 and expanded in April 1999.
These are intended by the government to be 'trailblazers' in developing
new approaches.

There is no shortage of guidance on how to 'do' partnership. The
Audit Commission's management paper, *A Fruitful Partnership* (Audit
Commission, 1998) begins by noting the growing importance of partnerships but adds that 'partnership working is difficult to do well and
making partnerships work effectively is one of the toughest challenges
facing public sector managers' (p. 5). The difficulties were felt to partly
come from an over-centralized political system but also from the practical problems of delivering partnership locally. These latter problems
were said to include:

- getting partners to agree on priorities for action;
- keeping partners actively involved;
- preventing the partnership from becoming simply a talking shop;
- making decisions that all partners endorse;
- deciding who will provide the resources needed to achieve the partnership's objectives;
- linking the partnership's work with partners' mainstream activities and budgets;
- monitoring the partnership's effectiveness;
- working out whether what is achieved justifies the costs involved; and
- avoiding 'partnership overload', particularly where agencies are involved in large numbers of partnerships. (Adapted from Audit Commission, 1998, p. 7)

The Department of Health discussion document *Partnership in Action (New Opportunities for Joint Working between Health and Social Services)* (Department of Health, 1998) provides advice for joint working at three levels:

- strategic planning;
- service commissioning; and
- service provision.

In their Foreword, the Minister of State for Health and the Parliamentary Under Secretary of State for Health insist that 'Instead of the fragmentation and bureaucracy of the internal market, we are building a system of integrated care based on partnership' (p. 3). The complexity of the task of building strong local partnerships is recognized but it is still regarded as necessary (although the reasons for this are asserted and not argued).

If we look at what this means 'on the ground' we would typically find an HImP reference group that comprises voluntary organizations and patient representation, health authorities and primary care groups, NHS Trusts, city councils, and county councils (for example, see Cambridgeshire Health Authority, 1999, internal HImP document). However, the Reference Group must be responsive to government priorities and has limited opportunities to establish its own priorities (these are laid down in the *National Priorities Guidance*). Furthermore, each of the constituent organizations also has both statutory obligations and its own commitments. District councils, for example, are being asked to commit resources to health improvement when they have already committed resources elsewhere.

Drilling down a little further into the Cambridgeshire HImP, we find one of the strands is the Health for Cambridgeshire alliance. Its 'Vision Statement' asserts 'Health for Cambridgeshire aims to reduce health inequalities and promote the health of people living in Cambridgeshire and Peterborough through a partnership approach to addressing the wider determinants of health.' It aims to address health issues 'upstream' and to align a range of statutory and voluntary bodies behind a shared project concerning accident prevention, healthier approaches to transport, education and housing, improved health information, Healthy Living Centres and so forth. It is therefore an ambitious attempt at both improved governance (inter-organizational collaboration) and governmentality (changing the thinking and behaviour of individuals and organizations).

It is too soon to assess the effectiveness of this strategy. It aims to encourage partners to work differently but it has a limited range of rewards and threats at its disposal if partners are reluctant. Partners have very different cultures, priorities and structures. They have different constituencies and operate within different statutory frameworks. It would be surprising if the new partnerships for health improvement did not become unstuck in at least some places.

In contrast, the Private Finance Initiative (PFI) is clearly a very different kind of partnership. In the 1992 budget speech, the Chancellor announced it as a new way of involving the private sector in investing in the infrastructure. Since 1993 any NHS Trust planning a capital programme must consider PFI. The intention was that private investment would be used to build and operate facilities which would then be leased back by the public sector. Labour came to adopt this policy in a fairly haphazard way. After the 1992 General Election defeat it was looking for a means to square the circle of improving public services without increasing taxation and PFI seemed to offer a way of achieving this (in the short run) in policy areas such as transport. Variations of this approach had been pursued in Labour-controlled local authorities (including apparently left-wing ones) during the 1980s (and roundly condemned by Conservatives and Labour moderates as the creative accountancy of the loony Left). By 1997 PFI had become an accepted part of Labour policy and with it the embracing of a particular style of public–private partnership.

As Corry, Le Grand and Radcliffe (1997) comment on the PFI: 'there is nothing wrong with stumbling upon a policy, but it can leave policy thinking undeveloped' (p. 1). They go on to suggest that there has been very little theoretical or empirical evidence to inform policy makers about when to use partnerships and what sort of partnerships are appropriate. But if the rise of PFI was not based on a very systematic weighing of the evidence it did have powerful affinities with elements of the 'Third Way' of New Labour. First, and for whatever reason, public sector capital projects were identified with deadlines missed and budgets broken. The Humber Bridge usually gets a deserved mention at this point – the product of political expediency and carelessness with public money. Secondly, it was believed that the private sector could bring with it project management skills which the public sector lacked while still giving the public sector the capacity to 'steer'. Let us consider this claim.

With PFI the private sector invests money in line with public sector goals but the public sector retains certain rights (typically that the facility will revert to public ownership after a given period of time such as thirty years). It is worth distinguishing between two types of PFI. In the first, the private sector charges the users and secures returns on its investment in that way (road users paying tolls on private roads would be an example of this). In the second, the private sector is reimbursed by the public sector in some guaranteed way. For example, a developer might build a hospital and operate the non-clinical aspects in return for public payments. The latter type is the most common throughout the public sector and especially in health care. The acronym commonly used to describe both approaches is BOOT, which stands for Build, Own, Operate and Transfer (where the facility is transferred to public ownership after a certain period of time). You might also read of BOO (where no transfer takes place) and the orally challenging DBFOT (Design, Build, Finance, Operate, Transfer).

In theory, PFI allows responsibility for managing risks to be placed where risk assessment and management can most effectively be made. (In this context, 'risk' has become a powerful discourse for changing behaviour: all health organizations have to undergo risk assessment but in addition individuals are constantly being encouraged to measure risk more 'sensibly' and properly to calculate the risks of being run over by a mad cow against the risks of accidents in the home with genetically modified carrots. The primary purpose of educating the public about risk is behavioural modification.) It is argued that where responsibility for managing financial risks is widely dispersed (as is typical in large public sector capital projects) risks are unlikely to be minimized, budgets will over-run and deadlines be missed. There are some grounds for this claim (see Heald, 1997). With the globalization and specialization of financial services there are also grounds for believing that the involvement of specialist financial services could support improved calculations and controls. The case for PFI is further strengthened by comparison with the historical experience of public sector investment. In the UK investment in the infrastructure has been low by international comparison and poorly managed. It has also suffered from narrow political interference. (These arguments are well reviewed in Heald and Geaughan, 1999.)

The original Treasury guidance requires public agencies entering into PFI arrangements to satisfy themselves that the advantages of this public–private partnership outweigh the higher cost of borrowing by the private sector, since the state can usually borrow at lower rates than private companies (HM Treasury, 1992). Despite this requirement, there is at least anecdotal evidence that the private sector regards PFI as a way of lending money to the government on a low-risk basis with the benefits of a long term contract which is hard to review and which offers only what the public sector could have got through normal contracting of services but on less favourable terms (see Flynn, 1997, p. 119). Behind the screen of commercial confidentiality it is impossible for either the public or MPs to know the full financial (and other) implications of PFI deals. The main problem, as far as the private sector is concerned, is the lengthy and complex process leading up to establishing the agreement.

The political motivations behind PFI are complex. Alongside some persuasive arguments are some clearly malodorous motivations. First it allows political gains to be made today and the costs imposed on future governments. This is despite the fact that the public sector is being encouraged in every other respect to adopt the resource accounting initiative. According to resource accounting rules, the costs of capital should be charged to the year in which it is being 'used' rather than the year in which the money was spent on it. This accounting on an accruals basis allows a more accurate assessment of the cost of providing a service in any particular year (see HM Treasury, 1995; Flynn, 1997, p. 118). PFI might therefore be viewed as a rejection of accepted accountancy practice in the name of political expediency.

A second motivation is that it is a way of keeping the Public Sector Borrowing Requirement artificially low; this has political benefits and it helps to achieve convergence criteria in the movement towards monetary union. It allows the pursuit of arbitrary political targets to distort the allocation of resources to the long term disadvantage of all. It is the sort of financial acumen that would bankrupt an average whelk stall owner.

A third is that it allows government to claim that it is involving the private sector in new and creative ways; it resonates, in other words, with the language of partnership. However, there is almost no evidence that the new pattern of motivations and risk spreading associated with the PFI has created genuine innovation in the financing, building or operating of capital resources. Indeed, the evidence is that it distorts resource allocation in many sub-optimal ways (for example, it encourages capital projects such as the Skye bridge where the benefits may be low but where toll charges are easy to levy, making third party payment for the project easier).

We can see, then, that comparing the HImP with the PFI demonstrates how wide the concept of 'partnership' is. We can use our typology outlined above to summarize these differences (see Figure 5.2).

We can see from this summary that the term 'partnership' covers a wide range of circumstances. It clearly has a function in mobilizing support behind a governmental strategy because partnership working is generally seen to be 'a good thing'. Does this mean that we should stop using the term in our debates about the new managerialism? This is the question I consider in my conclusion to this chapter.

Figure 5.2   *A summary of partnerships in the Health Improvement Programme*

Partnership members	Links between partners
• Individuals who follow the Chief Medical Officer's advice on healthy living • NHS trusts, primary care groups, health authorities, parts of local authorities, parts of voluntary groups and their local umbrella organizations	• Informal links with individuals, formal but non-contractual links within the HImP, and a statutory duty of partnership • High trust at outset (but will this be eroded by lack of progress?) • Non-hierarchical relationships • Focused on health but 'health' is redefined to be very inclusive • Voluntary groups and others forced to restructure and refocus in order to become partnership members
Scale and boundaries	**Context of partnership**
• Local boundaries • Around a dozen partners • Boundaries determined centrally; few local priorities	• Challenges existing non-health organizational interests by privileging the focus on health • Very new relationships which have not yet become mature • HImP is accorded legitimacy • Depends upon central government for resources • Its objectives are greater than its capacity to steer towards those objectives

Figure 5.3   *A summary of partnerships in the Private Finance Initiative*

Partnership members	Links between partners
• Companies, government departments, NHS Trusts	• Contractual • Low trust • Equal contracting parties • Focused on contract • Intended to encourage rapid change in public and private organizations but little evidence to support this
Scale and boundaries	**Context of partnership**
• Usually local • Two partners (concessioner and concessionaire) • Tight, negotiated boundaries	• 'Fits' well with existing institutional architecture • Relationships may eventually 'bed down' and mature • Commercial confidentiality • Anticipated improvements in steerage capacity yet to be delivered

8 Conclusion: partnership and the new (new?) managerialism

This chapter has revealed the sloppiness of the term 'partnership' and the often questionable political motives behind its use. However, this should not be taken to mean that it is either trivial or a façade behind which the 'real' action occurs. It is important for at least three reasons.

First, the rise of partnership charts the limits of elements of 1980s new managerialism. The reliance on contract culture, performance related pay, performance indicators and similar incentives never fully solved the problem of agency: how to be sure that when an organization or individual is recruited to pursue the interests of the purchaser, they do not use it as an opportunity to pursue their own interests. Contracts always have 'gaps', performance indicators can always be manipulated or used perversely, and, even worse, as 'contract culture' takes over from trust and good will, everyone looks to exploit these opportunities more forcefully. Partnership, on the other hand, seeks to address this problem of agency by mobilizing and aligning the values and culture of partner organizations, and using 'joined-up government' in pursuit of widely shared goals. It is therefore an essential part of managerialism at the start of the new millennium. It emphasizes the 'softer' skills of listening, inclusivity, sharing and generosity of spirit. It brings with it new facilitation techniques of visioning, hexagon mapping and work-shops with senior management teams which start with games or singing or other metaphors for co-operation.

But it also brings with it certain tensions. The HImP priorities are largely centrally determined. There is a statutory duty of partnership. There are few if any additional resources provided with it. Yet it is also driven by the pursuit of measurable improvement. It demands evidence of effectiveness not of the implicit form that volunteers have when they sense that they are helping someone, but in an explicit form which can be codified, formalized and used as evidence of the success of partnerships working. Without this, funding will not follow. Rightly or wrongly, there is insufficient trust in either the innate 'good will' of partners or the success of governmentality in creating a new set of motivations and behaviour. Consequently, those in the voluntary sector may feel that they are being driven in a direction not of their own choosing so that they can be 'fit partners'. Similarly, individuals may ignore the messages they are being given in an effort to encourage healthier lives. So although part-nership is an effort to mobilize and align with less bureaucracy, in its current centralizing version it will come up against resistance from below as well as practical implementation gaps.

Secondly, the rise of partnership reflects a genuine shift in the idea of what the appropriate purpose and limits of the state should be. The PFI continues because it is felt that even when it faces higher borrowing costs, the private sector brings a level of ingenuity and focus which the public sector cannot achieve. As we noted, there may also be less dignified motivations. But its persistence, despite the absence of comprehensive evidence to support the positive version of the PFI, reflects a genuine and deep ideological conversion on the part of the centre left in British politics. However, the case of the PFI suggests that this brand of partnership will also face practical limits. The commercial secrecy, the length of PFI negotiations, the difficulty of allocating risk in a mutually acceptable way all explain why the PFI has not taken off in a major way in health care.

Thirdly, partnership is significant because it provides us with a means for exploring the shift from governance towards governmentality. This is not the replacement of one paradigm by another. Rather it is the accretion of new responses to fundamental dilemmas of the British state. The growing difficulty of using the existing NHS structures to deliver the values of equity, efficiency, effectiveness and responsiveness (see Ling, 1999) has prompted a search for new techniques. In this sense, partnership should be viewed as a new element in the repertoire of public sector managerialism. It has important effects both in what the public sector does and in how it does it.

References

Audit Commission (1998) *A Fruitful Partnership. Effective Partnership Working*, London, Audit Commission.

Burchell, G., Gordon, C. and Miller, P. (1991) *The Foucault Effect: Studies in Governmentality*, Hemel Hempstead, Harvester.

Cambridgeshire Health Authority (1999) *Cambridgeshire Health Improvement Programme, 1999*, Cambridge, Cambridgeshire Health Authority.

Clarke, J., Cochrane, A. and McLaughlin, E. (eds) (1994) *Managing Social Policy*, London, Sage.

Corry, D., Le Grand, J. and Radcliffe, R. (1997) *Public/Private Partnerships: a Marriage of Convenience or a Permanent Commitment?* London, Institute for Public Policy Research.

Department of the Environment (1977) *Policy for Inner Cities*, Cmnd 6849, London, HMSO.

Department of Health (1998) *Partnership in Action (New Opportunities for Joint Working between Health and Social Services)*, London, Department of Health.

Department of Health (1999) *Saving Lives: Our Healthier Nation*, Cm 4386, London, The Stationery Office.

Etherington, S. (1999) 'Keys to success of the Third Way', *Health Care Today*, April/May, p. 16.

Finn, D. (1987) *Training Without Jobs: New Deals and Broken Promises*, London, Macmillan.

Flynn, N. (1997) *Public Sector Management*, 3rd edition, Hemel Hempstead, Harvester Wheatsheaf.

Handy, C. (1988) *Understanding Voluntary Organizations*, London, Penguin.

Heald, D.A. (1997) 'Accounting and accountability for infrastructure' in Lapsley, I. and Wilson, R.M.S. (eds) *Explorations in Financial Control*, London, International Thomson.

Heald D. and Geaughan, N. (1999) 'The private financing of public infrastructure', in Stoker, G. (ed.) *The New Management of British Local Governance*, London, Macmillan.

HM Treasury (1992) *Private Finance: Guidance for Departments*, London, HM Treasury.

HM Treasury (1995) *Better Accounting for Taxpayers' Money: Resource Accounting and Budgeting in Government*, London, HMSO.

Jessop, B. (1990) *State Theory: Putting the State in its Place*, Cambridge, Polity Press.

Ling, T. (1998) *The British State since 1945*, Cambridge, Polity Press.

Ling, T. (1999) 'The fragile context of health reforms', in Ling, T. (ed.) *Reforming Healthcare by Consent: Involving Those Who Matter*, Oxford, Radcliffe.

NCVO, Commission on the Future of the Voluntary Sector (1996) *Meeting the Challenge of Change: Voluntary Action into the 21st Century* (Deakin Report), London, NCVO Publications.

NHSME (1992) *Local Voices. The Voices of Local People in Purchasing for Health*, London, NHS Management Executive.

Osborne, D. and Gaebler, T. (1992) *Reinventing Government*, Reading, MA, Addison-Wesley.

Rhodes, R.A.W. (1991) *Local Governance*, Report to the Society and Politics Research Development Group, Swindon, Economic and Social Research Council.

Rhodes, R.A.W. (1992) 'Now nobody understands the system: the changing face of local government', in Norton, P. (ed.) *New Directions in British Politics*, Aldershot, Edward Elgar.

Rhodes, R.A.W. (1997) *Understanding Governance. Policy Networks, Governance, Reflexivity and Accountability*, Buckingham, Open University Press.

RSA (1997) *Tomorrow's Company*, Royal Society for the Encouragement of the Arts, Manufactures and Commerce, London.

Whitehead S.M. and Ray, K. (1999) 'Risks and limitations of user involvement', in Ling, T. (ed.) *Reforming Healthcare by Consent: Involving Those Who Matter*, Oxford, Radcliffe.

Wolfenden Report (1978) *The Future of Voluntary Organizations: Report of the Wolfenden Committee*, London, Croom Helm.

6

Health Care: New Labour's NHS

Lynne Poole

Contents

The impact of managerialism has been felt particularly strongly in the NHS. Throughout the 1980s and early 1990s the language of managerialism, managers and managerialist practices infiltrated all areas of the NHS resulting in both the managerialization of the NHS as a set of institutions *and* the managerialization of the workforce. However, whilst the Blair government recognizes the potential of a managerialist approach to welfare, especially in the context of its wider 'modernization' agenda, it has also been critical of the ways in which it had been interpreted and utilized by post-1979 Conservative governments. The chapter begins by summarizing the main problems associated with the New Right's approach to the reconstruction of health care as perceived by the New Labour government. It goes on to outline the Blair government's intentions in relation to the continued restructuring of health care in Britain. These policy developments and Blair's longer term agenda for health care are then briefly explored in the context of New Labour's wider modernizing agenda. The health care policy developments emerging since 1997, both north and south of the border, are then analysed in some detail. The chapter closes with a critical analysis of the reforms to date, highlighting the tensions, contradictions and uncertainties that they embody.

1 Against the grain

New Labour's critique of the Conservatives' managerialist approach can usefully be explored in relation to three interrelated aspects of health care restructuring: (1) organizational change, (2) the impact of managerialism on the workforce and (3) its impact on the health of the nation and key sections of the population.

1.1 Questions of organization

The introduction of managed markets into the NHS, following the NHS and Community Care Act, 1990, resulted in significant organizational change (LeGrand and Bartlett, 1993) and was accompanied and legitimated by a series of shifts in the language of health care to the more business-like language of competition, efficiency, providers, purchasers, consumers, effectiveness and markets (Clarke et al., 1994; Clarke and Newman, 1997). In addition, managers and managerialist practices were introduced at all levels of the service, not least primary health care with the development of GP fundholding, in the particular context of fixed budgets and with the explicit aim of containing health care spending. Finally, the relationship between different health care players was also increasingly mediated by the market, and by contracts in particular.

These reforms have been subjected to a barrage of critical commentary (Langan, 1998; Mohan, 1995; Ranade, 1997). Indeed the Labour Party itself, in opposition and since its election in 1997, broadly rejected the 1990 NHS reforms on the basis that they increased costs through the growth of administration, overheads and red tape, that they were imposed as opposed to negotiated with the medical profession and other experienced interest groups and thus went 'against the grain', that they created greater inequalities, with those not registered with a fundholding GP in particular experiencing a two-tiered NHS and greater delays, and that consequently they created service disruption, fragmentation and increased unaccountability (Light, 1998; Mohan, 1995).

1.2 Managing the workforce

In parallel with these organizational shifts, many of those working in the NHS were subjected to the principles of managerialism, whilst others have been encouraged to work at the interface of clinical practice and management, or cross that line altogether and become the new breed of NHS managers. The complex and often contradictory mix of both neo-Taylorist and New Wave Managerialist (NWM) approaches employed throughout this period reflects the diverse nature of the health care workforce.

1.2.1 The medical profession

The medical profession's first real brush with managerialist approaches came with the 1983 introduction of general management. This was increasingly paralleled with greater surveillance over medical practice coupled with a greater concern to evaluate outcomes through techniques like medical audit and performance indicators. Such methods reflected an early commitment to neo-Taylorist managerialist techniques. However, it is clear that this process of managerialization was a rather complex one. Walby and Greenwell argue that 'managerial control of the clinical agenda [was] more likely to be expressed through clinical budgeting and the management of case mix rather than through medical audit' (Walby and Greenwell, 1994, p. 62). In part, this reflected the profession's discontent about and resistance to managerial control over medical audit. It is perhaps then little surprise that the techniques of New Wave Managerialism grew in importance as the 1980s progressed. With its concern to utilize employees' capacity to treat work as a creative arena, it gave rise to a more people-centred approach to management with emphasis placed on decreased bureaucratic controls and a stronger focus on the motivation of individuals. In short, the medical profession was encouraged to improve the services it provided through these more flexible and innovative approaches. Moreover, the Department of Health's 1989 White Paper *Working for Patients*, and the subsequent NHS and Community Care Act also encouraged members of the medical profession into NHS management. Such an approach appeared to keep managerialism rooted within the profession and minimized the perception that doctors were being managed from outside by non-clinical specialists who understood little about the culture, ethics and practices of medicine. However, it also had the effect of reworking the role of doctors within the NHS in important ways. First, managerialist discourses refocused attention on financial considerations. Clearly, doctors have always made decisions regarding who gets access to what health care provision and they have always had some financial context within which to work (Langan, 1998), but increasingly this decision making became less focused on medical criteria and need as the salience of financial matters was recognized in the setting of priorities (Walby and Greenwell, 1994, p. 61). Secondly, those doctors who took up the role of health care manager became more removed from the 'coalface', and from both patient care and other members of the clinical team, not least their medical colleagues.

1.2.2 The nursing profession

In contrast to the experience of medical personnel working in the NHS, the highly feminized nursing profession was subjected to more systematic and sustained neo-Tayloristic managerial approaches. In effect, there was already a management hierarchy, a clear chain of command and responsibility and mechanisms for detailed supervision within the profession on which to build. Moreover, notwithstanding recent attempts by nurses and their governing bodies to evolve along more traditional professional lines, nursing practice has historically been rather task-oriented, making it more susceptible to neo-Taylorist techniques (Walby and Greenwell, 1994). However, there were differences in the nature and intensity of the neo-Taylorist strategies applied to the different grades. New grade health care assistants have been most at risk, giving rise to fears about the growing polarization of qualified and non-qualified staff and a subsequent downsizing of the qualified pool of workers.

1.2.3 Ancillary workers

The experience of ancillary workers has again been rather different. This group of NHS employees were amongst the first to experience the imposition of marketization, with the introduction of compulsory competitive tendering (CCT). This was a strategy which sought to control costs and improve efficiency through competition. However, managerialism was important here too as a tool through which to maximize efficiency gains within the tendering work group and thus increase its competitiveness in this new environment.

1.2.4 The managers

Driven by the need to ensure a successful reorganization of the NHS, managers charged with the task of restructuring local services were faced with sets of targets relating to efficiency savings, service performance and other outcome measures. As an incentive, they were placed on short term contracts and were increasingly subjected to performance related pay and rigorous accountability procedures.

The different experiences of each section of the workforce illustrate the complexities and diversities of managerialism as applied in the NHS. However, the pressure to perform was felt across the employee spectrum, albeit unevenly and, from New Labour's point of view, this reflected a culture of imposition as opposed to negotiation and co-operation. Indeed, for Blair such an approach to reorganization failed to draw upon the considerable skills and expertise of those working at the coalface and thus did not serve to get the most from the individual employee. The result was a health service which worked against 'common sense' and was informed principally by outdated ideology.

1.3   Managing inequality

Clearly, the range of managerial strategies employed in the NHS also impacted on service users in so far as they elevated and indeed facilitated increased individual responsibility for the 'health of the nation'. The relationship between welfare, the state, the market and the individual was effectively redefined within a context of cost control.

The Conservatives' focus on the three Es – efficiency, economy and effectiveness – and within that the prioritizing of the first two over the third, served to marginalize concerns about equality. Indeed, inequality in health care access and outcomes was seen to be almost entirely irrelevant to the New Right's welfare agenda, with critics being told that in the real world 'there is no alternative' to priority setting and working towards efficient managerial control. Granted only a narrow range of consumer-based procedural rights through the provisions of the Patient's Charter (Clarke, 1998; Lewis, 1998), individuals were increasingly responsibilized, that is expected to take care of themselves and their families, to engage in individualistic preventative strategies and, where possible, to purchase private health care insurance.

For New Labour, the drive for the increased responsibilization of the individual in relation to health was not problematic in itself. On the contrary, Blair has consistently called for rights to be accompanied by greater personal responsibilities. However, in the context of a growing unevenness of access and an emergent two-tier NHS, particularly in relation to the primary care reforms of the 1990s, New Labour has called for a rebalance of the roles of the NHS and the individual in maintaining and improving health and ensuring greater equality of opportunity. This has been coupled with a demand for the elevation of effectiveness to the status offered to the principles of efficiency and economy, legitimated by the discourses of 'best value' for the taxpayer and 'what works' for the health care consumer.

On being elected into office in May 1997, the New Labour government was faced with the task of addressing the very problems they themselves had identified whilst in opposition. Although they did not entirely reject the managerialist and marketized approaches of their Conservative predecessors, they placed a new emphasis on 'what works' and called for more money to be freed up for patient care. In addition they sought to re-engage all those working in the NHS in the drive to improve health care provision, tackle problems of inequality of access, service fragmentation and unaccountability on the one hand, and to gain the co-operation of newly responsibilized individuals to ensure that they played their part in the health of the nation on the other. In exchange, the Blair government promised to work towards an even more efficient yet effective NHS.

2   New Labour's modernizing project

In order to understand the modernizing project of the first New Labour government it is necessary to focus initially on what has been termed the 'Third Way'. According to Blair the 'Third Way' for social policy is, in essence, 'not dismantling welfare, leaving it simply as a low-grade safety net for the destitute; nor keeping it unreformed and underperforming; but reforming it on the basis of a new contract between citizen and state, where we keep a welfare state from which we all benefit, but on terms that are fair and clear' (Department of Social Security, 1998, p. v). This Third Way is conceptualized in relation to Blair's call for national renewal, itself a response to a changing world which for New Labour requires a restructured welfare and not simply an upgrading of benefits in the context of the post-war welfare framework.

2.1   New Labour's changing world

In conceptualizing the changing context of welfare New Labour draws on many of the issues highlighted by the early Thatcher governments: demographic change (and an ageing population in particular); rising expectations; social change in relation to the family and the gender roles within that; and the notion that changes at the level of global economy constrain the public expenditure ambitions of national governments. However, Blair claims that both the issue of public expectations and the so-called 'demographic time-bomb' have been given an exaggerated importance by New Right commentators (an assessment that the 1999 Royal Commission for Long Term Care agreed with). He outlines a somewhat different set of policy objectives which can be analysed by focusing on two key themes around which the modernizing agenda is organized. These are the importance of globalization and, closely related, the issues of efficiency and the cost of welfare and, secondly, the drive for national renewal which has at its heart the task of marrying values and responsibilities to the notion of rights.

2.1.1   Globalization, efficiency and the cost of welfare

Blair adopts a particular understanding of globalization, reading it as 'a single , uncontradictory, uni-dimensional phenomenon' which gives rise to inevitable outcomes everywhere and is uncontrollable by nation-states either individually or as a collective force (Hall, 1998, p. 11). This, then, is Blair's justification for the continued modernization of Labour and consequently of British society. Of key importance to this mission is the increased management of employees and social welfare to ensure the maximum flexibility, skill level and health of the workforce and thus meet the demands of a global economy. Perhaps rather ironically given the modernization claims of Blair's vision, there are clear parallels with the Beveridgean notion that certain types of welfare can be seen as productive expenditure, serving national renewal strategies and looking beyond the short-termism of certain sectional interests, particularly in the business world. Whilst the 'spin' is of the enabling or opportunity state, the objective continues to be to improve the workings of the capitalist system.

The significance of this specific reading of globalization is illustrated by a number of recently published policy documents, where emphasis is clearly placed on maintaining and improving competitiveness and squeezing out the inefficiencies in the economy, not least in relation to workers themselves. For example, the Green Paper *Our Healthier Nation* states that: 'There are sound economic reasons for improving our health. 187 million working days are estimated by industry to be lost every year because of sickness – a £12 billion tax on business' (Department of Health, 1998, p. 4). The main body of the document goes on to highlight the importance of a healthy population to a prosperous economy. Investing in health is therefore not only about working for a fair and decent society but is also part of the government's strategy to improve national economic efficiency and performance (pp. 12–13).

This particular task of government should also be viewed in the context of Blair's commitment to neo-liberal notions about taxation and incentives as illustrated by a continued decrease in income tax levels, with the recent introduction of the 10p rate, parallel reductions in business rates and the continued reluctance to raise income tax levels for higher earners.

New Labour's policy focus, therefore, calls for the development of welfare strategies which enhance the economy but require rather modest injections of extra money relative to the overall cost of the NHS and the increased and more diverse demands now placed upon it. Hence whilst

Labour's approach draws on a rather different welfare discourse (and set of justifications) to that of the Thatcher governments it results in at least one similar key objective, that of managing public services in an effort to get more for less. For example, *Our Healthier Nation* and its Scottish counterpart both highlight the efficiency gains that can potentially be achieved by a continued focus on preventative strategies which curtail the need to spend scarce resources on preventable illnesses such as those related to smoking. Such a policy focus releases resources for targeting non-preventable illness – seen as a more effective use of funds. Similarly, whilst both *The New NHS* (Department of Health, 1997) and *Designed to Care* (Department of Health/Scottish Office, 1997) commit New Labour to increasing spending in real terms year on year, for example by 5 per cent per annum until the year 2004 (Elliott, 1999), cash injections are likely to remain small relative to the size of the overall NHS budget and may be eaten up by commitments other than patient care (Brindle, 1999). Indeed the government implicitly acknowledges its reliance on funding released by planned cuts in red tape.

2.1.2 National renewal and active citizenship

The second organizing theme at the heart of Blair's modernizing agenda is the notion of national renewal. This centres on a reconceptualization of the role of the state. In place of the more traditional social democratic state which concerns itself with tackling class inequality and issues of redistribution is the enabling or 'opportunity' state: a state which marginalizes notions of class as old fashioned and centres on the nurturing of active citizenship. Intrinsic is a denial that 'there might be structural interests preventing our achieving a more equitable distribution of wealth and life chances' (Hall, 1998, p. 10). Indeed, as Hall notes, there is no 'sustained reference to power' in the Blair discourse, which means that there is neither a recognition of income and wealth inequalities (Hills, 1995) nor a developed strategy for dealing with them. Here poverty is 'respun' as social exclusion, a multidimensional, multifaceted concept which can only be solved through the redistribution of opportunities (to participate in paid employment), managed by the state. Self-advancement and self-investment in 'human capital', partly enabled by the 'opportunity' state which works in partnership with individuals and families themselves bound together in communities, is at the heart of this new Blairite vision. It speaks to a national renewal agenda and assumes a national interest. Similarly then, in the way that class inequalities are marginalized, so too are other inequalities – for example those around gender and 'race'/ethnicity. In this approach the nation and 'the people' are understood as undifferentiated, uncontested concepts.

The strategy centres on the activation of partnerships as if they involve equally powerful players, all striving for the same outcome.

Hence, in the Foreword of *Our Healthier Nation* (Department of Health, 1998), Dobson and Jowell state that the focus of New Labour policy is 'tackling the root causes of avoidable illness' for the benefit of the individual, society and the economy through what is termed a 'contract for health'. Such an approach, which centres on notions of partnership at the local or community level and the management of individual health behaviours, elevates equality of opportunity above equality of outcome. As Sullivan (1996) notes, it marks the replacement of a concern with class with a concern for communities, at the heart of which are individuals and their families. This Jordan (1998) terms the 'communitarian turn'. So, despite the well documented relationship between material deprivation, class and ill health (Whitehead, 1988), even acknowledged by the government itself in its recent consultative documents on public health, poverty will not be tackled directly through an upgrading of benefits on a general level or the introduction of a decent minimum wage. Rather, Blair's approach is to facilitate the reactivation of values and responsibilities and breathe new fire into the notion of civic virtue. Drawing on Christian and ethical socialist traditions, he argues that moral obligation and duty run alongside social rights, and the granting of the latter is conditional on the fulfilment of the former. Citizens are expected to take responsibility for themselves, their families and neighbours. Self-help is central, and the state's role is largely one of managing the partnerships through which this is to be achieved. The spirit of partnership embodies the notion of stakeholding, the 'something for something society' (Blair, 1996, p. 298).

In the area of health care this approach is captured in recent policy documents which highlight the parallel roles and duties of all stakeholders working in partnership to achieve a set of common objectives. For example, Dewar summarizes the role of government as one of co-ordinating and managing co-operative action between portfolios, but goes on to stress that in return the Scottish people have a role to play, as do Scottish institutions, agencies and companies, in both the public and private sector. He concludes that what is required are 'personal and community efforts' (Department of Health/Scottish Office, 1998, p. v). The state will monitor and regulate these efforts to ensure a fully functioning partnership. The key objectives of the Blairite agenda, as illustrated above, are reflected in the NHS reforms planned and implemented since 1997.

3   Partnerships and the NHS

The Labour government has clearly stated its commitment to developing an NHS for the twenty-first century based on the principles of a national service, local responsibility, partnership, efficiency, excellence and public confidence. The government seeks to foster a co-operative partnership between itself, the NHS and those who work in it and draws upon three strategies to achieve these aims: the limited restructuring of the NHS; the continued application of a range of managerialist strategies to the workforce; and the reworking of the relationship between the state, the community and the public.

3.1 'What works' for the NHS

The Labour government has outlined plans to replace the internal market and move from a system of health care based on competition to one based on partnership and co-operation and characterized by the increased integration and co-ordination of budgets and services and a redressing of health inequalities, albeit in the context of a continued devolution of responsibility as close to patients as possible (Blair, 1996, p. 182). Whilst it is beyond the remit of this chapter to chart the historical differences that exist in the organization and delivery of health care in England and Scotland in any great detail, where the differences are significant in relation to the introduction of 'managed partnerships' – central to the reform agenda across Britain – they will be highlighted.

3.1.1 Primary care groups

In England, Primary Care Groups (PCGs) comprising GPs and other primary care providers, mainly nurses, will be set up to replace the system introduced following the 1990 Act. PCGs will work primarily with Health Authorities in the drawing up of Health Improvement Programmes, although they will also consult with providers including Trusts. The Health Authorities will then be responsible for setting the unified budget to cover the cost of financing those services commissioned by the PCGs. The chain of responsibility and of service and financial accountability runs from PCGs, who enter into longer term service agreements with the providers, to Health Authorities and finally to the Department of Health/NHS Executive.

Despite Labour's claims that it intends to phase out GP fundholding, the English reforms in particular clearly embody many of its principles, including devolved budgetary responsibility and a GP role in purchasing and commissioning (Klein, 1998). Indeed on a more general level the extent to which all the main features of the internal market will actually be replaced is hotly contested, given the continued separation of the commissioning/purchasing and providing functions (now called the planning/provision distinction), the continued existence of contracts (albeit in their new guise as service agreements, a term which captures the partnership theme in so far as it implies a process of negotiation and co-operation), and hence a degree of competition between providers. However, the situation is somewhat different in Scotland. Scottish

Health Boards will develop Health Improvement Programmes, in consultation with other stakeholders, and then commission services. In place of PCGs, Primary Care Trusts, incorporating localized groups of GPs, and Acute Hospital Trusts, will then use their fixed budgets to develop and provide primary and acute hospital services respectively, in line with Health Board plans. *Designed to Care* (Department of Health/ Scottish Office, 1997) has thus effectively removed GPs from the process of health care commissioning. These differences are, in part, a result of GP fundholding being relatively less well developed in Scotland (Turner, 1998) and mean that the make-up of local and regional partnerships will vary north and south of the border.

However, despite these differences in the organization and delivery of health care, what is emerging both in England and in Scotland is a 'Third Way' which combines elements of competition, particularly between providers, *and* co-operation. The notion of co-operation has already been illustrated in relation to PCGs and can be further explored with reference to the role of Trusts.

3.1.2   NHS trusts

Whilst Trusts retain their status as semi-autonomous providers they will be granted a consultative role in the drawing up of Health Improvement Programmes across Britain. In return they are required to accept a new *statutory duty* to work in partnership with service commissioners and planners, as well as their own clinical staff, with the explicit aim of providing a high quality service for the population they serve. The state, however, will define what is expected of Trusts in terms of quality and outcome. Coupled with the close and detailed monitoring and inspection of professional activity at all levels, these processes mark the effective management of Trusts by the state (Flynn, 1994). This approach is seen as providing a number of benefits in comparison with the one it replaces, not least that of reducing transaction costs, service overlap, gaps and uncertainty, all of which are viewed as giving rise to inefficiencies. In addition it marks the elevation of partnership at the level of service delivery in that Trusts are now required to work *with* clinicians and in harmony with state-controlled bodies at a local, regional and central level in the provision of health care.

3.2   'What works' for the workers

In relation to the workforce, many of the managerialist features introduced by the post-1979 Conservative governments (Walby and Greenwell, 1994), including the extension of performance related pay for managers (Waine, Chapter 14 in this volume), are being retained by New Labour. In addition, the Blair government has worked to convince frontline NHS employees that not only is their approach one of negoti-ation and co-operation but it is one that recognizes the skills of those who deliver care on a day-to-day basis. This is illustrated particularly clearly in relation to nurses through the development of new pay and incentive packages, designed to attract disaffected nurses back to the service, attract new individuals to the profession and persuade them that Labour's primary concern is to improve patient care. In relation to the medical profession it is the promise of consultation and involvement which is seen as the main carrot. However, whilst many of the reforms introduced since 1997 have been welcomed by the medical profession in so far as they are seen to embody a rebalancing of professional–manager relations, the response to more recent plans to change consultants' contracts in relation to private practice and thus redefine the respon-sibilities they must meet in exchange for newly granted rights, is less certain. This commitment to co-operative working, at least on the face of it, is also illustrated by the elevation of clinical governance.

3.2.1   Clinical governance

Under Blair's leadership the rhetoric of quality is elevated alongside a continued commitment to increased efficiency. Once again the govern-ment, in partnership with the medical profession in particular, has a key role to play. National Service Frameworks and a National Institute for Clinical Excellence are being set up to focus on clinical effectiveness, developing clinical guidelines and identifying and disseminating good practice. In addition, a Commission for Health Improvement will have the role of monitoring quality in the delivery of services, with the power to intervene in 'failing' services where the Secretary of State deems it necessary. These initiatives are being introduced in an attempt to enhance the importance of evidence-based medicine and achieve a better quality of service. They effectively mark the rise of 'clinical governance' (Jarrold, 1998, p. 7), which will be complemented by continuous review and a clear managerial focus on quality, both of which will draw on clinical expertise. Indeed *all* management teams at all levels (Trusts, PCGs and Health Authorities in England, and PCTs, ACTs and Health Boards in Scotland, as well as the national bodies listed above) will have clinician input. Professionals have been well and truly brought 'on board' as part of the process of commitment building (Clarke and Newman, 1997, p. 72). This marks the expansion of New Wave Managerialism whilst allowing the government to present management as partnership – something to be welcomed, not feared and resisted.

Even nurses, traditionally neglected in terms of power and voice, will be incorporated into these new partnerships. They will be more visibly valued and be offered healthy work environments, training and staff development coupled with support for good practice and a role in

planning, in exchange for working to maximize quality and accountability. In this way the state is continuing to disperse particular sets of
responsibilities and duties, especially at the local level, and build stake-
holder commitment while also managing and attempting to control that
dispersal through processes of surveillance, evaluation and regulation.
This approach is not limited to state–worker relations but extends into
the business community and the voluntary sector as well as working to
reshape the relationship between the state, the public and health care.

4   Shifting health care relations

4.1   Business and community agencies

At the level of service provision mixed-economy-type partnerships will
feature. Here, too, managerialism retains its status as the organizing
principle. This can be illustrated by looking at the recent Green Papers
dealing with prevention. Whilst the specific health improvement targets
in Scotland and England differ and lifestyle can be seen to play a more
prominent part in health discourses north of the border, in both settings
the central and, in particular, the local state will work in partnership
with business and community agencies with the aim of facilitating and
managing change largely at the individual and community level. This
gives rise to a range of community-based health initiatives. For example
the initiative on smoking involves community programmes, sparked by
local agencies with the support of government finance and aimed
principally at encouraging and supporting individuals in their quest to
quit. At the national level, the partnership approach involves the
government banning tobacco advertising.

   Such health initiatives require co-ordination and management.
Moreover, they centre on providing a framework of support for individual effort, as opposed to directly addressing the structural barriers to
equality and good health. Of course, running parallel to these health
initiatives are a number of measures designed to increase opportunity in
terms of education, housing, environment and employment. Indeed the
notion of co-ordinating the policies and action of different departments
to equalize and increase opportunities and thus combat the circumstances which affect health is a key aspect of New Labour's total welfare
package. Once again the focus on removing the barriers to equality of
opportunity as opposed to outcome is obvious. Where life circumstances
are referred to, the pronouncements are vague and centre on calls for the
strengthening of communities as a tool of improvement. As such they
are highly problematic.

   Turning from community-based and voluntary sector agencies to the
role of the private sector, the Private Finance Initiative (PFI) stands out
as a clear example of how the Labour government intends to maintain

the central role for business interests introduced by its Conservative predecessors, in the shape of public–private partnerships. In the sphere of health, PFI is designed to utilize private capital in the building and equipping of hospitals which are then rented or leased by the NHS at a long term cost to the taxpayer likely to be much greater than the investment required in the first place (Kerr, 1998; Pollock and Dunnigan, 1998 and Ling, Chapter 5 in this volume). Labour has embraced it enthusiastically as a way to control public spending (and borrowing) in the shorter term.

Each of the examples explored in this section reflects the continued dispersal of provider roles and of finance, though the state continues to regulate that dispersal. The last piece in the jigsaw is the role of the individual within this framework of reform.

4.2 Individual responsibilization

In relation to health care, the responsibilities of individuals centre on the prevention of ill health first and foremost, through a combination of active engagement in healthy behaviours, re-education and moral pressure. In addition, the individual has a responsibility to participate in government and NHS initiatives where possible, for example through community representation on different health care bodies. In exchange they are promised a limited set of rights expressed in customer charters, access to open information systems and a more transparent NHS which guarantees efficient, quality, responsive service provision for all, irrespective of geographical position. Where children and young people are concerned it is the parents who are expected to take responsibility. The increasingly authoritarian approach of Blair's government in promoting these responsibilities raises the question of whether those deemed to be acting irresponsibly in relation to their own health and that of their families will be seen as undeserving of NHS resources and will subsequently be rationed out. In this sense Labour's managerialist strategies can be interpreted as a tool of remoralization.

4.3 The managerial state

Through the growing regulatory role of the state and a continued central role for managers accountable to the local state and ultimately central government, New Labour seeks to ensure quality of service. Under Blair, the state has a key role in preparing stakeholders for partnerships as well as managing those that are instituted between itself in all its organizational forms, the individual and community agencies including businesses. Through this partnership approach Blair seeks to manage and facilitate a cultural shift in the longer term at the individual and institutional level, which will serve the agenda of national renewal.

5 New Labour, new health care

There is a continued focus on efficiency, mirroring the cost concerns of both the Thatcher and Major governments. But in addition the state has a newer, more developed role in the pursuit of quality and increased standards of health care, for which it is prepared to provide more money, as illustrated by recent announcements from the Treasury. Indeed, a concern with the performance of the public sector is much more evident in New Labour discourses than it was in those of the Thatcher governments, with emphasis being placed on the state monitoring, surveillance and regulation of the NHS. This, in essence, is the Blairite hands-on approach to NHS managerialism. Far from a 'rolling back' of the state we can discern an extension of its involvement and ultimately its power, despite the rhetoric of partnership and co-operation.

Similarly, the employment of New Wave Managerialist (NWM) strategies is still very much in evidence, but with a new emphasis on teamwork and co-operation alongside individual performance. Indeed, with clinicians getting increasingly more involved in the commissioning and management of services at all levels these strategies will grow in importance. However, placed in the context of the new partnership frameworks within which they will operate, these NWM strategies have the potential to exclude as well as include. In terms of the relationship between the state, health care professionals and the individual, we can see that in place of the state as guarantor of universal social rights for passive recipients of welfare, the Blair project seeks to act as a persuading and often coercive force working to activate citizens and workers alike. Basic rights are now granted only to those with a proven commitment to the fulfilment of individual obligations and duties. In effect this approach shifts the burden of responsibility away from the state – service users (and providers) who are excluded can be blamed for not taking up their opportunities or for seeking to get 'something for nothing'. They can be constructed as undeserving on the grounds that they are unwilling to invest a stake in society for the good of themselves, their communities and the nation as a whole. Individual advancement is in the hands of individuals once the state fulfils its more limited responsibilities to enable or provide opportunity. In this vision the welfare state acts as a springboard to opportunity – a hand up rather than a hand out (Commission on Social Justice, 1994) – and in this way the state and its institutional forms are recast as enabling, opportunity creating, managerial. What exactly the New Labour government means by the term 'partnership' begins to emerge. And with it comes a realization of the limitations of state responsibility as conceived by Blair.

It is clearly the case that the New Labour government is committed to extending managerialism within the NHS in important ways. However, there is more to Blair's strategy than simply reproducing the policies of the New Right. Rather, the government seems to be building on some of the strategies introduced by the Thatcher governments, while also reworking the managerialization of the NHS in an attempt to gain the support and co-operation of the medical profession and the public in particular. At the heart of this reworking is what could be termed 'managerialism as partnership'. And, whilst this shift has been accompanied by changes in the language of management, the reforms cannot simply be understood as 'spin'.

In some cases we *can* see points of continuity, despite some changes in the language they are dressed up in – a simple rephrasing of essentially Thatcherite strategies. Elsewhere, as in, for example, *The New NHS* (Department of Health, 1997), we can see perhaps a genuine effort to work 'with the grain' and thus move away from New Right approaches. However, these new managerialist strategies bring with them their own contradictions, uncertainties and potential conflicts. The questions we are left with then are, how successful will such a strategy be? What are its key strengths and weaknesses? And what problems do the reforms leave unsolved?

6 Health care partnerships under scrutiny

6.1 Sustaining partnerships

How meaningful the involvement of stakeholders will be is contested. It will probably be incredibly uneven and will need to be seen in the light of a continued concern to increase efficiency. The 'spin' is of accountability, joint working, co-operation and bottom-up change, but partnerships are still both statutory and imposed. The distribution of power within them is still unclear given the early stages of development, but signs seem to point to a powerful state – one which seeks to monitor, regulate and control not only individual professions but also local agencies (Boyne, 1998, p. 47). If Trusts are deemed to be 'failing' on the basis of performance measures, hit squads will be sent in. In this sense the pursuit of 'what works' serves to strengthen 'central sovereignty and hierarchy rather than consumer sovereignty and markets' (ibid.). So, whilst responsibility has been dispersed, the power to ensure the fulfilment of those responsibilities rests with the state. The vertical relations which are cemented in managed partnerships subject NHS organizations and their employees to the demands of government and those of consumers in more visible and sustained ways than was the case under the Thatcher governments. At one and the same time the horizontal relations associated with the marketization of health care (Clarke, 1996) are diluted through the restructuring of the NHS and the introduction of PCGs in particular. The notion of partnership suggests an empowerment of stakeholders. Yet with a strong, dispersed state how much real space is there for participation, consultation and renegotiation?

Secondly, to what extent can partnership stakeholders force a responsibilization of the government in relation to its own part of the bargain? So far the government has not been particularly convincing in relation to enforcing or managing changes at the level of business, as the examples of the tobacco advertising fiasco and the issue of genetically modified foods illustrate. Ellison (1997) argues that although Blair seeks to match economic investment with social investment to empower both individuals and communities, this is done in the context of an overarching concern for maintaining business confidence and supporting economic growth. This limits the amount of structural change and regulation that is deemed desirable by the government. It also leads to a renewed emphasis on local authorities as lead agencies in area regeneration – the co-ordinators and managers of individual and community change through targeted strategies – as opposed to a reliance on increased funds and business regulation alone.

Thirdly, Blair's partnerships are also about disciplining stakeholders through regulation, surveillance and fiscal control by the increasingly authoritarian state (Jordan, 1998). They are statutory yet rely on the effective performance and co-operation of the workforce. Hence, whilst partnership is constructed as being about creating a more organic set of relations not dominated by the state, in reality it can be seen as a set of relations imposed by an authoritarian government (Hall, 1998). Such a situation is inherently unstable. There is scope for partnerships to break down, resulting in the imposition of 'hit squads'. This may lead to professional resistance and disagreement between state and professional bodies. The issue of 'ownership' is central here in relation to the question of who has responsibility for the breakdown of services – the government as a result of fiscal constraints, or professional bodies, because of their underperformance and incompetence? These issues raise questions of democracy and accountability.

At a more day-to-day level there is enormous potential for disagreement about the co-ordination and management of disparate partnerships. There are significant differences of opinion and method both within and between the professions brought together in PCGs. Yet the government's approach forces co-operation between many partners on the basis of geographical proximity and relies on the self-discipline of professionals and provider agencies to work together for the good of the NHS, which the state then regulates and polices.

6.2 Unstable power relations

Just as Walby and Greenwell (1994) note how the contested processes of complex managerialist changes pulled in opposite directions after 1989, creating pressures for both centralization (through neo-Taylorism) and decentralization (through New Wave Managerialism) on the one hand

and bureaucracy and flexibility on the other, so too will these pressures be a feature of the 'new' NHS. To date, the government's policy plans have been positively received by the medical profession in particular. However, in the longer term they may come to resent and resist being policed by others and questioned about their clinical practice, especially if the pendulum swings towards increased centralized control and professionals are constructed as the problem as a result of their perceived failure to meet the challenges of self-discipline. There is a definite potential for tension resulting from the tendencies towards both centralized control and managerialized dispersal of responsibility, and in some cases power.

6.3   Balancing 'what works' with 'best value'

New Labour policy documents have placed a strong emphasis on 'what works'. However, effectiveness, like quality, is a difficult thing to measure (Keaney and Lorimer, 1999). New Labour may be tempted to use abstract standards in the search for effectiveness, just as governments throughout the *whole* of the 1980s and 1990s used them in the search for efficiency.

Yet it is not just a question of measurement. 'What works' must be seen in the context of a parallel and ongoing commitment to efficiency and 'best value', and more concretely the imposition of fixed NHS budgets. Partnerships and co-operative working cannot solve the problem of limited earmarked resources in an era of growing demand. Thus the message of the NHS White Papers is to redistribute the 'pie' away from administrative and contracting costs and towards patient care (Goddard and Mannion, 1998, p. 117). But, what if 'what works' demands a larger pie? Is evidence-based practice as a new mode of managerialism to be followed as a matter of principle or will the Blair government flout it where it does not concur with its more pressing objectives?

6.4   Contesting the people

At the heart of Blair's modernizing project are the concepts of partnerships, stakeholding, the nation, 'the people' and national renewal. These concepts conjure up images of a united British people and government working together with a shared set of objectives. The main weakness in such an approach centres on the undifferentiated nature of the key concepts used. Blair's implicit denial that there is an unequal distribution of power between stakeholders and that the 'people' are diverse and not homogeneous creates a fertile environment for sustained challenges from the margins: disputes and struggle around the unstable relations of welfare. Government policy is bound by a narrow conceptualization of the nation and its people, reproducing existing inequalities and divisions as well as creating new ones. And, just as the New Right sought to use the concept of consumer choice to justify its actions, Blair seeks refuge in the voice of the 'people's choice'.

7 Conclusion: cultivating negotiated change?

This chapter has focused on Labour's recent NHS reforms in Scotland and England. It has argued that Blair's approach draws on managerialization as the connecting thread between the reforms. Moreover, it has explored the ways in which managerialism has been reworked since 1997 in an attempt to improve the NHS as well as solve the problems created by the earlier Conservative reforms. Whilst it has not been my aim to argue that partnerships are inherently 'bad', the analysis presented suggests that how they are conceptualized, set up and on what terms they are evaluated will have a profound effect on the NHS as a set of institutions and its workers, but more generally on the relationship between the individual, the state and welfare and the intensity and form of the struggles that are generated.

Given the tensions inherent in attempting to sustain partnerships, as conceived by the New Labour government, maintaining what are essentially unstable power relations and balancing 'what works' with 'best value', what space is there for the development and negotiation of counter-discourses? Clearly, contestation and struggle will continue to be a feature of health care policy in the twenty-first century, but to what extent will Blair's team listen and respond positively in an attempt to cultivate negotiated change? The answer to these questions will depend in part on the extent to which New Labour genuinely wants to build a new welfare 'settlement' for the new millennium and is prepared to abandon its authoritarian approach to change. Early indications suggest that we should not hold our breath.

References

Blair, T. (1996) *New Britain: My Vision of a Young Country*, London, Fourth Estate.
Boyne, G.A. (1998) 'Public services under New Labour: back to bureaucracy?' *Public Money and Management*, July–September, 18 (3), pp. 43–50.
Brindle, D. (1999) 'Nurses are warned of staff cuts', *Guardian*, 19 April, p. 5.
Clarke, J. (1996) 'The problem of the state after the welfare state', in May, M., Brundon, E. and Craig, G. (eds) *Social Policy Review* 8, London, SPA.
Clarke, J. (1998) 'Consumerism', in Hughes, G. (ed.) *Imagining Welfare Futures*, London, Routledge.
Clarke, J. and Newman, J. (1997) *The Managerial State*, London, Sage.
Clarke, J., Cochrane, A. and McLaughlin, E. (eds) (1994) *Managing Social Policy*, London, Sage.
Commission on Social Justice (1994) *Social Justice: Strategies for National Renewal*, London, Vintage.

Department of Health (1989) *Working for Patients*, Cmnd. 555, London, HMSO.

Department of Health (1990) *NHS and Community Care Act*, London, HMSO.

Department of Health (1997) *The New NHS: Modern, Dependable*, Cmnd. 3807, London, HMSO.

Department of Health (1998) *Our Healthier Nation: A Contract for Health – A Consultation Paper*, Cmnd. 3852, London, HMSO.

Department of Health/Scottish Office (1997) *Designed to Care*, Cmnd. 3811, Edinburgh, Scottish Office.

Department of Health/Scottish Office (1998) *Working Together for a Healthier Scotland: A Consultation Paper*, Cmnd. 3854, Edinburgh, Scottish Office.

Department of Social Security (1998) *New Ambitions for Our Country: A New Contract for Welfare*, Cmnd. 3805, London, HMSO.

Elliott, D. (1999) 'Blair plans health and education spending pledge', *Guardian*, 19 April, p. 1.

Ellison, N. (1997) 'From welfare state to post-welfare society', in Brivati, B. and Bale, T. (eds) *New Labour in Power: Precedents and Prospects*, London, Routledge.

Flynn, N. (1994) 'Control, commitment and contracts', in Clarke, J., Cochrane, A. and McLaughlin, E. (eds) *Managing Social Policy*, London, Sage.

Goddard, M. and Mannion, R. (1998) 'From competition to co-operation: new economic relationships in the National Health Service', *Health Economics*, 7, pp. 105–19.

Hall, S. (1998) 'The great moving nowhere show', *Marxism Today*, Special Issue, November–December, pp. 9–14.

Hills, J. (1995) *Inquiry into Income and Wealth*, York, Joseph Rowntree Foundation.

Jarrold, K. (1998) 'The new NHS', *Public Money and Management*, July–September, 18 (3), pp. 5–7.

Jordan, B. (1998) *The New Politics of Welfare*, London, Sage.

Keaney, M. and Lorimer, A.R. (1999) 'Clinical effectiveness in the National Health Service in Scotland', *Journal of Economic Issues*, 23 (1), pp. 117–39.

Kerr, D. (1998) 'The Private Finance Initiative and the changing governance of the built environment', *Urban Studies*, 35 (12), pp. 2277–301.

Klein, R. (1998) 'Why Britain is reorganizing its National Health Service – yet again', *Health Affairs*, July–August, pp. 111–25.

Langan, M. (1998) 'The restructuring of health care', in Hughes, G. and Lewis, G. (eds) *Unsettling Welfare: The Reconstruction of Social Policy*, London, Routledge.

LeGrand, J. and Bartlett, W. (eds) (1993) *Quasi-markets in the Welfare State*, Bristol, SAUS.

Lewis, G. (1998) 'Coming apart at the seams: the crises of the welfare state', in Hughes, G. and Lewis, G. (eds) *Unsettling Welfare: The Reconstruction of Social Policy*, London, Routledge.

Light, D.W. (1998) 'Managed care in a new key: Britain's strategies for the 1990s', *International Journal of Health Services*, 28 (3), pp. 427–44.

Mohan, J. (1995) *A National Health Service? The Restructuring of Health Care in Britain since 1979*, Basingstoke, Macmillan.

Pollock, A.M. and Dunnigan, M. (1998) 'Public health and the Private Finance Initiative' (editorial), *Journal of Public Health Medicine*, 20 (1), pp. 1–2.

Ranade, W. (1997) *A Future for the NHS? Health Care in the 1990s*, Basingstoke, Macmillan.

Royal Commission on Long Term Care (1999) *With Respect to Old Age: Long Term Care – Rights and Responsibilities* (Sutherland Report), Cmnd. 4192–I, London, HMSO.

Sullivan, M. (1996) *The Development of the British Welfare State*, Hemel Hempstead, Harvester Wheatsheaf.

Turner, M. (1998) 'Health services', in English, J. (ed.) *Social Services in Scotland*, 4th edition, Edinburgh, Mercat.

Walby, S. and Greenwell, J. (1994) 'Managing the NHS', in Clarke, J., Cochrane, A. and McLaughlin, E. (eds) *Managing Social Policy*, London, Sage.

Whitehead, M. (1988) *The Health Divide*, London, Penguin.

7

Local Government: Managerialism and Modernization

Allan Cochrane

Contents

There is a widely agreed, and commonly accepted, story about contemporary local government in the UK. It can be summarized relatively briefly:

> everybody knows that local government faces a number of very serious, even fundamental problems. It is no longer what it was. It lacks electoral legitimacy because hardly anybody bothers to vote in local elections any more; the calibre of councillors and local government officers is pretty low; the self-interest of senior politicians and the complexity of committee systems increasingly gets in the way of effective decision making; councils are producer-driven and bureaucratic – run in the interests of their professional staff rather than the needs of local residents; local government is highly resistant to change.

This is a story that seems to have entered into the common sense (see Clarke and Cochrane, 1998) of public discourse. It is taken for granted and rarely challenged, but has regularly been reinterpreted, reworked and mobilized in different ways to fit with the range of strategies to reshape the UK's welfare system and welfare state that have been attempted since the 1960s. In some ways, it's a very familiar story. If the official reports and government statements justifying new legislation are anything to go by, then local government has been in crisis and in need of restructuring at least since the 1960s. But – even if the complaints sound familiar, and there has been a recurrent stress on making local government more business-like – it is important to recognize that the process of restructuring has been uneven and uncertain, and that local government has generally played a bit part in the wider drama of welfare state restructuring.

In this chapter, we shall explore some of the ways in which local government has 'reformed' since the 1960s. Three key periods are identified to highlight the different phases of restructuring, which we have labelled: modernization as big business (1965–75); modernization as markets (1976–89); and modernization through managerialization (1990 onwards). Clearly there are no fundamental divisions between these periods, and the organizational and political agendas being pursued in them often overlap, but they are distinctive enough to illustrate how the same sort of story can be mobilized to support quite different policy conclusions, and to highlight some of the key features of the present phase of restructuring.

1 Modernizing as big business: size does matter (1965–75)

The first phase of major local government reform was pursued within a wider reform programme as Britain's 'long' post-war boom gradually stuttered to an end in the 1960s. The rhetoric of modernization which was at the heart of the programme was espoused by politicians and pundits alike (see, e.g., Wilson, 1964; Shanks, 1961). And it explicitly drew on lessons from big business – the welfare state was to become more business-like. But for those of us familiar with the more recent rhetoric of modernization, associated with the Blair government elected in 1997, it is – perhaps – important to stress that the modernization which was promised was of a rather different type. In this case, modernization was driven by a powerful belief in the value of technical expertise (rather than narrow professionalism) and a belief that bigger organizations were necessarily more efficient and effective than smaller ones. The big private sector corporations provided the model from which lessons were to be learned.

An increased role for the state in the planning (although not necessarily the ownership) of the economy was at the heart of this vision – there was what Middlemass (1979) has described as a 'corporate bias' in which state, big business and trade unions were expected to come to together to manage 'Great Britain Limited'. Despite differences of emphasis, this approach was largely shared across the main political parties. The welfare state (and local government within it) would be made more efficient and effective because different aspects would be integrated into more unified (and larger) bodies. So – for example – between the mid-1960s and mid-1970s:

- government departments were merged into super-ministries;
- consultative bodies were set up at national and regional level to incorporate the major economic interests into networks of economic planning;
- the Manpower Services Commission was set up to co-ordinate training for employment;
- regional water authorities were created;
- the structures of the National Health Service were reformed in ways that were intended to reduce local fragmentation by creating regional health authorities;
- new universities (including the Open University) were created;
- the last wave of new towns was designated from on high;
- social security was reformed with the introduction of the State Earnings Related Pensions Scheme (SERPS), supplementary benefit and the creation of a Supplementary Benefits Commission;
- and the spread of comprehensive schools was sponsored and encouraged by successive governments.

In the 1960s, most discussion of local government started by empha-sizing that it handled large budgets and was 'a multi-million pound' business, in order to show that it was an important part of the UK state system. Even then it was recognized that turn-out in local elections was low, but it was believed that there was nevertheless something about the very localness of local government that made it especially democratic (see the summary in Dearlove, 1979, pp. 28–50). A clutch of official reports and royal commissions at the end of the 1960s and the beginning of the 1970s concentrated on suggesting ways of improving managerial efficiency and 'streamlining' decision making, within larger (more business-like) authorities. The reports were generally known by the names of those who chaired the relevant committees: Maud (1967) on management, Mallaby (1967) on staffing, Redcliffe-Maude (1969) on local government in England and Wales, Wheatley (1969) on local government in Scotland, Macrory (1970) on local government in Northern Ireland, Bains (1972) on management and internal organization in England and Wales, Paterson (1973) on organization and management structures in Scotland.

The main criticisms focused on the calibre of councillors and officers. The legacy of the past (including its democratic basis) was blamed for the perceived inefficiencies of the system. Dearlove neatly summarizes these arguments: 'Most commentators have described the system as demo-cratic, inefficient, subject to massive and increasing central control, and dominated by councillors (and officers) of declining calibre' (Dearlove, 1979, p. 22). What was needed, it was argued, was better management and more appropriate organization in larger units to meet the technical requirements of service delivery. What was needed, in other words, was reorganization. This was reflected in the Local Government Acts passed in 1972 for England and Wales, and for Scotland in 1973. In Northern Ireland, the reforms went further still with the creation of Area Boards responsible for education, housing, health and social services, with only limited electoral representation and a greater emphasis on the importance of experts and 'public-spirited individuals'.

Bigger organizations were created, and it was assumed that they would, therefore, be able to attract better staff and more ambitious councillors. As the 1970 White Paper on the reform of local government in England put it:

> Unless local government is organized to meet the needs of the future, and in particular is organized in units large enough to match the technical and administrative requirements of the services which it administers, its powers must diminish, and with it the power of local democracy. . . . Radical change is overdue. And only if such change occurs, and local government is organized in strong units with power to take major decisions, will present trends towards centralization be reversed, and local democracy secure its place as a major part of our democratic system. (HMSO, 1970, paras 10, 97, quoted in Dearlove, 1979, p. 23)

The Bains Report (1972) on the management and structure of the new (post-reorganization) local authorities in England and Wales, and the Paterson Report (1973) on the organization and management structures of the new Scottish local authorities pointed in similar directions. As part of the move away from old local government administration, with a chief officer generally drawn from the legal profession and committees based around specialist professional divisions, what was needed, it was argued, were chief executives, senior officer groups (or management teams) and policy and resources committees that could look right across the work of the authority, alongside the creation of major directorates each with responsibility for a significant area of the council's services. The academic orthodoxy of the time pointed towards the value of corporate planning – that is the need to run the council as a whole – a corporation – rather than as merely the sum of its disparate parts (see, e.g. Greenwood and Stewart, 1974; Stewart, 1974). Critics complained that this represented an attack on community politics, because it promised the management of people as much as of the organization and literally threatened to make local government 'big business' with little possibility of input from backbench councillors who would be excluded from the groups of senior officers and councillors who were determining council strategy (Benington, 1976; Cockburn, 1977).

Whatever the specific charges laid against local government, these changes reflected a wider agenda of organizational restructuring, reform and 'modernization'. Indeed, it might be argued that the changes which had the biggest effects on local government were not those associated with local government reorganization, but those being pursued at the same time in areas of the welfare state for whose delivery local government was actually responsible. So, for example, this was the period in which social services departments were created in England and Wales and social work departments in Scotland, drawing together the different aspects of personal social services which had previously been distributed across a range of smaller departments. This was the moment in which the public sector social work profession was created. It was also a time of major reform in town planning – which separated strategic or structure planning from development control or local planning – as well as a period of major change in education policy with the move towards large comprehensive schools.

Underpinning these reforms was the fundamental belief (what might be described as a Fordist logic) that what was required was large scale organizational units, coupled with rational planning driven by technical experts. The reforms were not particularly aimed at reducing costs – indeed costs rose following reorganization – but were oriented towards improved efficiency. In one sense, this was the last major attempt to reform the welfare state – the social democratic state – in its own terms. This was a modernization in which the existing structures were to be strengthened and developed. It was an attempt to build on the logic of state welfarism, rather than to undermine and question it.

2   Modernization and markets: dismantling the social democratic state (1976–90)

Almost as soon as the new structures were in place, the ground rules had changed. Famously, in 1975, Tony Crosland (the Labour government's Secretary of State for the Environment) announced that cuts were needed in local government spending: 'We have to come to terms with the harsh reality of the situation which we inherited. The party's over' (quoted in Crosland, 1983, p. 295). The new authorities were in defensive mode almost as soon as they came into being. Now the (same?) problems were reinterpreted as waste, the need to cut spending.

After the mid-1970s local government became the focus of major debate throughout the UK and had an increasingly high profile not only at local level, but in the national newspapers, radio and television. By the early 1980s 'excessive' council spending was identified as one of the factors to blame for the country's economic problems, councillors were heavily criticized for financial irresponsibility and local government officers attacked for inefficiency and constructing 'bureaucratic empires' on the basis of self-interest (see, e.g., Butler and Pirie, 1981; Forsyth, 1981). Central government increasingly set out to control and limit the spending of councils. A series of reform packages was introduced to achieve this, to redirect the priorities of service departments and to encourage the creation of alternatives to local authority provision. A layer of councils (the metropolitan counties and the Greater London Council) was abolished in England in the mid-1980s, and 'ratecapping' was introduced in one form or another across the UK at around the same time. This gave departments of central government final say over levels of local taxation. At the end of the decade the community charge (or poll tax) was imposed as a replacement for the old rating system everywhere in the UK except Northern Ireland, and in England and Wales the old commercial rating system was replaced with a nationally levied business rate.

But these changes were not simply about saving money or reducing state expenditure – indeed levels of spending by local government did not fall significantly in the 1980s (the reduction that took place can largely be explained by the decision to give polytechnics – all of which are now universities – and further education colleges their own corporate status, but, of course, they are still publicly funded). Again, reform flowed from a wider political and organizational agenda, although local government made a particularly juicy target for the Thatcher government, since councils were largely controlled by Labour and could be used as powerful symbols of all that was perceived to be wrong with British politics and society.

The political and social meaning of Thatcherism has been a matter of much debate (see, e.g. Gamble, 1985; Hall, 1988), but its emphasis on the superiority of markets as the best form of economic and social organization is not in doubt. It promised a genuine and powerful alternative to what were seen as the orthodoxies of social democracy and the welfare state. Instead of accepting the notion that that the state had a key role in providing welfare services, the Thatcher governments started from the opposite assumption – namely that it was state involvement that was the problem, creating welfare dependency and undermining individual responsibility. This understanding fed into a series of reforms explicitly aimed first at undermining and then at replacing the welfare state with something better. So, for example, this was a time in which a range of nationalized industries – some of which had made claims to being public services – were privatized and became public limited companies (British Gas, British Telecom, National Power, and – finally – British Rail are all examples of major privatizations) and the regional water authorities were sold off, too. Within the National Health Service, although full scale privatization was not attempted, an attempt was made to create an 'internal market' with the help of a whole series of Health Service Trusts. Within central government, a range of relatively autonomous agencies was set up with the aim of moving them closer to commercial approaches, as contracted agencies of government – these include the Benefits Agency, the Passport Agency and the Child Support Agency.

Some of the key welfare state reforms directly affected local government because of its important role in service delivery in those areas. So,
for example, council housing was made available for sale to sitting
tenants, and there were increasingly severe constraints on the building
of further social housing, except through housing associations. The shift
of housing subsidy from capital subsidy (i.e. subsidy of the costs of
house construction) paid to local authorities, to housing benefit paid
through tenants to their landlords to cover their rents had dramatic
effects, gradually forcing rents higher and making owner-occupation
more attractive. Moves towards the local management of schools
following the Education Reform Act, 1988, shifted responsibility for
running schools to governing bodies and ensured that funds were
distributed between schools according to a formula based on pupil
numbers. A form of market based on parental choice was expected to
drive development. The introduction of legislation on community care
(through the Community Care and NHS Act, 1990) was intended to
transform the operation of adult social services by creating a mixed
economy of care in which social workers were to be the purchasers of
care on behalf of, rather than providers of care to, those in need.

The overall approach to local government was consistent with this.
Traditional local government was accused of 'operating in the interests
of those who administer it' (Forsyth, 1981, p. 1). Legislation was used to
increase central control of local government spending, but – more
importantly – it was also used to force councils to contract out services,
so that they were purchasing services from the private sector or from
agencies that behaved as if they were in the private sector. There were
moves towards the market, if not yet the creation of genuine markets.
The notion of the 'enabling authority' entered the language of central
and local government. It offered a model which effectively sponsored
the enabling (or even 'empowering') of appropriate others (such as
voluntary organizations, trusts, partnerships and privately owned
companies) to do the things that local government had previously
done. In other words, instead of local authorities being primarily concerned with the delivery of services, a range of other agencies would be
doing so (Ridley, 1988). According to one interpretation of this model,
local government would have 'a more modest role as specifier,
purchaser and regulator of community services' (Mather, 1989, p. 216),
although others saw the model as creating new opportunities for
councils as orchestrators of a mixed economy of community governance,
co-ordinating and leading the other agencies through their broader
strategic vision (Brooke, 1989).

Although ultimately a political failure, which helped to bring down
Margaret Thatcher as Prime Minister, the introduction of the community
charge (more popularly known as the 'poll tax') at the end of the decade
represented the most developed version of the market approach as it was
applied to local government. The principal aim of the community charge

(first introduced in Scotland, and then rolled out to England and Wales) was to transform electors into consumer citizens, who would vote on the basis of the packages of services provided by councils and the costs (in terms of community charge) associated with them (Adam Smith Institute, 1989). They would, it was firmly believed, vote in favour of those political parties who promised (and delivered) low charges and 'good services', and against those who had a record of high costs and poor efficiency and were therefore likely to levy high charges. Comparisons between local authorities and their efficiency would be made possible through the reports of the Audit Commission, which had been set up in 1983. As a result of this, it was predicted that performance would improve, bureaucracy would be reduced and costs and (ultimately) public spending would be cut. The very notion of a 'community charge' rather than a local tax was intended to highlight the extent to which this was like a commercial relationship (even if the only way to opt out was actually to move to another area) (see Cochrane, 1993, pp. 59–67).

By contrast with the previous period of reform, this was one in which the emphasis was on dramatically challenging the fundamentals of Britain's post-war settlements (see Hughes and Lewis, 1998, particularly Chs 1 and 2) and setting the basis for a new settlement based on rather different assumptions – particularly questioning the role of the state (and specifically local government) as welfare provider and substituting an emphasis on market, family and voluntary sector. In a sense, it is less important whether the reforms achieved their stated ends – the effective marketization of welfare services, the destruction of Labour local government, the reduction of public spending – because they did not, and rather more important whether they succeeded in shifting the ground rules and expectations of local government. The Thatcher period is sometimes presented as one of universal top-down 'attack' on local government, but its more significant legacy has been in the ways of thinking which have come to be accepted by many of those working in local government as well as those seeking to 'reform' it from the outside. The moves to an enabling authority, towards an increased role for a strategic core capable of managing a mixed economy of care, and towards governance (rather than government), in which stress is put on the management of networks rather than the delivery of direct services by councils, had become a new orthodoxy at the start of the 1990s, ready for reinterpretation in the next wave of modernization (see e.g. Stoker, 1999).

3 Modernization through managerialization (since 1990)

Some of the critics of Thatcherite modernization have associated it with a management style – a top-down approach – that was all too easily replicated in local government (see e.g. Stoker, 1999, pp. 1–21). It encouraged an overemphasis on measuring performance through inputs rather than outputs, and on a confrontational style in managing staff. In other words, the management style being borrowed from the private sector was an authoritarian (or Taylorist) one. To use the language of value for money, in practice there was an overemphasis on economy (cuts) at the expense of efficiency and effectiveness. And, of course, there was an ideological belief that any activity undertaken by the private sector was necessarily more efficient than any activity performed by local government.

However, the impact of Thatcherism went beyond its immediate achievements. In the case of local government it has played a significant part in reshaping the terrain on which debates now take place – in creating the context for what Hughes and Lewis (1998) describe as a resettlement. Although this may never have been expressed as an explicit ambition by central government, either in the 1980s or even during the Major years of the 1990s, in practice the emergence of a rather different approach to management was encouraged. Clarke and Newman (1997) chart the complex process by which a 'managerial state' was constructed across the public sector in these years, building both on the neo-liberal agenda of privatization and markets, and on the need to manage more complex mixed economies of care. They remind us of the importance of managerialism as an ideology with which many professional and organizational actors actively engaged, to the extent that its features were increasingly internalized within the organizational structures of local government. Pollitt, too, highlights the power of managerialism as an ideology because of the way in which it emphasizes the importance of managers in all organizations, whether in the public or private sectors (Pollitt, 1993). It links the public and private sectors in ways that help to give local government managers external and personal legitimacy in the new public sector climate.

The move away from the notion of local welfare state as self-sufficient provider to that of local government as 'enabler' has increasingly been reimagined as a positive move creating the possibility of something called 'community government' (or sometimes governance) (Stewart, 1995). Local authorities – their senior managers and senior councillors – are offered the possibility of somehow embodying the overall interests of their areas (and 'communities') in order to manage the contributions of a range of agencies and interests to achieve the best possible outcomes for their local residents – 'enabling communities to define and meet their needs' (Clarke and Stewart, 1991, p. 62). In that sense the new arrangements for the organization of welfare appeared to provide a genuine alternative to the old arrangements, which were defined as patronizing, bureaucratic, and run in the interests of the professionals who worked in them (teachers, social workers, environmental inspectors and town planners). What was needed instead was a customer orientation, or – at any rate – an approach based on 'community governance', rather than merely service delivery.

Many of those within local government were themselves sympathetic to this view. Senior managers in local government (and chief executives, in particular) were now able to claim a powerful role with a higher status than that of the welfare professionals they had had to manage so frustratingly since the 1960s. In this version, management became a means of escaping from some of the narrow (Taylorist) forms of control that had seemed so central in the early 1980s. The customer orientation helped to link the private and public sectors, and to erode the older hierarchies of welfarism, while recognizing the importance of those who could manage the rather more fluid realities of life after the welfare state.

Again, of course, this has been part of a broader set of changes across the public sector, charted elsewhere in this book. During the 1990s, and into the twenty-first century, there has been a continuing process of adjustment and readjustment as attempts have been made to reach an organizational settlement capable of encompassing those areas previously associated with the welfare state. The redefinition of citizens as consumers or customers, as providers as well as receivers of care, as active as well as passive, as having responsibilities as well as rights, has affected local government as much as any other part of the public sector.

In the early 1990s, this was reflected at national level in the Citizen's Charter initiative, which encouraged the spread of an approach to public service in which a series of promises were set out (in a quasi-contractual) form and consumer-citizens were invited to complain or challenge providers who did not meet the targets specified in the charters. William Waldegrave (1993) (the Minister responsible) argued that the search for democratic accountability was irrelevant to the operation of the local welfare state; what mattered to people was the quality of the services they received – a rather different form of accountability. Not only were local authorities themselves expected to develop their own charters, but a new wave of local government reorganization was launched. This time the agenda reflected the new managerialism agenda, focusing on the perceived need to reduce overlap between levels of government which left consumers confused about responsibility and made moves towards accountability more difficult to achieve. In Scotland and Wales, legislation was simply introduced to remove one tier of local government and create a series of what were called unitary authorities (i.e. with overall responsibility for all local authority services). In England matters were rather more complicated, as a Local Government Commission toured the country, redrawing the boundaries of some counties and creating a series of unitary authorities in some places, but not in others. By the end of the process most urban areas outside London were governed by unitary authorities.

What is most interesting about this, however, was not the creation of new authorities themselves, but the context within which it took place. In principle the new organizational structures might have been consistent with almost any welfare regime, but in this case they were associated with a move towards different ways of working, which drew on a managerialist agenda. 'Best practice' guidelines on 'new patterns of organization and management' were produced in 1993 within the local government sector by the Local Government Management Board (LGMB) – a body funded by a top slice of local authority budgets and with extensive institutional involvement by local authorities. These guidelines were taken up enthusiastically by many of the new councils and were reinforced by specific guidance issued to the new councils by the LGMB (1995a, 1995b) and the Audit Commission (1995). The key aims included 'developing a strategic direction', 'providing effective community leadership', 'being responsive to the public as customers and consumers', as well as sustaining local democracy', which was defined as 'strengthening accountability to the public as citizens' (LGMB, 1993, 1.8). As Keen and Scase (1998, p. 170) conclude, any attempt to revert to the more traditional structures of bureaucratic and professional organization associated with the welfare state 'would be resisted by practising local government managers. For the majority of them, the "new managerialism" is no longer rhetoric but the reality of their employment'.

All of this – of course – long pre-dated the election of the Blair government in 1997, yet the themes are consistent with those taken further by that government. Similar points were raised in the White Paper *Modernising Government* (Cabinet Office, 1999, p. 6) which identified three aims – 'Ensuring that policy making is more joined-up and strategic', 'Making sure that public service users, not providers, are the focus, by matching services more closely to people's lives' and 'Delivering public services that are high quality and efficient'. This is more than mere rhetoric. It reflects a wider (if not always coherent) agenda (sometimes labelled the 'Third Way' – see Giddens, 1998, and Chapter 1 in this volume). It questions the extent to which services should be provided by the state, emphasizes the role of other organizations (including voluntary organizations and business groups) and seeks to draw a range of agencies together into 'partnerships' whose operation is held to produce better outcomes than the sum of the work of the same agencies (see Chapter 5 in this volume). By encouraging their participants to work together such partnerships are also intended to reduce conflict over policy outcomes because of the way in which they incorporate key professional, user and business interests.

This has also been translated into the local government context. In England, local government has been allocated its very own modernization White Paper, *Modern Local Government. In Touch with the People* (DETR, 1998) and has, of course, also been affected by a series of other reforms relating to particular services, as well as by the devolution of power to Scotland and Wales. The White Paper follows the familiar route of stressing the need for change – 'The old culture of paternalism and inwardness needs to be swept away' (p. 7) – and spells out a series of incentives intended to encourage this. Above all, it focuses on the need for new political structures intended to reflect and encourage this cultural shift. Possible models include directly elected executive mayors, cabinet government with a leader elected by the council, and directly elected mayor with a council manager. In all of these models, the role of backbench councillor is principally expected to be to scrutinize the operation of the strategic executive, which links the political leadership and senior managers. Stress is placed on the importance of responsiveness and consultation – on exploring new forms of accountability including referenda – but it is also promised that the reforms will lead to higher levels of voting in local elections (we are promised electronic voting, more postal voting, voting on different days, etc.). Alongside these changes, a policy of 'best value' is to be pursued, which requires councils to review their service and to ask why it is being provided as it is; to compare their performance with that of others; to consult local 'stakeholders' (taxpayers, service users and business) on how the service might be improved; and to 'embrace fair competition as a means of securing efficient and effective services' (p. 9). All of this – as in so many other areas – will be overseen and regulated by external regulators and inspectors.

The management emphasis on responsiveness and consultation, and on inter-agency working (or, to use the political rhetoric favoured by the Blair government, 'joined-up working') effectively undermines the traditional role of local politicians. It becomes increasingly difficult to relate the old structures of representative democracy (through committees and sub-committees) to the new managerial structures. As Lowndes (1999, p. 37) argues, 'many "new management" developments . . . were destabilising power relations within the locality. . . . New approaches to local governance management were . . . restructuring constraints and opportunities for the exercise of local democracy and citizenship.' She points to the need to develop new political institutions in local governance and this is reflected in the modernization proposals. So, in a sense, the rise of new managerialism *within* local government is seen as one of the key drivers for political change at local level.

Stress is placed on the need for dramatic cultural change within local government. This has been particularly apparent in the arguments developed by the Local Government Network – a campaign organization that draws together academics, local councillors and local authority managers – but it is also disseminated more widely, for example through the Improvement and Development Agency (whose ambitions are well expressed in its title) which has been formed out of the restructuring of the old Local Government Management Board. This emphasis on culture echoes the wider language of managerialism in the private and public sectors, which often starts by emphasizing the extent to which a culture change is needed if broader change is to be achieved and an organization is to be successfully transformed. The new approach requires commitment from within local government, since 'Local authorities must own the need to change' (Dromey et al., 1998, p. 5), but the implied threat is also clear – if that ownership is absent, then central government will bypass the councils. Above all, it is argued, new forms of political leadership are required, which will shift the emphasis from leading (or managing) the council and its (in-house) service delivery towards leading their communities.

At times the language is almost messianic, and there is no doubt that those who are not modernizers (and see 'modernization' as a threat) are part of the problem that needs to be overcome (see, e.g. Filkin et al., 1999). In a speech to the Local Government Association in 1999, Hilary Armstrong (minister responsible for local government) argued that 'Those who oppose modernization are setting themselves up as conservatives with a small "c", defending an institution that is as outdated and in need of reform as the hereditary peerage' (quoted in Hetherington, 1999). Corrigan (1999) uses the arrival of the new millennium to construct a vision of electronic communication in which fully wired backbench councillors are in constant touch with their local communities, which means that they are able to scrutinize the work of the strategic executive effectively. 'The new millennium successful councillor', he writes, 'will be the one that can demonstrate that their ability to scrutinize is based firmly upon their close contact with local people.'

The extent to which existing arrangements are actually being transformed remains a matter of some contention, and there is evidence of resistance from some local authority leaders who remain to be convinced of the value of the new approaches. But the lines along which the restructuring and resettlement are expected to take place are clear enough. This time modernization is about what is to follow the social democratic welfare state, rather than about seeking to strengthen it (as was the case in the first period we discussed) or to attack it (as in the second period). This time the issue is about supersession, about what comes next, with local government acting as one of the key sites on which the negotiation and conflict over the building of a new welfare regime or welfare settlement is taking place.

References

Adam Smith Institute (1989) *Wiser Counsels: The Reform of Local Government*, London, Adam Smith Institute.

Audit Commission (1995) *Seize the Day! Guidance for Incoming Unitary Authorities*, Local Government Reorganization Paper 3, London, HMSO.

Bains Report (1972) *The New Local Authorities: Management and Structure*, London, HMSO.

Benington, J. (1976) *Local Government Becomes Big Business*, London, Community Development Project.

Brooke, R. (1989) *Managing the Enabling Authority*, Harlow, Longman.

Butler, E. and Pirie, M. (eds) (1981) *Economy and Local Government*, London, Adam Smith Institute.

Cabinet Office (1999) *Modernising Government*, London, The Stationery Office.

Clarke, J. and Cochrane, A. (1998) 'The social construction of social problems', in Saraga, E. (ed.) *Embodying the Social: Constructions of Difference*, London, Routledge, pp. 3–42.

Clarke, J. and Newman, J. (1997) *The Managerial State: Power, Politics and Ideology in the Remaking of Social Welfare*, London, Sage.

Clarke, M. and Stewart, J. (1991) *Choices for Local Government from the 1990s and Beyond*, London, Longman.

Cochrane, A. (1993) *Whatever Happened to Local Government?* Buckingham, Open University Press.

Cockburn, C. (1977) *The Local State: Management of Cities and People*, London, Pluto.

Corrigan, P. (1999) 'Local democratic power in the new millennium', *Network News*, February/March.

Crosland, S. (1983) *Tony Crosland*, London, Coronet.

Dearlove, J. (1979) *The Reorganization of Local Government: Old Orthodoxies and a Political Perspective*, Cambridge, Cambridge University Press.

DETR: Department of the Environment, Transport and the Regions (1998) *Modern Local Government. In Touch with the People*, London, The Stationery Office.

Dromey, J., Filkin, G. and Corrigan, P. (1998) *Modernising Local Government*, London, Fabian Society.

Filkin, G., with Lord Bassam, Corrigan, P., Stoker, G. and Tizard, J. (1999) *Starting to Modernise*, London, Foundation for the New Local Government Network.

Forsyth, M. (1981) *Re-servicing Britain*, London, Adam Smith Institute.

Gamble, A. (1985) *Britain in Decline. Economic Policy, Political Strategy and the British State*, 2nd edition, London, Macmillan.

Giddens, A. (1998) *The Third Way. The Renewal of Social Democracy*, Cambridge, Polity.

Greenwood, R. and Stewart, J. (1974) *Corporate Planning in English Local Government*, London, Charles Knight.

Hall, S. (1988) *The Hard Road to Renewal. Thatcherism and the Crisis of the Left*, London, Verso.

Hetherington, P. (1999) 'Abrupt end to the honeymoon', *Guardian, Society* supplement, 7 July, p. 5.

HMSO (1970) *Reform of Local Government in England*, Cmnd 4276, London, Her Majesty's Stationery Office.

Hughes, G. and Lewis, G. (eds) (1998) *Unsettling Welfare: The Reconstruction of Social Policy*, London, Routledge/Open University.

Keen, L. and Scase, R. (1998) *Local Government Management: The Rhetoric and Reality of Change*, Buckingham, Open University Press.

Local Government Management Board (1993) *Fitness for Purpose. Shaping New Patterns of Organization and Management*, Luton, LGMB.

Local Government Management Board (1995a) *Gearing up to Govern*, Luton, LGMB.

Local Government Management Board (1995b) *Shaping Future Authorities*, Luton, LGMB.

Lowndes, V. (1999) 'Management change in local governance', in Stoker, G. (ed.) *The New Management of British Local Governance*, London, Macmillan.

Mather, G. (1989) 'Thatcherism and local government: an evaluation', in Stewart, J. and Stoker, G. (eds) *The Future of Local Government*, London, Macmillan.

Middlemass, K. (1979) *Politics in Industrial Society: The Experience of the British System since 1911*, London, André Deutsch.

Paterson Report (1973) *The New Scottish Local Authorities: Organization and Management Structures*, Edinburgh, HMSO.

Pollitt, C. (1993) *Managerialism and the Public Services*, 2nd edition, Oxford, Blackwell.

Ridley, N. (1988) *The Local Right. Enabling not Providing*, London, Centre for Policy Studies.

Shanks, M. (1961) *The Stagnant Society: A Warning*, Harmondsworth, Penguin.

Stewart, J. (1974) *The Responsive Local Authority*, London, Charles Knight.

Stewart, J. (1995) 'A future for local authorities as community government', in Stewart, J. and Stoker, G. (eds) *Local Government in the 1990s*, London, Macmillan.

Stoker, G. (ed.) (1999) *The New Management of British Local Governance*, London, Macmillan.

Waldegrave, W. (1993) *The Reality of Reform and Accountability in Today's Public Service*, London, Public Finance Foundation.

Wilson, H. (1964) *The New Britain: Labour's Plan Outlined by Harold Wilson. Selected Speeches 1964*, Harmondsworth, Penguin.

8

Social Housing: Managing Multiple Pressures

Roberta Woods

Contents

Social housing has undergone major changes over the last twenty years. It has come to occupy much more of a residual role, with tenants increasingly concentrated among people with low incomes. The size of the council housing sector has shrunk since the 1980 Housing Act introduced the tenant's 'right to buy', often resulting in the sale of better parts of the housing stock. Many estates have effectively become welfare ghettos, leading Flynn (1997, p. 85) to comment that housing management 'becomes less of a housing management job and more of a social welfare and crisis intervention one'. Despite this, the past twenty years has seen the application of public sector management innovations to social housing in the local authority and housing association sectors. This chapter considers how the new managerialism has developed in these sectors (Clarke and Newman, 1997; Newman, 1998). In particular it considers what the impact of New Labour's 'Best Value' approach is likely to mean for the providers of social housing.

There is now widespread agreement that the strategy of New Labour is in many respects a continuation of the reform agenda started under previous Conservative administrations (Alcock, 1998; Blackman and

Palmer, 1999). The main aspects of the New Public Management agenda introduced under the Conservatives have been extensively rehearsed in the academic literature and the key aspects of this agenda are briefly reviewed below. The chapter then considers the extent to which there is continuity or change in the management of social housing under the 1997 Labour government.

The primary shift in public sector management during the 1980s involved redirecting managerial effort towards performance rather than administrative routines based on conformity with rules and regulations. Policies were introduced to concentrate managerial effort on the most efficient use of resources, a commitment to targets and striving to achieve results which could be demonstrated by outcome measures. These policies included exposing public services to market forces through compulsory competitive tendering or various forms of internal market involving a split between commissioning and providing services. This became known as the 'contract culture'.

Result-orientated management emphasizes the use of indicators to provide feedback to managers about the efficiency and effectiveness of services. A range of management techniques was employed to do this, many borrowed from the private sector, such as performance standards, complaints procedures and 'customer care'. The initial emphasis was on reducing costs and improving efficiency, tending to give rise to a pre-occupation among housing managers with financial and volume indicators such as rent arrears and unlet properties. But towards the end of the 1980s more emphasis was placed on 'quality', defined as consumer satisfaction with services. This reflected a growing public dissatisfaction with the way public services were managed and delivered, summed up by Hambleton (1992, p. 5) as 'concern about the remoteness of centralized decision making, irritation with the insensitivity and lack of account-ability of at least some officers, and frustration with the blinkered approach often associated with highly departmentalized organizations'.

This dissatisfaction reflected the way consumerism was spreading from the private to the public sector (Blackman, 1995). Paternalistic attitudes to the customer had been common in the private sector until recession in the 1970s intensified competition and saw customer care develop as a competitive strategy. By the beginning of the 1980s, 'close-ness to the customer' was the hallmark of excellence and innovation in private companies (Peters and Waterman, 1982). But change was not imported wholesale from the private sector. A public service orientation marked the various initiatives, especially in local government. The best examples involved users in setting standards and assessing value, rather than being passive recipients of services. The Conservative government's Citizen's Charter, launched in 1991 as a high profile initiative to force local councils to publish indicators of their performance service by service, was in fact preceded by Labour-controlled York City Council's annual citizens' charters which began in 1989.

User consultation, user participation, staff consultation and service evaluations all aimed to bring services closer to the needs of users. Decentralization initiatives such as neighbourhood offices sought to achieve greater responsiveness to service users, but like many of the changes these were double-edged. Moves to decentralize management retained accountability for the centre, isolating the ownership of performance with regard to both standards and spending within budget, and thus strengthening central control (Farnham and Horton, 1992; Ferlie et al., 1996). In addition, a new framework for independently validating the performance of services was put in place, focusing attention on performance indicators defined by central government rather than priorities decided locally.

In summary, the wider ideological agenda of Conservative governments in the 1980s and 1990s was concerned with an attack on welfare bureaucracy, reducing public expenditure, and using markets and competition as the preferred catalyst for change. The public sector was required to reform and open up its services to competition, and much of the council housing stock was privatized (Flynn, 1997). Housing associations became the preferred method of providing a much-reduced output of new social rented housing, and they were increasingly expected to raise private finance, with consequent pressure to increase rents. However, the period also saw the emergence of new expectations about user involvement, with tenants wanting a say in how their estates were run.

1   The arrival of Best Value

Over the past twenty years the management of social housing has been subject to three major changes in managerial practice that have sought to reshape the delivery and consumption of social housing. The first of these was introduced by the Local Government and Housing Act, 1986, which enabled the ownership and management of local authority housing to be transferred to registered social landlords (RSLs). This in practice usually meant a transfer to a housing association. The main vehicles for this were large scale voluntary transfer (LSVT) and the 'Choose a Landlord' scheme. The main difference between these two schemes was that the local authority as landlord could initiate LSVT whereas tenants could initiate 'Choose a Landlord'. Both approaches required a ballot of tenants.

The second main change was the extension in 1996 of compulsory competitive tendering (CCT) to the management of local authority housing. Local councils' own housing management organizations were forced to compete with other organizations such as housing associations and private companies for contracts to manage the housing stock.

The third change has been the replacement of CCT with the regime of Best Value following election of the New Labour government in 1997.

Best Value is a core part of a new discourse of modernization which places increased emphasis on partnership, community consultation and service improvement, without necessarily requiring service providers to compete in the market place. The link between Best Value and these three aspects of the modernizing agenda is considered below.

Housing organizations hailed the introduction of Best Value as an improvement on CCT and support, albeit muted at times, was widely reflected in the housing and local government press. It is likely, however, that this indicated a distaste for CCT rather than a warm-hearted embrace of the new regime, as important details of the scheme were not made available until publication of draft legislation in December 1998.

2   Service improvement

Key aspects and details of how Best Value should work in practice are still being developed. Indeed, many operational issues are to be left for local authorities to determine (DETR, 1999a). The government has sought to fill in some of the gaps by establishing forty-two 'Best Value pilots' across a range of local authorities and establishing a Best Value in housing steering groups. It has also responded to requests for more information from local authorities by providing some framework papers and has published the *Best Value and Audit Commission Performance Indicators* (DETR, 1999c). The government is keen to present the approach of Best Value as an inclusive one and points to the range of membership on the steering group and, in particular, the inclusion of tenant representatives.

Much of the language used by government ministers, civil servants and some local authority commentators presupposes that what is currently delivered by local authorities is not as good as it should be in terms of quality and efficiency. The Best Value bill states: 'The need is for local authorities to provide services which bear comparison with the best . . . this is not simply a question of poor performing local authorities needing to pull up their performance substantially; other authorities also need to raise their sights and achieve continuous improvement' (DETR, 1999a).

The challenge to local authorities is considerable. They are exhorted to examine whether existing services deliver high standards; consult with local people in determining this; explore areas for improvement; respond to community aspirations; work effectively in partnership; have clear organizational objectives; and embrace performance management.

The guidance accompanying *The Local Government Act, 1999: Part 1, Best Value* sees informed comparison as the basis of performance management and effective review. Authorities will be expected to set targets within the range specified by the national Best Value indicators

(DETR, 1999e). The targets will reflect where an authority is placed nationally in comparison with others of a similar nature in respect of cost and efficiency. Authorities will also be expected to compare their current and prospective performance against other public sector bodies and the voluntary and private sectors. Selective and informed benchmarking and the use of quality schemes are mentioned in the Act as further aids to improving performance.

Research undertaken by the Local Government Centre at Warwick University and by Oxford City Council has provided evidence that this is a huge and complex task (Bovaird, 1998). Local authorities can spend a long time agreeing common definitions and sharing these with partner agencies before benchmarking can be undertaken. For example, one issue that preoccupied a series of meetings between some Best Value pilot local authorities was the definition of housing benefit overpayment. Other problems have arisen over what might seem to be straightforward performance measures, such as the value and volume of rent arrears, number of voids, empty properties and waiting list turnaround. Additionally, there is evidence that local authority pilots are having to invest considerable resources to develop usable benchmarking data (IRRV, 1999). The results of the Best Value pilots will enable other local authorities to apply benchmarking more quickly and easily, but the complexity of the benchmarking system remains.

If a local authority service does not achieve Best Value standards, the service will have to be contracted out to an external supplier. Authorities are as yet uncertain how many of their services will meet government requirements in this respect. Public sector unions and many elected members are naturally suspicious that Best Value could lead to compulsory competitive tendering by another route.

The framework for Best Value can be summarized as involving the setting of objectives, establishing a programme of performance reviews, publishing a performance plan, undergoing independent inspection and audit, and ultimately being subject to intervention by the Secretary of State if services fail. Regular review of the performance of services is required, together with wide consultation with users in drawing up a performance plan that will set out the framework for continuous improvement in service delivery. Improving service delivery is closely allied with the need to increase efficiency. The desire by the government to improve efficiency is spelt out in clear managerialist terms in the Best Value Act: 'As far as possible comparisons should be made on the basis of outcomes, although detailed comparisons of inputs and outputs will be required to assess the scope for greater efficiency consistent with the government's overall target of 2 per cent p.a. efficiency for local government as a whole' (DETR, 1999e, p. 11).

The Audit Commission is to develop a new branch within the Best Value inspectorate – a Housing Inspectorate – solely for the purpose of evaluating housing management performance. The Audit Commission was established by the Conservatives in 1982 to keep the management of local authorities under review (see Chapter 15 by Clarke, Gewirtz, Hughes and Humphrey). But in addition to the three Es of economy, efficiency and effectiveness – which were the catch-words of the 1980s – Best Value has its four Cs: challenge, compare, consult and compete. Local authorities are required to challenge how and why services are being provided, to compare performance with other authorities on a range of performance indicators and user views, to consult with tenants and the wider community in the setting of performance measures, and to embrace fair competition. Authorities that fail to do this will be deemed to be failing to operate a Best Value regime: 'We look to see continuous improvement even among the best. We will tackle vigorously those authorities that are persistently poor performers and will have the power, ultimately, to remove their responsibilities from them should they fail to improve' (DETR, 1998c, p. 3).

However, the reforming zeal does not end there. Local authorities are also expected to develop corporate visions which apply 'joined-up thinking' to service planning and delivery, tackling social exclusion, creating sustainable communities and supporting vulnerable people. So is this simply managerial-speak run rampant or can deeper ideological and political objectives be discerned in this agenda? Best Value reflects important aspects of the new managerialist agenda – the 'excellence' approach, consumerism, quality and entrepreneurship (Newman, 1998). To this we can perhaps add another discourse of 'partnership'.

3 Partnership

The current attention being placed on partnerships by the government means that the fact that partnership working is not new to local government tends to be overlooked. Since the mid-1980s the Estate Action scheme had required private sector involvement in renewing and diversifying local authority housing estates. In inner city areas, the City Challenge initiative, launched in 1992, required local authorities to have urban regeneration partnerships in place between the statutory, private and voluntary sectors as a condition for receiving funding for regeneration projects. This initiative marked a shift away from the property-led regeneration typical of urban policy in the 1980s and attempted to target training, job creation, housing and social projects so that disadvantaged local residents benefited directly. City Challenge also required targets to be established and monitored.

Nevertheless a new emphasis has been placed on the development of partnerships. To some extent this has been applied to all levels of government. In 1997 a DETR discussion paper *Building Partnerships for Prosperity* (DETR, 1997) stressed the importance of central government working in partnership with local government, the voluntary sector, education and training agencies, local communities and the business sector to achieve economic, social and physical regeneration. The new Charter programme Service First has produced guidance to enable all public sector agencies to work more effectively with the private sector. The stress on partnerships is also reflected in the modernizing local government agenda.

Guidance for the Local Government Act, 1999 (DETR, 1999e), establishes that partnerships should be developed within a corporate framework. The need for clarity in the expectations of each partner is emphasized as is the need for local government to develop new management structures that 'recognize the challenge that working with others brings' (p. 5). Partnership working should be far-reaching and extend to the commissioning and procurement of services. In addition the Local Government (Organization and Standards) draft Bill contains new powers for local authorities to form partnerships and encourages authorities to use these to promote the economic, social and environmental well-being of their areas. It also includes the provision of a general power to enable councils to form companies. When introducing the Local Government (Best Value and Capping) Bill for its second reading in the House of Commons, the Minister for Local Government and Housing stated:

> Best value will encourage local authorities to work in partnership with other bodies – pooling budgets, making better use of assets and ending some of the false boundaries between different deliverers of public service. At the same time, however, best value will encourage partnerships with private enterprise and voluntary organizations to secure new expertise and greater investment, and to promote innovation. (Armstrong, 1999a)

An evaluation of the Best Value pilots (Martin, 1998) showed that 79 per cent of those selected as pilots had included the development of new partnerships with the private sector as part of their bid, and 71 per cent proposed new partnerships with the voluntary sector. The bids included a wide range of models – multi-agency steering or advisory groups, community partnerships, strategic alliances with Trusts and not-for-profit organizations, new contracting systems, partnerships with other public sector agencies and between different tiers of local government.

Best Value is also about managing housing through partnerships. The idea of delivering services in this way is not new for local authority housing departments (Rogers, 1990; Bemrose and MacKeith, 1996; NCVO, 1993). However, as we noted above, the modernizing agenda of the government raises the profile of partnerships in the delivery of local as well as national services (DETR 1998a, 1998b). Emphasis is placed on this as an important way in which services can be improved for the benefit of local communities.

However, the effort required in developing, setting up, servicing and maintaining partnerships across institutional boundaries may have been seriously underestimated by the government. Reading City Council's

Best Value pilot shows what can be achieved, but not all the partnerships they pursued were successful (Bovaird, 1998). Partnerships are
subject to institutional rivalries and different policy agendas, and are
clearly not a straightforward panacea for improving service standards.
As Blackman (1997, p. 138) observes, 'Partnerships can have the benefit
of achieving very focused, jointly funded work, but can blur the process
of democratic accountability because no single player has overall
responsibility and often most of the resources are from the private
sector, giving primacy to commercial considerations such as the rate of
return on projects.'

4 Consultation

Best Value guidance to local authorities insists that they consult with
their community and involve tenants and residents in the drawing up of
performance plans (DETR 1998a, 1998b, 1999a, 1999b, 1999e). Whilst
there is some acknowledgement that communities for many authorities
are not homogeneous entities and that unequal power relations exist
that might lead to some voices being heard and others marginalized, the
complexities of the situation are to a large extent glossed over (Gilliver,
1999). Similarly, much decision making is being devolved to tenants
without widespread evidence that they wish to be involved in the
management of their estates (Winchester, 1999). Indeed, one of the Social
Exclusion Unit action teams concludes that: 'Local people do not usually
want to sit in meetings and on landlords' committees. Instead the focus
should be on helping communities to come together for themselves'
(Bright, 1999).

   The government's housing consultation document on Best Value
requires authorities to consult with tenants within a National Framework for Tenant Participation (TP) Compacts (DETR, 1999b). The
framework sets out the need for local authorities to inform, consult and
involve tenants in the drawing up of consultation strategies and in
undertaking fundamental performance reviews, reaching judgements
about priorities, targets and outputs, setting, monitoring and reviewing
performance targets and standards, and agreeing service standards and
methods for achieving them. In other words, tenants are expected to
think and act like local housing managers. As Kemp (1999) argues, these
compacts may simply mean a transfer of responsibilities from councils
to tenants:

> It is clear that New Labour are committed to empowering tenants through
> enabling them to be involved in virtually every aspect of the housing service.
> TP Compacts represent a major shift towards a consumer focused orientation
> in council housing and away from a producer orientated one. However this
> greater involvement also represents a partial offloading of responsibility from
> councils to tenants.

5   Demunicipalization?

The Best Value regime is not the only managerial change to be applied to local authority housing services. The government has announced that housing budgets are to move to a new system of resource accounting from the financial year 2001–2. Resource accounting will change the basis for accounting for the cost of capital. It will enable depreciation of housing stock to be taken into account, introduce stock evaluation and will remove the cost of rent rebates from the Housing Revenue Account. The new system will also contain a major repairs allowance to enable authorities to tackle some of the repairs backlog.

For some it appeared initially that this change might amount to a reversal of the demunicipalization of council housing and a major commitment by central government to local authority housing (LGIU, 1999). It has, however, become obvious that the Labour government does not see the backlog of investment in local authority housing as being met wholly from public sector resources (Perry, 1999). Whilst simply by switching finances from capital to revenue the new system will lever in more money, this may not be enough in itself to keep housing in the council sector. Perry argues that yet more resources are needed to make the finances add up for a number of authorities. The move to Best Value, coupled with resource accounting, may also be paving the way for a transfer of local authority housing stock to new landlords on a greater scale. The government's tacit support for stock transfer was recently stated by the Deputy Prime Minister, John Prescott (*Guardian*, 19 January 2000). Currently, large scale voluntary transfers are at their highest level ever. This could increase further as resource accounting sets out in clear terms the value of a housing stock and the total value of repair work that needs to be undertaken. Faced with this information, some local authorities may decide to transfer their stock rather than tackle its problems themselves, even with some additional resources from central government. To that end, the new managerialism may be contributing to the demunicipalization of social rented housing, a process begun under the Conservatives (Kemp, 1999).

6   Tackling the cross-cutting issues

The major problems facing housing managers at neighbourhood level are often different from the topics reflected in performance management indicators (Power and Tunstall, 1995; SEU, 1998; Power and Mumford 1999). Many estates face huge problems of crime, poverty, isolation, neighbour nuisance, racial and other forms of harassment, anti-social behaviour, lack of choice of affordable housing and a backlog in investment. It is widely acknowledged that these problems are insurmountable without a multifaceted approach. It was noted earlier that part of the government's wider agenda for local authorities is that they should generate a corporate vision and apply 'joined-up thinking' to service planning, tackle social exclusion, create sustainable communities and support vulnerable people. A key question to ask, therefore, is whether the changes facing housing make addressing these issues easier or more difficult.

The managerial developments we are seeing in social housing may provide the tools for change identified by Newman (Chapter 3 in this volume) as needed in order to replace ideology as the main motivator for change. It is necessary to consider whether the modernizing reforms of New Labour will enable area-based initiatives to be more successful than previously, providing for the creation of sustainable communities and hence delivering the wider-based social policy objectives of the government. The government's Social Exclusion Unit sets out a key role for local government in meeting these objectives. The modernizing agenda is about achieving these aims. Best Value and a new duty to be placed on local authorities to promote the social, environmental and economic well-being of their areas are examples of how local government is being prepared for this role. Additional aspects of the work that local authorities must do are finding effective ways of linking with other agencies and organizations locally, and promoting more neighbourhood management. The goal set for Action Team 17 – 'Joining It Up Locally' – is: 'to reach an agreed plan for building on existing area initiatives and local government reform so that in the long term broad based local strategies to prevent and tackle social exclusion become the norm' (Social Exclusion Unit, 1998, p. 76).

The Best Value scheme, with its emphasis on community consultation, partnership working and improved service delivery, could support the aim of tackling social exclusion. What appears to be missing are clear mechanisms to support local authorities in their strategic leadership role to produce a broad-based package of measures. Newman (1998) describes managerialism as the glue which holds together the increasingly fragmented field of social welfare, but for local authorities delivering the new agenda the glue may not have set. Some components are in place, such as the expectation placed on local authorities to produce a community plan; and the provision of additional powers and the duty to promote the economic, social and environmental well-being of their areas. These should enhance their local leadership role but duties may have to be placed on other agencies to encourage a real commitment to improving service delivery through partnerships.

The Local Government (Organization and Standards) draft Bill (DETR, 1999d) encourages local authorities to lead in drawing up a community plan for their areas. The *Modernising Local Government* White Paper states:

> It is essential that there should be a clear and understandable strategy for every area based on an analysis of the area's needs and priorities for future

action. It should be developed with local people, local business and with public and voluntary sector bodies who operate in the local area. The government will not impose on councils any particular approach to the task – councils will have . . . flexibility over the precise nature, scope and coverage of the strategy, the level of detailed action it contains and over how they go about preparing it in partnership with other organizations. (DETR, 1998a, p. 81)

This could be an effective tool for drawing up strategies to tackle neighbourhood problems and needs and for placing them within a council-wide strategy. The weakness is that duties are not being placed on other organizations or public bodies to co-operate with the planning process or to deliver on implementation.

Rather than being given additional powers to bring organizations together, local authorities are having their leadership roles strengthened through internal organizational reforms. A government consultation paper, *Local Leadership, Local Choice* (DETR, 1999f) and the Local Government (Organization and Standards) draft Bill, discuss new forms of political governance at local level, raising the possibility of directly elected mayors and cabinet-style government with scrutiny committees. The government takes the view that local political leaders in the form of directly elected mayors, and more transparency in decision making, will enhance the standing of local government. Local government, however, although generally approving of the changes to political structures, continues to argue the case for greater powers and local financial flexibility (Beecham, 1998). So whilst the government acknowledges the need for improved local leadership, its approach to delivering this is very cautious and centres on the availability of some limited additional powers.

7 The modernizing agenda and housing

The Local Government and Housing Minister, Hilary Armstrong, considers housing to be central to the government's strategy for tackling social exclusion:

> housing could become the pivotal service in the successful delivery of the new forms of cohesive integrated neighbourhood management. . . . We will be looking to develop the approach to a wide range of deprived areas, where the main form of tenure might be home ownership, or private renting or housing association, or where there is a mix of tenures. (Armstrong, 1999b)

Traditionally, attempts to tackle the most disadvantaged areas have concentrated almost exclusively on council housing, but this agenda is changing. The Social Exclusion Unit (1998) has acknowledged that the problems of social exclusion belong to areas of private renting and owner occupation as well as council housing. That having been said, council housing estates do dominate the list of most disadvantaged areas (SEU, 1998). Tenants in these areas may be resistant to stock transfer as a way of improving their areas, while the view that who the landlord is does not matter is reflected by some tenants' organizations (Cooper, 1999).

The policy emerging is based on the argument that strategies to tackle social exclusion need to be wider than an approach based solely on areas of council housing. This is coupled with the view that the demunicipalization should continue. This includes encouraging transfers to RSLs where tenants support this: 'The transfer of housing stock to Registered Social Landlords has helped to separate out responsibilities, and this programme will continue. It gives local authorities the scope to transfer their stock to specialist housing providers and to lever in significant private investment where they consider it sensible to do so' (DETR, 1998c, p. 3)

So where does this leave local authorities in developing solutions to joined-up problems? Clearly it is not essential for local authorities to have a direct management function in order to deliver inter-agency solutions to the problems facing some estates. But is success in tackling these problems possible without countering the discourse of welfare dependency that residualizes council housing? The government wants to rebrand council housing, but measures to achieve inclusion of the tenure as a normal type of housing and not an option for those with no other choice are not yet evident. The government is beginning to discuss the future of council housing (Armstrong, 1999b), and in doing so it acknowledges the important role this housing tenure has played in improving living standards during this century, but it also recognizes its current lack of popularity. It sees a need to have council housing develop a new modern image to go with the wider modernization agenda for local government: 'Even when the ownership of housing remains with the local authority, we should consider options for rebranding council housing to create a modern image to go with the more modern styles of management that are being pursued' (Armstrong, 1999b).

Undoubtedly this will not be as easy as it sounds. It may be made more difficult by having a policy that considers RSLs to be the preferred providers of social housing. It may be the case that part of a strategy to tackle social exclusion will involve a transfer of housing stock to new landlords and a degree of privatization, redevelopment and stock investment, but is this process to be led by a desire to achieve Best Value or a desire to tackle social exclusion? It is unclear how multi-agency approaches at local level will be made to work without a strengthening of the strategic role of local authorities. At present a Green Paper on housing is awaited and a major review of the future of social housing is being undertaken by the Institute for Public Policy Research. This review, at the government's request, is on a 'nothing ruled out' basis. It must be concluded from this that the government intends to consider a wide range of options for the future of council housing, including a complete transfer to other social landlords, transfer to the private sector, or the establishment of housing companies.

8 Conclusions

It would seem on the face of it fairly convincing to argue that Best Value is merely an extension of the competitive management and perform-ance measurement culture introduced by the Conservatives. It extols managerialism's values of quality improvement, benchmarking and corporate strategy. However, Best Value also encompasses a commit-ment to consultation and partnership. Managers do not have the right to manage with unbridled executive power: they are accountable for their performance in an increasing number of ways. A key issue, therefore, is whether management will end up being pulled in different directions. On the one hand, the expectations of central government are becoming more detailed and prescriptive, as the large number of Best Value and Audit Commission performance indicators demonstrate. On the other hand, local authorities are expected to be open to their communities, involving local people in making decisions that reflect local rather than central priorities. Local authorities are also expected to be developing partnerships that will deliver joint objectives, planning and directions. The extent to which this produces a contradictory and unmanageable framework for local government to operate within remains to be seen.

Clarke and Newman (1997) argue that the welfare state has experi-enced a new settlement based on managerialism. In housing, whilst the ideological quest to demunicipalize services may have disappeared, the pragmatism associated with managerialism has created conditions for the continuing withdrawal of local authorities from managing social housing. At the same time, authorities are being urged to tackle social exclusion, but lack both the powers and the resources to make major changes in their localities.

References

Alcock, P. (1998) 'Labour in power: New Labour social policy one year on', *Community Care*, Nov–Dec, pp. 17–24.

Armstrong, H. (1999a) *Hansard*, 12 January, p. 130.

Armstrong, H. (1999b) 'A lever long enough', *Labour Housing*, January, pp. 6–7.

Beecham, J. (1998) *Response of the Local Government Association to the Modernisation White Paper*, London, Local Government Association.

Bemrose, C. and MacKeith, J. (1996) *Partnerships for Progress*, Bristol, Policy Press.

Blackman, T. (1995) *Urban Policy in Practice*, London, Routledge.

Blackman, T. (1997) 'Urban planning in the UK', in Pacione, M. (ed.) *Britain's Cities: Geographies of Division in Urban Britain*, London, Routledge.

Blackman, T. and Palmer, A. (1999) 'Continuity or modernization? The emergence of New Labour's welfare state', in Dean, H. and Woods, R. (eds) *Social Policy Review 11*, Luton, Social Policy Association.

Bovaird, T. (1998) *Achieving Best Value through Competition, Benchmarking and Performance Networks*, Warwick, The Local Government Centre, University of Warwick.

Bright, J. (1999) 'Residents should help themselves', *Inside Housing*, 23 April, p. 3.

Clarke, J. and Newman, J. (1997) *The Managerial State*, London, Sage.

Cooper, P. (1999) 'Value added?', *Roof*, May–June, pp. 23–5.

DETR (1997) *Building Partnerships for Prosperity*, London, Department of the Environment, Transport and the Regions.

DETR (1998a) *Modernising Local Government: Local Democracy and Community Leadership*, London, The Stationery Office.

DETR (1998b) *Modern Local Government in Touch with the People*, Cm 4014, London, The Stationery Office.

DETR (1998c) 'Housing and regeneration policy', A statement by the Deputy Prime Minister and Secretary of State for the Environment, Transport and the Regions.

DETR (1999a) *Local Government (Best Value and Capping) Bill*, London, The Stationery Office.

DETR (1999b) *Best Value in Housing*, Framework Consultation Paper, London, DETR.

DETR (1999c) *Best Value and Audit Commission Performance Indicators*, vols 1 and 2, London, DETR.

DETR (1999d) *Local Government (Organization and Standards) Draft Bill*, London, The Stationery Office.

DETR (1999e) *Guidance for the Local Government Act 1999, Part 1, Best Value*, Circular, 10/99, London, DETR.

DETR (1999f) *Local Leadership, Local Choice*, Cm. 4298, London, DETR.

Farnham, D. and Horton, S. (1992) *Managing the New Public Services*, Basingstoke, Macmillan.

Ferlie, E., Ashburner, L., Fitzgerald, L. and Pettigrew, A. (1996) *The New Public Management in Action*, Oxford, Oxford University Press.

Flynn, N. (1997) *Public Sector Management*, London, Harvester Wheatsheaf.

Gilliver, D. (1999) 'Living hell', *Housing*, May, pp. 20–1.

Hambleton, R. (1992) *Rethinking Management in Local Government*, Papers in Planning Research 130, Department of City and Regional Planning, University of Wales College of Cardiff.

IRRV (1999) *Revenues and Benefits in the Best Value Pilots: The Lessons to be Learned from the First Year*, London, Institute of Revenues, Rating and Valuation .

Kemp, P. (1999) 'New Labour and the housing question', in Dean, H. and Woods, R. (eds) *Social Policy Review 11*, Luton, Social Policy Association, pp. 166–86.

LGIU (1999) *Breathing New Life into Public Housing*, Special Briefing 51, London, Local Government Information Unit .

Martin, S. (1998) *Bidding for Best Value: an Analysis of English Best Value Bids*, Warwick Best Value Series, Local Government Centre, Warwick and the DETR.

NCVO (1993) *Building Effective Local Partnerships*, Luton, Local Government Management Board.

Newman, J. (1998) 'Managerialism and social welfare', in Hughes, G. and Lewis, G. (eds) *Unsettling Welfare*, London, Routledge/Open University.

Perry, J. (1999) 'Investment in council housing – the options', *Housing*, May, pp. 22–3.

Peters, T.J. and Waterman, R.H. (1982) *In Search of Excellence: Lessons from America's Best Run Companies*, New York, Harper and Row.

Power, A. and Mumford, K. (1999) *The Slow Death of Great Cities? Incipient Urban Abandonment and Urban Renaissance*, York, Joseph Rowntree Foundation and London School of Economics.

Power, A. and Tunstall, R. (1995) *Swimming Against the Tide: Progress or Polarisation on Twenty Unpopular Estates*, York, Joseph Rowntree Foundation.

Rogers, S. (1990) *Performance Management in Local Government*, London, Longman.
SEU: Social Exclusion Unit (1998) *Bringing Britain Together: A National Strategy for Neighbourhood Renewal*, Cm 4045, London, The Stationery Office.
Winchester, R. (1999) 'Sanctions will cost tenants dear', *Inside Housing*, 30 April, p. 4.

9

Social Services: Managing the Third Way

Mary Langan

Contents

THE THIRD WAY: NEW POLITICS FOR THE NEW CENTURY
In the key public services, the Third Way is about money for modernization –
new investment of £40bn over the next three years driving reform and higher
standards . . . .

In all areas, monitoring and inspection are playing a key role, as an incentive to higher standards and as a means of determining appropriate levels of intervention. (Blair, 1998, p. 16)

MODERNIZING SOCIAL SERVICES: PROMOTING INDEPENDENCE, IMPROVING PROTECTION, RAISING STANDARDS
High quality and good value services can only be achieved if there are sound management, information and performance systems in place. Checks are needed both locally and nationally to make sure that people are getting the modern and dependable social services that they deserve. (Department of Health, 1998a, p. 108)

The commitment to 'modernize' the institutions of British society, particularly public services, has guided the rapid implementation of the programme to reform the delivery of social services under the New Labour government. Management is the key instrument of the reform process and its buzzwords are standards and performance indicators, monitoring and inspection, audit and accountability.

After a flurry of policy statements and initiatives in 1998, the reform programme was implemented at a hectic pace over the following two years (Hirst, 1999). By the summer of 1999, some sixteen social services departments (10 per cent of the total) had been deemed to be performing badly and were being 'closely monitored' by the government's expanded Social Services Inspectorate (SSI). As staff complained about the 'unremitting pace of change', the government made clear its determination to impose payment by results on the social services: 'outcomes' rather than 'ideology' would now drive the activities of social workers (Inman, 1999).

1   The Third Way

When Tony Blair's New Labour came to power in May 1997, the world of social services was still reeling under the impact of the 'revolution' initiated by the community care reforms of the early 1990s (Langan, 1998). The 'purchaser–provider split' and the resulting extension of market forces and the shift from state to voluntary, private and informal agencies had transformed social workers into care managers administering a 'needs-led' service with cash-limited resources. An apparently endless series of scandals involving physical and sexual abuse by staff in children's homes, violent deaths of children in families under social services supervision and murders committed by former psychiatric patients discharged into 'community care' focused public attention on the defects of social services.

The new administration also inherited a series of more than thirty reviews undertaken at the behest of the previous government jointly by the Social Services Inspectorate and the Audit Commission. These reports provided, according to the White Paper *Modernising Social Services: Promoting Independence, Improving Protection, Raising Standards*, 'a comprehensive picture of social services performance' (Department of

Health, 1998a, p. 108). Whilst acknowledging 'many examples of good practice', the joint reviews had also found 'too many examples of poor services, widespread inefficiency, and a worryingly high number of authorities with serious and deep-rooted problems' (p. 108).

The message was categorical: 'This situation must change. Improvements are needed in the quality and value of social services and to ensure that local people are receiving the services that, as taxpayers, they should expect' (p. 109).

The White Paper proposed that the government should establish 'clear objectives' for social services, 'creating a clear expectation of the outcomes social services are required to deliver'. It should set medium-term 'key targets', in the form of 'National Priorities Guidance', and provide resources to support the achievement of these targets. The White Paper also proposed that the government should put in place 'effective systems to monitor and manage performance' (p. 110).

In his foreword to the White Paper, Health Secretary Frank Dobson singled out the issue of performance standards, announcing the introduction of regional 'commissions for care standards' to regulate residential and domiciliary care, a stronger role for SSI/Audit Commission joint reviews and 'new tough powers for the secretary of state to step in when standards are not met' (p. 2). He also emphasized the government's commitment to raising professional and training standards through the replacement of CCETSW with a General Social Care Council to regulate training.

The managerialist thrust of the social services White Paper was also apparent in a series of official documents on different aspects of welfare that appeared in the first two years of the New Labour government. These included health (with additional reports on mental and public health), social security, and local government. Numerous modernizing initiatives affected social services: for children in care, there was 'Quality Protects'; for children in the community, 'Sure Start'; for everybody else there were 'National Priorities Guidance' and 'Best Value' projects.

The notion of 'modernization' is a key rhetorical figure in the discursive strategy of the Third Way (Clarke and Newman, 1998). New Labour has sought to distinguish itself from 'Old Labour', which it characterizes as committed to centralized, bureaucratic, hierarchical – and inefficient – modes of service delivery: 'the near-monopoly local authority provision that used to be a feature of social care led to a "one size fits all" approach where users were expected to accommodate themselves to the services that existed' (Department of Health, 1998a, p. 8). It has also repudiated what it regards as the extreme attachment of the Thatcher regime to the virtues of the free market: 'the last Government's devotion to privatization of care provision put dogma before users' interests and threatened a fragmentation of vital services' (p. 8).

Under Tony Blair, New Labour offers a Third Way, which is something new and, above all, something modern. In social services this takes the form of a commitment to quality: 'Our Third Way for social care moves the focus away from who provides the care, and places it firmly on the quality of services experienced by, and outcomes achieved for, individuals and their carers and families' (p. 8).

The key agency through which this modernizing, improving mission is to be accomplished is not the old welfare professionals (at least not *qua* traditional professionals) but the new force of managers. In preparing the way for its reform programme, it was important for the government to establish that the existing arrangements in social services had proved a failure.

2 The failures of the old order

Social services are often failing to provide the support that people should expect. (Department of Health, 1998a, p. 5)

In its introductory section on the theme 'the need for modernisation', the White Paper *Modernising Social Services* provides a lengthy indictment of the record of social services.

2.1 The indictment

The failings of the social services are detailed under six headings:

Protection
All too often children and vulnerable adults have been exposed to neglect and abuse by the very people who were supposed to care for them . . .

Co-ordination
Sometimes various agencies put more effort into arguing with one another than into looking after people in need . . .

Inflexibility
Although social services help many people to live fuller and more active lives, they sometimes provide what suits the service rather than what suits the person needing care . . .

Clarity of role
Up to now, neither users, carers, the public, nor social services staff and managers have had a clear idea which services are or should be provided, or what standards can reasonably be expected . . .

Consistency
. . . in some authorities one in five children in care are moved three times or more in one year, while the best authorities manage to keep this down to one in fifty . . .

Inefficiency
An important finding of the Joint Reviews so far is that there is scope for many authorities to get more for what they spend on social services. (Department of Health, 1998a, pp. 5–7)

2.2   The record

These criticisms are familiar, but many participants in social services over the preceding decade would contest them. The White Paper notes in passing that there may be 'various reasons' for the 'failings of the system', but all its proposals appear to assume that these failings are the exclusive responsibility of the social services. In a study of 'quality development' in social services across Europe, Evers comments on the tendency to 'blame the victim – an individual personal social services unit or manager – for problems which are set by the economic or social policy environment' (Evers, 1996, p. 5). Evers points in particular to the not unfamiliar situation where the low quality of a service is attributable to outside decisions which result in understaffing. As 'the community' became the solution to every social problem in the 1980s and 1990s, those burdened with the responsibility of turning political rhetoric into the reality of services on the ground for those in need – without additional resources – also carried the burden of the inevitable ensuing disappointments.

The trend towards victim blaming is apparent under each of the above headings. In the sphere of child protection, social services have been at the centre of a national controversy running for the past two decades, a controversy characterized by a high level of ambivalence about whether social workers should be more or less interventionist. The demonization of social care workers reached a new extreme in cases arising out of children's homes scandals in the late 1990s, with mounting allegations that serious injustice had been done to a number of social workers, if not the system as a whole (Webster, 1998). Many social workers in child protection felt that they were 'in a "no win" situation, "damned if they did, damned if they didn't" interfere' (Langan, 1998, p. 163; Franklin and Parton, 1991, pp. 16–19).

In the course of the 1980s and 1990s, social services departments had to grapple with the consequences of major administrative and organizational changes in other welfare agencies. One of the main influences on the community care legislation was the perverse incentive towards institutional care created by government subsidies to private residential care for the elderly (Langan, 1990). In a similar way, social services had to deal with pressures from health authorities to redefine the boundary between 'medical' and 'social' care by discharging highly dependent elderly people from hospital into 'the community'. The accelerated closure of long-stay psychiatric hospitals and the discharge of their patients into 'the community' was another source of problems for social services departments.

Furthermore, there is some contradiction between the charge of inflexibility and that of inconsistency. If social services respond in a flexible way to the needs of the local community – needs which are diverse – this will result in inconsistent patterns of provision both within and among local authority areas. Evers (1996, p. 9) notes that 'in many countries personal social services units, or parts of them, are intertwined with local communities, subcultures and networks; they are finely tuned with demands rising from there, the respective values and aspirations'.

The charge of inefficiency, based on comparisons of unit costs, raises the question of the applicability of 'value for money' criteria derived from the world of business to the world of social care, which we consider further below. In this context, however, it focuses attention on the difficulties created for the 'care manager' by the contradictory demands imposed on her by the community care reforms. On the one hand, she is responsible for assessing the client's needs and for ensuring that these needs are met. On the other hand, she is responsible for allocating resources for these needs – and for the needs of her other clients – within the constraints of the budget she has been allocated. She thus has to reconcile the tension between her responsibility to her client and her responsibility for rationing social services resources (Lewis et al., 1995, 1997; Langan, 1998, p. 168).

2.3   The discourse of failure

Though the arguments continue, the aura of failure hangs over the old local authority social services departments. This is nowhere more apparent than in the sphere of community care for the mentally ill, the subject of the White Paper *Modernising Mental Health Services: Safe, Sound and Supportive*:

> Care in the community has failed because, while it improved the treatment of many people who were mentally ill, it left far too many walking the streets, often at risk to themselves and a nuisance to others. A small but significant minority have been a threat to others or themselves. (Department of Health, 1998b, p. 4)

The conviction that 'community care has failed' has been proclaimed by the Secretary of State. It recurs throughout the White Paper and has been repeated so frequently in television reports and newspaper articles that it has acquired the status of conventional wisdom.

The discourse of 'failure' stands in symbolic contrast to that of 'modernization'. Indeed the legitimacy of the Third Way depends on the success of its advocates in discrediting the record of the – retrospectively constructed – previous two ways. What is striking is that, despite the contested character of the indictment of social services and community care, the perception of failure is shared not only by politicians and the media, but also apparently by social services staff. The readiness of workers at every level of the system to endorse a comprehensively critical judgement of previous standards of social care reflects a crisis of confidence among social care professionals (Langan, 1999).

The factors that have contributed to this crisis of confidence are wider than the list of failings provided by the 'modernizing' White Paper, though these are undoubtedly significant. The wider context is the breakdown of the consensus that sustained the post-war welfare state, and the impact of globalized market forces that have eroded old solidarities without providing any replacement (Exworthy and Halford, 1999, pp. 7–11). The resulting state of disorientation and demoralization in society at large has had a particular influence on those whose professional concern is to sustain what *Modernising Social Services* refers to as 'the fabric of a caring society'. In their current state of low self-esteem, social workers are highly receptive to new strategies – even in the unlikely forms of commissions, councils and inspectorates, or national service frameworks offering service models and national standards, the key innovations in the 'modernizing' proposals.

3   Managerialism before New Labour: the New Public Management

All the soundbites about innovation and modernization notwithstanding, managerialism was scarcely new to the world of social services in the late 1990s. After a number of false starts and hesitant beginnings in various public services in the 1980s, 'the New Public Management' really took shape in the early 1990s. It was already well established before Labour came to power in May 1997.

3.1   Reinventing government

The ideological impetus of the New Public Management came from the US, in the form of Osborne and Gaebler's 1992 book *Reinventing Government*, which, according to one British commentator, 'effectively translates private sector managerial ideas about quality into the context of public administration (Power, 1997, p. 43). In social services the key legislation was the NHS and Community Care Act, 1991; the key policy document the Audit Commission's *The Community Revolution*, published in 1992.

The mission of the New Public Management is to replace the presumed inefficiency of old-style 'bureau-professionalism' with the presumed efficiency of the market. There are four key principles. First, austerity: the New Public Management is committed to cost control and financial transparency. The creation of organizational sub-units with budgetary autonomy is a key device for rationing scarce resources. Secondly, market forces: the introduction of the purchaser/provider split and the formation of an internal market in welfare, in which state providers were obliged to compete with the voluntary and private sectors, was the major innovation of the 1991 community care reforms. Thirdly, the decentralization of managerial authority means making a distinction between strategic management (challenging the old order, removing middle management, imposing a commercial outlook) and operational management (managing budgets, ensuring collaboration with other agencies, utilizing information technology). Finally, the need to satisfy consumer demands for greater accountability in public services has led to a concern to define standards of performance and to establish mechanisms for consulting and involving services users, carers and the public.

3.2   A new workplace culture

The progress of what the Audit Commission dubbed a 'cultural revolution' in social services in the course of the 1990s has been widely discussed (Langan and Clarke, 1994, 1998; Hadley and Clough, 1997). Based on research carried out in 1995, Harris has described the emergence of a 'new managerialist social work labour process' characterized by pervasive managerial control. He has identified a 'new workplace culture' with a number of distinctive features (Harris, 1998, pp. 856–8).

Harris's research confirmed that the authorities had met with some success in promoting a more commercial outlook in social services. He noted that a 'business orientation' had emerged at operational management level as a consequence of devolved budgetary responsibility. Furthermore, 'scrupulous gate-keeping and strict rationing of scarce resources' had become 'the major activities of social workers'. He also observed that social workers' discretion had been 'curtailed by information technology systems which prioritize budgetary considerations in the allocation of services' and that these IT systems were 'coupled with close supervisory control'. As a result, 'human and information technology surveillance' could be 'combined with workload measurement and integrated into the worker's routine on-line recording', allowing supervision sessions to focus on social workers' 'productivity'.

4   Managerialism after New Labour: the drive for accountability

MODERNISING SOCIAL SERVICES
While allowing authorities the freedom to manage their social services as they think best, the Government intends to monitor these arrangements as part of the performance management arrangements described earlier. (Department of Health, 1998a, p. 123)

It is clear that, of the four principles of the New Public Management, the first three – austerity, market forces and decentralization – were well established in social services by the mid-1990s. The innovations of New Labour have concentrated on the fourth principle – that of account-ability. The modernizing White Paper proposes initiatives in a number of areas to render social services more answerable to the mythical taxpayer/citizen who ultimately foots the bill, to the clients and carers who rely on social care – and to the rest of us who may well, at different times, or indeed at the same time, occupy any of these categories.

4.1   Performance

Having proclaimed the need for clear objectives and priorities, for performance standards and effective systems for monitoring them, the White Paper offers extensive tables and flow charts and even a table including examples of possible performance indicators. The system begins with a list of 'national objectives for social services', subdivided into objectives for children's and adult services and common objectives. These objectives have a fairly general 'mission statement-type' quality, for example: 'to ensure that children are protected from emotional, physical, sexual abuse and neglect'. However, the White Paper recog-nizes the ambitious character of these objectives and emphasizes that 'there is a need to prioritise'. Another table presents 'national priorities for health and social services', in which the social services' priorities are 'children's welfare', 'inter-agency working' and 'regulation'.

How are these objectives to be attained? Here the social services White Paper refers to another modernizing White Paper, *Modern Local Government* (Department of the Environment, Transport and the Regions, 1998) which 'sets out the Government's proposal for Best Value, a rigorous and systematic approach to improving local govern-ment performance', a 'regime' which 'will apply to all local government functions, including social services' (p. 113). Another flow chart explains how 'the Best Value performance management framework' will ensure continuous improvements in performance.

The plan in the *Modernising Social Services* White Paper is that local authorities will establish *authority-wide objectives* and performance measures (reflecting national objectives and priorities). They will then carry out *fundamental performance reviews* of all their services over a five-year cycle which will inform *local performance plans* which will identify targets for annual improvements against locally defined performance indicators. The local planning process will be supported by information from a new statistical *performance assessment framework* (incorporating the Best Value National Performance Indicators). The Department of Health will carry out *annual reviews* of the social services aspects of the local performance plan. The Social Services Inspectorate will carry out *independent inspection*, informed and underpinned by the data in the performance assessment framework. It will also conduct *joint reviews* with the Audit Commission of every authority, every five years.

The final proposal of the modernizing White Paper to make social workers perform better is that most traditional of managerial techniques – the carrot and the stick. Authorities which are deemed successful according to these standards 'will be able to apply for beacon status'. This means that they 'will be recognized as centres of expertise and excellence that everyone should look up to'. On the other hand, the government 'will not hesitate to intervene where services are failing' (Department of Health, 1998a, p. 118).

4.2   Standards

The key feature of the government's plans to reform the system of regulation and inspection is the establishment of eight regional Commissions for Care Standards. These will be independent statutory bodies, each with its own chair and management board, including representatives from local authorities and health authorities.

The Commissions will take over responsibility for regulating the full range of residential and domiciliary services from the poorly co-ordinated network of national, local and health authorities currently undertaking these tasks. Services to be inspected include residential care homes for adults, nursing homes, children's homes, domiciliary care providers, independent fostering agencies, residential family centres and boarding schools. Inspection teams will have powers to serve improvement notices, to prosecute, and where necessary to deregister, including temporary closure.

The object of this comprehensive framework of regulation is to provide 'greater assurances that high standards will be met every-where', and, in particular, to provide 'stronger protection for vulnerable adults and children' whether they are cared for in institutions or at home (Department of Health, 1998a, p. 67).

4.3   Training

The main reform proposed in the sphere of staff training and development is the replacement of CCETSW with a new General Social Care Council. This is chaired by a lay person appointed by the Secretary of State and half the members are appointed so that service users and lay members form a majority. This long-anticipated initiative is the culmination of the shift in power over social work education from academic and professional agencies to state and managerial authorities. It also reflects the abandonment of the consensus of the 1970s that social workers needed a broad education in social sciences and psychology in favour of a narrower training emphasizing practical and administrative skills. Though the scandals involving child protection and children in care have encouraged the development of a post-qualification specialist 'child care award', the basic social work training is to retain its generic, competence-based, character.

For Mark Lymberry, who has critically appraised the impact of the community care reforms of the early 1990s on social work with older people, the shift towards a managerial rather than a professional approach in practice is mirrored by the trend in social work education towards an 'increasingly narrow, uncritical, competence-based model of learning' (Lymberry, 1998, p. 875).

The two key objectives for the General Social Care Council defined by the *Modernising Social Services* White Paper are that it should strengthen public protection and that it should ensure that social services staff are equipped to provide social care 'which allows and assists individuals to live their own lives' (Department of Health, 1998a, p. 88). It adds that the practical help offered by social workers should be based 'on research and other evidence of what works' and that it should be 'free of unnecessary ideological influences', though it does not specify what these might be.

4.4   Consultation

A recurrent theme of the *Modernising Social Services* White Paper is that 'people should have a say in what services they get and how they are delivered'. For example, in the section on services for adults, the White Paper states that: 'the Best Value regime will place a requirement on local authorities to find out what local citizens' service needs are, and what they think of how the council is doing' (p. 34). Local surveys of user and carer experience and of satisfaction with social services are to be part of the new monitoring arrangements. The White Paper emphasizes a 'user-centred' approach to social services that provides clear information, easy access (for example, through 'one-stop shops'), better choice based on user feedback, and effective methods of consultation.

The abandonment of the principles and methods of Old Labour is indisputable: the White Paper takes for granted the ascendancy of the market-oriented system of welfare introduced in the early 1990s over the traditions of state socialism. The distinction between the New Labour approach and that of the previous government is more difficult to discern: the White Paper's emphasis on quality and its regulation marks a development of the managerialist agenda that was so forcefully implemented under the Conservatives, rather than a radical departure from it. Despite all the rhetoric about innovation, continuities are more apparent than change in the direction of social policy under New Labour.

5   Problems and conflicts

Many of the problems arising from New Labour's plans to reform social services are not new – they are the set of problems that arose in the 1990s associated with the strategy of transforming social services along business lines. The modernizing proposals raise additional difficulties associated with attempts to extend user involvement and the measures to improve accountability.

5.1   Social services as a business

The question of whether market principles can be directly applied to public services, such as health or social services, has inevitably attracted a great deal of controversy. In his survey of 'quasi-markets' in the NHS, for example, LeGrand observed that there was no consensus on whether these had led to an increase in quality, or even choice and responsiveness to patients (LeGrand, 1994). Flynn has described the persistence of problems of information asymmetry (consumers lacking the knowledge to make informed choices), barriers to the entry of alternative providers to the internal markets, a paucity of information on outcomes on which to base evaluations of quality and a tendency for 'cream-skimming' (the selection by providers of the most valuable/least costly clients) (Flynn, 1999).

According to Nicky Stanley, who has studied 'user–practitioner transactions' in the process of care assessments in one local authority, the new culture of community care embodies 'consumer choice' rather than 'user choice' (Stanley, 1999). This study revealed that users and carers who can articulate their needs clearly have more 'choice' than those who lack a forceful voice and are uncertain how their needs might be met.

There is a fundamental conflict between the impersonal and formal relations of contract which prevail in the market, and the relationships which prevail in social services and which place a high premium on personal and informal contacts (Evers, 1996). Factors which play a very limited role in commerce – the helping and caring roles of individuals, family members and local networks – are the essence of the work of social services. The statutory responsibilities of official agencies are also a crucial part of the social services framework, in a way they are not for a normal commercial enterprise.

Another key distinction arises from the fact that social services departments provide *public* rather than *consumer* goods. Whereas the ordinary entrepreneur needs to satisfy only the customer, workers in social services have a 'multidimensional agenda': they have to satisfy service users (who may have carers or families with conflicting interests and needs), but also have important responsibilities to the common, public, interest. In child protection cases, for example, social workers have to reconcile responsibilities to the child, to the child's parents and other family members – and satisfy statutory duties. In some mental health cases, social workers have to balance the needs of the individual patient and the risk to the public – and again satisfy the requirements of the law. It is clear that the judgement of the quality of service varies according to the perspective of the person making the judgement.

5.2   User involvement

Emphasizing the contribution of the 'new social movements' around gender, race, ethnicity, sexuality, disability and age to the emergence of a new politics of welfare, Fiona Williams proposes, as one of her 'new principles for the millennium' that welfare subjects should have a *voice* to challenge the power of expert knowledge (Williams, 2000). Drawing on the traditions of the new social movements, she calls for the 'demo-cratization' of the relationship between user and provider, opening the way to a politics of differentiated universalism. The conception of user involvement advanced in the social services White Paper appears to fall short of these millennial aspirations.

Pollitt observes that the characteristic 'pathology' of business approaches to investigating consumer satisfaction is 'manipulative managerialism' – the use of superficial consultation methods which have little or no effect on practice (Pollitt, 1996). Though there is no evidence of such a pathology afflicting consultation procedures in social services, there are some indications of what might be described as a morbid predisposition (Priestley, 1998).

In their account of user involvement in personal social services in the UK, Beresford and colleagues note that there has been an expansion of independent service users' organizations in Britain and that this has received 'strong encouragement from the Department of Health' (Beresford et al., 1996). They are concerned at the evolution of rival discourses around user involvement. On the one hand there is a 'service agency' discourse which seeks to involve users as a 'data source to manage restricted resources, to inform rationing and targeting decisions'; on the other, there is a 'service users' discourse which is concerned with 'the wider life problems affecting clients, with civil and human as well as welfare rights'. Their conclusion is that, in practice, user involvement is 'still shaky, and genuine involvement on the basis of equality is still very rare'.

Forbes and Sashidharan are also concerned about the danger that user involvement may lead to incorporation and to the moderation of an oppositional position by individuals, or by advocacy or self-help groups. They note the 'uncritical approach to the definition of "users", which equates them with purchasers/consumers in a market, when, in reality many users of social services have little scope for choice': 'It is sometimes forgotten that the majority of service users within social work and psychiatry are not actively choosing to be in that position but are often inducted into service usage as a result of particular life experiences or the social context in which they find themselves.' Furthermore, where there is a coercive element in service provision, they warn that 'it could be argued that the concept of user involvement in these services is little more than an attempt to facilitate the smooth running of existing care provision' (1997, p. 486).

Despite all the rhetoric about autonomy, choice and empowerment, there are real limits on direct consumer control for frail elderly people, children, people with severe learning difficulties and for marginalized groups, who make up a substantial proportion of social services clients (Clarke, 1998). There may be some conflict here between the interests of that minority of service users who are able to participate in service users' organizations (people with physical disabilities or mild and moderate learning disabilities, people with HIV/AIDS, some former psychiatric patients) and those who are not.

5.3   Quality

Pollitt has questioned the applicability of fashionable business approaches to quality improvement – such as 'total quality management', 'benchmarking' and 'business process engineering' – to personal social services (Pollitt, 1996). He notes that such approaches assume an executive line management capable of imposing changes. This may work in business in conditions of major crisis, when everybody recognizes the need for drastic measures usually involving mass redundancies, but is unlikely to succeed in social services departments. Furthermore, such evangelical methods carry high risks and may themselves prove to have a destabilizing effect. He also comments that they rely on accurate performance data, which are, at present, lacking in social services.

The quest for objective standards of quality and ways of measuring performance is largely the result of the breakdown of the rather understated, but nonetheless authentic, 'community spirit' which in the past provided an informal framework for promoting good practice. Unfortunately, the techniques of quality assurance proposed by the *Modernising Social Services* White Paper are likely to exacerbate this underlying problem rather than help to overcome it. Evers reports on the conclusion drawn by a survey in the Netherlands on the effects of introducing such a scheme into social services:

> Enumerating quality benchmarks will neither give a coherent mission to the organization to be contracted in, nor will it work as the only point of departure for quality control, unless one creates a more basic presupposition which helps to safeguard a kind of general mutual understanding and some basic trust. (Evers, 1996, p. 9)

Can contract and control approaches compensate for the loss of this 'corporate spirit of community'?

6 A question of trust

The *Modernising Mental Health Services* White Paper (Department of Health, 1998b) specifically emphasizes the need to 'build confidence in our mental health services'. The elaborate mechanisms of audit, inspection and regulation proposed in this document and the *Modernising Social Services* White Paper are in large part a response to the perception that the public has lost confidence and trust in social welfare professionals. The question that arises is – can such mechanisms restore trust?

Power has warned of the dangers of the 'audit society': 'Assumptions of distrust sustaining audit processes may be self-fulfilling as auditees adapt their behaviour strategically in response to the audit process, thereby becoming less trustworthy' (1997, p. 135). He points to evidence that 'the very quality of service or output which the audit process is intended to enhance is itself damaged, even though goals of efficiency and cost-effectiveness are achieved'. The peculiar 'pathology of the audit society' is that 'in place of reflection on the need for auditable account giving, there are increasingly formalized rituals of accounting and verification. And this means that trust in auditing may be risky' (p. 138).

As Taylor-Gooby puts it, 'trust takes time to establish, but is easy to destroy' (1999, p. 101). Reviewing the results of surveys conducted by economic psychologists, he notes that contrary to the predictions of rational choice theory, people's decisions in welfare markets are strongly influenced by a normative framework in which trust plays a key role. It appears that markets in welfare depend more on trust because of the importance (and inscrutability) of professional decisions and because of the difficulty of assessing future risks. Taylor-Gooby wonders to what extent current welfare markets are sustained by the moral legacy of the welfare state – and how the erosion of this legacy might compromise efficiency. His conclusion is that welfare markets should be designed to foster rather than erode inclusive normative frameworks which assist them in achieving welfare goals.

Many commentators have expressed concern about the consequences of the current ascendancy of managerialism for social work as a profession. In his study of the effects of the community care reforms, Lymberry (1998) warns of 'the potentially serious consequences for the continuation of a distinctive social work role in relation to services for older people'. He notes some contrary trends – uncertainty about whether current developments will be successful, the emergence of more critical research, the attempts to reclaim professionalism by some teachers and researchers, grass roots resistance to the 'top-down' character of the reform process. However, he concedes sombrely that his own research suggests a negative response to the question – is there a future for the 'professional project' of social work?

The question that must be answered by the proponents of more managerialism as the solution to the problems of social services is whether such methods are likely to weaken still further the local and moral economy that still prevails and, arguably, still sustains the best social work practice.

References

Audit Commission (1992) *The Community Revolution: The Personal Social Services and Community Care*, London, HMSO.

Beresford, P., Croft, C., Evans, C. and Harding, T. (1996) 'Quality in personal social services: the developing role of user involvement in the UK', paper presented to International Seminar, Developing Quality in Personal Social Services, Helsinki, April.

Blair, A. (1998) *The Third Way: New Politics for the New Century*, London, Fabian Society.

Clarke, C. (1998) 'Self-determination and paternalism in community care: practice and prospects', *British Journal of Social Work*, 28 (June), pp. 387–402.

Clarke, J. and Newman, J. (1998) 'A modern British people? New Labour and the reconstruction of social welfare', paper presented at the Discourse Analysis and Social Research Centre, Copenhagen Business School, 24–26 September.

Department of the Environment, Transport and the Regions (1998) *Modern Local Government. In Touch with the People*, London, Stationery Office.

Department of Health (1998a) *Modernising Social Services: Promoting Independence, Improving Protection, Raising Standards*, London, Stationery Office.

Department of Health (1998b) *Modernising Mental Health Services: Safe, Sound and Supportive*, London, Stationery Office.

Evers, A. (1996) 'Quality development: part of a changing culture of care in personal social services', lecture delivered at the International Seminar, Developing Quality in Personal Social Services, Helsinki, 12–14 April.

Exworthy, M. and Halford, S. (1999) 'Professionals and managers in a changing public sector: conflict, compromise, collaboration', in Exworthy, M. and Halford, S. (eds) *Professionals and the New Managerialism in the Public Sector*, Buckingham, Open University Press.

Flynn, R. (1999) 'Managerialism, professionalism and quasi markets', in Exworthy, M. and Halford, S. (eds) *Professionalism and the New Managerialism in the Public Sector*, Buckingham, Open University Press.

Forbes, J. and Sashidharan, S.P. (1997) 'User involvement in services – incorporation or challenge?' *British Journal of Social Work*, 27, pp. 481–98.

Franklin, B. and Parton, N. (eds) (1991) *Social Work, the Media and Public Relations*, London, Routledge.

Hadley, R. and Clough, R. (1997) *Care in Chaos: Frustration and Challenge in Community Care*, London, Cassell.

Harris, J. (1998) 'Scientific management, bureau-professionalism, new managerialism: the labour process of state social work', *British Journal of Social Work*, 28, pp. 839–62.

Hirst, J. (1999) 'Pulled everywhichway', *Community Care*, 19–25 August, pp. 18–21.

Inman, K. (1999) 'Changing roles', *Community Care*, 3–9 June, pp. 20–1.

Langan, M. (1990) 'Community Care in the 1990s', in *Critical Social Policy*, 29, Autumn.

Langan, M. (1998) 'The personal social services', in Ellison, N. and Pierson, C. (eds) *Developments in British Social Policy*, London, Macmillan.

Langan, M. (1999) 'The management myth', *Community Care*, 28 January–3 February, pp. 24–5.

Langan, M. and Clarke, J. (1994) 'Managing in the mixed economy of care', in Clarke, J., Cochrane, A. and McLaughlin, E. (eds) *Managing Social Policy*, London, Sage.

Langan, M. and Clarke, J. (1998) 'Review', in Langan, M. (ed.) *Welfare: Needs, Rights and Risks*, London, Routledge.

LeGrand, J. (1994) 'Evaluating the NHS reforms', in Robinson, R. and Le Grand, J. (eds) *Evaluating the NHS Reforms*, London, Kings Fund Institute.

Lewis, J., Bernstock, P. and Bovell, V. (1995) 'The community care changes: unresolved tensions in policy issues and implementation', *Journal of Social Policy*, 24 (1), pp. 73–94.

Lewis, J., Bernstock, P., Bovell, V. and Wookey, F. (1997) 'Implementing care management: issues in relation to the new community care', *British Journal of Social Work*, 27 (February), pp. 5–24.

Lymberry, M. (1998) 'Care management and professional autonomy: the impact of community care legislation on social work with older people', *British Journal of Social Work*, 28 (December), pp. 863–78.

Osborne, D. and Gaebler, T. (1992) *Reinventing Government*, Reading, MA, Addison-Wesley.

Pollitt, C. (1996) 'Business and professional approaches to quality improvement: a comparison of their suitability for the personal social services', paper presented to International Seminar at the European Centre for Social Welfare and Research, Helsinki, April.

Power, M. (1997) *The Audit Society: Rituals of Verification*, Oxford, Oxford University Press.

Priestley, M. (1998) 'Discourse and resistance in care assessment: integrated living and community care', *British Journal of Social Work*, 28 (October), pp. 659–73.

Stanley, N. (1999) 'User–practitioner transactions in the new culture of community care', *British Journal of Social Work*, 29 (June), pp. 417–35.

Taylor-Gooby, P. (1999) 'Markets and motives: trust and egoism in welfare markets', *Journal of Social Policy*, 28 (1), pp. 97–114.

Webster, R. (1998) *Care in the Community: Illusion or Reality*, London, Orwell Press.

Williams, F. (2000) 'Principles of recognition and respect in welfare', in Lewis, G., Gewirtz, S. and Clarke, J. (eds) *Rethinking Social Policy*, London, Open University/Sage.

10

The Criminal Justice System: New Labour's New Partnerships

Eugene McLaughlin and John Muncie

Crime was crucial to both the ideological rebirth of the Labour Party as 'New Labour' and its landslide victory in the 1997 General Election. Indeed, it could be argued that one of New Labour's most remarkable political achievements is to have successfully challenged the idea that social democratic political parties are by definition 'soft on crime'. This chapter traces the emergence of New Labour's 'Third Way' project on crime and moves on to evaluate the nature and impact of the proposed modernization of the criminal justice system. The final sections focus on youth justice, since reducing youth crime and radical reform of the youth justice system are the issues that New Labour has proclaimed as pivotal to realizing its long term objective of commanding the centre ground of law and order politics. Our overall perspective is that New Labour is engaged in a high stakes balancing act. An amalgam of managerialist, communitarian and authoritarian populist ideas has been pulled together under the phrase 'modernization'. This has created the basis for assembling a settlement on law and order and the long-held vision of an integrated or 'joined-up' criminal justice system operating

within a commonly agreed philosophy. However, the tensions and contradictions generated by this 'tough on crime and tough on the causes of
crime' project will require careful political management.

1 The managerialization of crime control

During the 1979 election campaign the Conservative Party accused the
then Labour government of presiding over fifteen years of rising crime
and growing disrespect for the rule of law. To reverse this situation, the
Conservatives promised to spend more on fighting crime, even if this
meant diverting resources from other public services. No matter what
the mountain of academic research findings said about what worked
and what did not work in the field of crime control, the Conservatives
were wedded to the ideological truth that criminals could be deterred by
sufficient numbers of police officers armed with the necessary legal
powers, and backed by punitive sentencing and harsh penal regimes.
However, as the 1980s progressed, despite the fact that the criminal
justice agencies enjoyed an unprecedented period of growth in overall
resourcing and systemic empowerment, the official crime rate and the
public's fear of crime escalated to unparalleled levels. The period also
witnessed outbreaks of urban rioting and industrial conflict which,
although not unprecedented, underlined the depth of racial and social
division in Britain. To cap it all, a series of high profile miscarriages of
justice undermined public confidence in the ability of the criminal justice
system to identify the guilty and protect the rights of the innocent.

The political reverberations of this ignominious 'failure to deliver'
and a much starker financial backdrop compelled a radical rethink of the
assumptions underpinning the Conservatives' law and order policies
and the uncritical support traditionally given to the criminal justice
agencies. Home Office officials, under growing pressure from the
Treasury to account for the dramatically increased 'law and order'
budget, began to make headway in persuading ministers and key
members of the policy community that a self-generated crisis of morale
and legitimacy was engulfing the criminal justice system. The sheer
number of individuals entering and re-entering the system was threatening to paralyse the functioning of the courts. The knock-on effects of
punitive sentencing were overcrowding in the prisons and Prison
Service demands for more resources. The experience of incarceration
was entrenching patterns of offending and increasing the likelihood of
more serious offending upon release. Spiralling rates of re-offending
were increasing levels of victimization and the public's fear of crime and
growing intolerance generated demands for more police officers,
tougher policing strategies and harsher sentences, which in turn thrust
even more people into the system. As far as Home Office officials were
concerned a pragmatic settlement had to be pieced together which

would reallocate responsibility for crime control and remove questions of crime causation, criminality and punishment from the political arena. The proposed criminal justice settlement consisted of:

- situational crime prevention strategies;
- punishment in the community;
- the managerialization of the criminal justice agencies;
- transforming the demoralizing and fatalistic 'nothing works' culture of criminal justice agencies;
- the quasi-marketization of certain criminal justice functions;
- the responsibilization of individuals.

The overall purpose of this sea-change in policy was to create a cost-effective, efficient and unified criminal justice system which would work within nationally agreed sets of guidelines and standards to:

- reduce the crime rate and the fear of crime to 'acceptable' levels;
- ensure that demands for a scarce resource – 'justice' – were kept within economically manageable levels.

Throughout, the principles of new public managerialism were identified as the tailored pathway to economical criminal justice. It became increasingly apparent to commentators that, taken collectively, these policy proposals heralded the most sweeping and radical reforms of the criminal justice system in over a century. In the long term, the unfolding mixed economy of criminal justice would lead to the state radically reworking its traditional responsibility for preventing, detecting and punishing crime (see Fowles, 1990; Tuck, 1992; Jones, 1993; McLaughlin and Muncie, 1994; Garland, 1996).

However, even before the new settlement was put into practice it came under intense attack. First, senior members of the judiciary, magistrates and police officers voiced grave misgivings about the underlying philosophy of the sentencing reforms. Secondly, the attempt to inject new public managerialist ideas provoked considerable resistance from criminal justice professionals who argued that criminal justice – a public sector good – could not be run like a business selling products to customers in a competitive market. Thirdly, the nature of the law and order debate in England and Wales shifted dramatically during 1992–93. The appointment of Tony Blair as shadow Home Secretary in June 1992 marked a decisive shift in the Labour Party's stance on law and order. Opinion polls indicated that unless the Party persuaded 'Middle England' that it was not 'soft on crime and soft on the causes of crime', Labour could not win a general election. Against the backdrop of the highest crime levels in western Europe, an escalating tabloid newspaper panic about the seemingly relentless surge in juvenile crime and increasingly conflictual relations between the Conservatives and core criminal justice professionals, Tony Blair found the critical space to present New Labour as the party of law and order.

1.1   The 'Third Way' on law and order

In January 1993 the soundbite 'Tough on crime and tough on the causes of crime' was coined by Tony Blair to signal a new 'Third Way' approach to law and order. In various speeches and position papers, Blair spelt out the importance of moving beyond what he described as ideologically blinkered 'Old Left' and 'New Right' understandings of the problem of crime (Blair, 1993, 1994, 1996). He argued that rising crime rates were not inevitable and that the restoration of law and order could be achieved by rebuilding the foundations of a strong civic society, self-regulating families and cohesive communities and by re-establishing the moral values of mutual obligation, self-discipline and individual responsibility. 'Old' Labour's liberal thinking on penal affairs would have to be 'modernized' by giving equal rights to victims and the needs of law-abiding citizens. Crime was morally wrong and 'New Labour' would not seek to excuse or condone it. Individuals would be held to be responsible for their own behaviour and be brought to justice and punished if they committed a criminal offence (Blair, 1996). In a highly volatile political context, Blair's determination to play the crime card for electoral advantage stoked an emergent Conservative backlash. At the Conservative Party conference in October 1993, an ever-more-desperate Michael Howard vacated the centre-Right ground of British politics and shifted government policy resolutely to the right, unveiling a 27-point law and order package of new criminal sanctions, tough minimum sentences and plans for more prisons.

With the appointment of Jack Straw as shadow Home Secretary in 1994 it became clear that New Labour was willing to go to considerable lengths to 'out-tough' the Conservative government on law and order. For example, in order to politically undercut the impact of the drop in recorded crime and an emergent post-recession economic boom, Straw attempted to expand the crime debate by highlighting the need to implement 'zero tolerance' policing strategies to tackle what he described as a rising tide of 'low level' disorder, incivility and anti-social behaviour. Furthermore, New Labour lent tacit parliamentary support to increasingly illiberal Conservative proposals contained in the Criminal Justice and Public Order Act, 1994; the Crime (Sentences) Act, 1997; and the Police Act, 1997. The reward for this 'new realist' crusade against crime and disorder and the tailoring of its policies towards 'Middle England' was a series of opinion polls which indicated that for the first time in the post-war period New Labour was consistently ahead of the Conservatives on the issue of law and order (Anderson and Mann, 1998).

But what of the commitment to be tough on the causes of crime? Commentators are agreed that in the countdown to the election the relentless repetition of the 'tough on crime' part of its favourite soundbite closed down the space for any meaningful political discussion of New Labour's position on the causes of crime (Bowring, 1997; Brownlee, 1998; Johnson and Bottomley, 1998). The discourse of tackling the causes of 'social exclusion' gave New Labour a politically acceptable way to effect a subtle shift in emphasis that proved highly acceptable to criminal justice professionals and pressure groups. For example, the briefing paper *Tackling the Causes of Crime* (Labour Party, 1996) identified poor parenting; educational underachievement; school truancy; drug and alcohol abuse; lack of facilities for young people; unemployment; low income; poor skills, homelessness and deprivation as the key contributory factors. This document argued that New Labour's broader social and economic policies would address the structural causes of crime. It also stressed that crime prevention policies were central to New Labour's aim of increasing social inclusion.

However, given its fears about the social fragmentation wrought by neo-liberalism and the emergence of a substantial 'underclass' where informal social controls and norms of respectability had all but collapsed, New Labour also flagged up the urgent need to implement crime and disorder reduction strategies in 'dysfunctional, disorderly communities'. The Conservatives were berated by both Blair and Straw for under-resourcing crime prevention and for ignoring the recommendations of the Home Office-commissioned Morgan Report, which concluded that real progress would only be forthcoming if local authorities were empowered by statute to prevent crime and promote community safety (Home Office, 1991). The Conservatives' ideological position on local government and public expenditure and their belief in the primacy of voluntary effort and market forces ruled out acceptance of such a stance.

Labour local authorities who had been involved in police monitoring and community safety in the mid to late 1980s enthusiastically embraced the key findings of the Morgan Report. In contrast to situational crime prevention, which had become almost synonymous with locks, bolts, CCTV and a large dog, the term 'community safety' facilitated acknowledgement of the impact of broader social and economic factors and suggested greater community participation and representation (McLaughlin, 1994; Crawford, 1997; Hughes, 1998). Because these local authorities were at the forefront in developing pilot projects they were also forced to think about effective inter-agency partnerships and the setting of strategic objectives and the evaluation of outcomes. Thus, prior to the 1997 General Election, as the result of local authority initiatives, New Labour was able to commit itself to delivering a nationally co-ordinated, evidence-based programme to reduce crime and prevent re-offending.

One other important issue needs to be discussed here. Although both Tony Blair and Jack Straw had made considerable political capital out of their opposition to the Conservatives' proposed managerialization of criminal justice, they were aware that the criminal justice system they were inheriting was marked by 'complexity, confusion, overlapping areas of responsibility and a fundamental lack of organizational structure and accountability' (Addison, 1998, p. 1). If New Labour was to make real progress on its commitment to be 'tough on crime and the causes of crime', it would have to embark on radical reform of the criminal justice system. The positive citation of the conclusions and recommendations of Audit Commission reports in various New Labour policy documents and statements indicated that the 'modernization' of criminal justice would be achieved by the reworking and intensification of the new public managerial disciplines working their way unevenly through the various parts of this policy environment.

1.2   A 'modern' criminal justice settlement

In government, New Labour has been keen to demonstrate to 'Middle England', through a series of well-publicized crackdowns on various 'deviant' groups and lifestyles, that it is taking its fear of crime and disorder seriously. It has also been able to legitimize its policy proposals through extensive consultation with Home Office officials, criminal justice organizations and pressure groups who are committed to 'evidence-based' approaches. The intention is to ensure that its 'flagship' criminal justice legislation, the Crime and Disorder Act, 1998, can stand as the basis for 'the most co-ordinated and coherent attack on crime in a generation' (Straw, 1999). The cornerstones of the new criminal justice settlement are:

- consistent and mutually reinforcing aims and objectives;
- enhanced use of existing resources ('Best Value');
- evidence-based approaches to crime reduction which embed a 'what works' occupational/professional culture;
- modernization of the structure and operation of criminal justice agencies;
- improved performance management.

The objectives for the criminal justice system are as follows:

- to reduce crime and fear of crime and their social and economic costs;
- to dispense justice fairly and efficiently and to promote confidence in the rule of law.

Virtually every Home Office document stresses that this will be achieved through continual auditing, setting priorities and targets, monitoring, evaluation and inspection. Moreover, a considerable amount of time and energy has been spent inducting criminal justice professionals into understanding how they can manage, improve and account for perform-ance levels (Home Office, 1998a, 1998b, 1999; Hough and Tilley, 1998; Audit Commission, 1999).

Teasing out the long-term implications of government policy is inevitably fraught with difficulty. However, because the multiple trans-formations signalled by the Crime and Disorder Act, 1998, and unfolding crime reduction agenda both reflect and reinforce New Labour's much wider 'modernization' project, it has the potential to produce several fundamental changes in the nature of local crime control. First, imple-mentation of the Act will require extensive changes in the working practices and thinking of all the criminal justice and partner social policy agencies. Because the partnerships are expected to work across a series of institutional barriers and further blur and mix the boundaries between private, public, voluntary and community spaces, they have the potential to produce entirely new organizational configurations/networks with their own distinctive managerialized culture. And secondly, the com-munities within which the partnerships are working are being subjected to, in the words of Edwards and Stenson (1999), unprecedented 'weeding and seeding' strategies. As a result of the recognition that effective crime control strategies must be rooted in the dynamics of local communities, and New Labour's fixation with clamping down on disorder, we are witnessing the intensive reterritorialization and remoralization of crime control strategies. Taken together they have the potential to:

- produce new conceptualizations and discourses of crime causation;
- construct new criminal subjects and new model law-abiding citizens;
- deepen and intensify managerialization processes;
- rewrite the script of local governance and civil liberties.

These shifts mark the difference from previous Conservative admin-istrations. In order to explore some of these emergent issues in more depth, the remainder of this chapter focuses on the modernization of youth justice, arguably the most important part of New Labour's crime and disorder agenda and a central part of its contract with the electorate.

2   The modernization of the youth justice system

Within New Labour's approach to law and order there are marked divergences from the past, and a series of recurring and familiar themes. Most importantly, because the problem of crime continues to be officially documented as primarily a problem of young people, the vast majority of the clauses in the Crime and Disorder Act, 1998, are directed specifically to this particular age group. It continues to relocate responsibility for their regulation and control from central government to local authorities, local communities and parents. However, the new statutory duty for local authorities to develop partnerships with a wide range of agencies specifically to reduce levels of youth crime and nuisance significantly adds to the depth of managerialist intervention. The legislation promotes a 'Best Value' ethos in youth justice by creating a series of organizations, such as Youth Offending Teams, with their own targets that are amenable to the logic of the quantifiable audit. To justify this 'modernization' all previous youth policy has been reassessed and condemned as 'failure'. Furthermore, traditional philosophical justifications for a separate system of youth justice – whether grounded in principles of welfare or justice – are effectively bypassed. The 1998 Crime and Disorder Act seeks to draw a line under the 'failures' of past decades by:

- defining the principal aim of the youth justice system as the prevention of offending and re-offending by children and young persons;
- enabling offenders and their parents to take responsibility for their offending behaviour;
- deploying early effective interventions for first offenders;
- implementing fast-track, efficient procedures from arrest to sentence;
- building partnerships between the various youth justice agencies.

But what exactly does this agenda signify for those working in the youth justice system given that it is to be operationalized through further managerialization?

2.1   Identifying and constructing the problem

There is certainly nothing unique in New Labour's identifying young people as the major source of the 'problem of crime'. Such official concerns date at least as far back as the origins of a separate system for juveniles in the early nineteenth century. However the prognosis of the problem has shifted dramatically. For example, in the 1960s a welfare lobby was able to conflate delinquency with parental neglect, whilst, as we have seen, in the 1980s the New Right promoted a popularly received view of crime and criminality as indulged in by individuals with no self-control and lacking any sense of individual responsibility. Not surprisingly, New Labour's 'Third Way' view would seem to be something of an amalgam of these polar positions. The key cause of youth crime is identified as lack of parental responsibility at an early age.

But however youth crime is explained, it is clear that by the mid-1990s New Labour was convinced that it was a massively growing problem: this despite the fact that between 1987 and 1997 there was a 30 per cent fall in the number of those aged 10–17 found guilty of indictable offences. Custody rates of young people also fell, sometimes dramatically, particularly between 1986 and 1994. Much of this has been explained as the result of the growing confidence of magistrates in rigorous and innovative community disposals (such as intensive inter- mediate treatment) and a tendency on the part of the police to caution informally rather than through official record (Muncie, 1999a, p. 283). For some it had already amounted to a successful 'quiet revolution' in youth justice policy (Allen, 1991). However, during 1992–93 the tabloid press managed once more to place the issue of youth crime at the top of the law and order agenda following a series of disturbances on housing estates, often associated with joy riding, and, most pertinently, following the murder of James Bulger by two 10-year-old boys in Liverpool. This latter event, more than any other, seemed to galvanize politicians and commentators of all persuasions to give the issue of out-of-control juveniles and children their renewed critical attention (Muncie, 1999a, pp. 3–9). A number of authoritarian measures – secure training centres for 12–15-year-olds, boot camps, mandatory minimum sentences, aboli- tion of the presumption of innocence for 10–14-year-olds – quickly followed. Whilst all of this appeared to be driven as much by political posturing as by any concern for effectiveness and responsibility, it was noticeable that by 1995 the numbers of under-18s facing custody had already begun to rise (Goldson, 1999).

By 1996 the Audit Commission had entered the fray and much of the impetus for the reform of the youth justice system stems from its influential report *Misspent Youth* (Audit Commission, 1996). This comprehensive, independent review of the youth justice system esti- mated that 26 per cent of known offenders were under 18, accounting for some seven million offences a year. It recommended a two-pronged strategy – targeting persistent offenders to get them to change their behaviour and discouraging those 'at risk' from getting involved in offending in the first place. The report was significant in side-stepping the long-standing and thorny debate over crime causation (wilfulness, deprivation, poverty, neglect and so on), instead identifying a series of 'risk conditions', such as drug use, school exclusions and inadequate parental supervision, which were 'known' to correlate with recorded offending. Whereas in the past, neglect or lack of self-control had been conflated with delinquency, now misbehaviour and crime were viewed as coterminous. As a result a risk management strategy based on pro- moting parenting skills, restructuring under fives' education and supporting teachers was proposed. In addition, the Audit Commission noted that the problem also lay in the inefficient, uncoordinated use of resources. Its key proposals were to implement statutory time limits – to reduce the length of time taken from arrest to sentence – and perform- ance targets to ensure that the many different agencies involved (courts, education, probation, social services, prison, health) agreed and acted upon the main objectives (Audit Commission, 1998). The aim was to make serious inroads into the £1 billion a year spent processing and dealing with young offenders.

The Audit Commission finding that key parts of the existing youth justice system were inefficient, expensive and failing to prevent young people from offending was enthusiastically embraced by New Labour. The Home Secretary, Jack Straw, constructed the 1980s and early 1990s as years of failure, stating that the entire youth justice system was in disarray and gave the impression that a 'hard core' of young people was offending with impunity because of fundamentally flawed policies and practices (Straw, 1998, p. 4). The White Paper preceding the 1998 Crime and Disorder Act dwelt on the 'failures' of the past and ominously insisted that from now on there would be 'no more excuses' (Home Office, 1997). In office New Labour's rewriting of the failed contemporary history of youth justice has continued, with Jack Straw insisting that:

> by the time of the last election . . . repeat cautioning encouraged young offenders to believe that they could get away with their crime without punishment, and even when the system did intervene, it was slow, inefficient and largely ineffective. If a case got to court, the young offender would, at best, be a spectator in court – spoken over, round or about, but rarely spoken to, still less asked to explain his or her behaviour. (Straw, 1999)

2.2   Partnerships – joined-up youth justice

Both the Morgan Report on crime prevention and the Audit Commission report on youth justice had stressed that for successful outcomes to be achieved, responsibility for law and order should be devolved from a central state to a series of semi-autonomous local partnerships, voluntary agencies and privatized bodies. Their recommendations also emphasized the need to act primarily on evidence-based research which revealed 'what works' and to ignore any alternative approaches considered uneconomic and inefficient. As a result such 'transformative' issues as individual need, diagnosis, rehabilitation, and reformation have tended to be replaced, or subsumed within a range of 'actuarial' techniques of classification, risk assessment and resource management (Feely and Simon, 1992; Muncie, 1999b). Evaluation of success or failure has come to rest on indicators of internal systems performance. The Audit Commission, for example, argued that systems should be established to allow sharing of information, that social services, schools and police should work together to establish local crime audits and crime reduction strategies and that local authorities should continuously review how they allocate resources: 'Practitioners need to see the value of the multi-agency approach. . . . Joint training of practitioners working in the target areas can help promote shared understanding and help identify shared problems' (Audit Commission, 1996, p. 104).

The 1998 Crime and Disorder Act carried forward much of this ethos of solving problems through partnership and joint ownership by effectively nationalizing youth justice. A Youth Justice Board, sponsored by the Home Office, began operating in October 1998 to support, monitor and evaluate the performance of youth justice nationwide and to encourage 'what works' and 'best practice'. As Lord Warner, head of the Youth Justice Board, warned, youth justice workers 'will not be able to stay in the professional trenches defending themselves against change' (1998, p. 2). The board has an extremely wide strategic remit, overseeing all aspects of the youth justice system, advising the Home Secretary on how the new statutory aim of preventing offending can be achieved, assessing how far that objective is being met at a local level, commissioning research, awarding grants to develop good practice and acting as a central source of promotion and publishing. It is also the budget holder and quality controller for the entire penal estate for young offenders in England and Wales.

At a local level, the Crime and Disorder Act, 1998, imposes a statutory duty and responsibility on all local authorities 'to prevent offending by young people' and requires all agencies – police, probation, social services, health authorities, the Crown Prosecution Service, defence solicitors, the Prison Service, the courts – to have regard to that aim. All aspects of local authority work are now infused with crime prevention responsibilities. Every local authority with social service and education responsibilities is required to formulate and implement an annual youth justice plan setting out how youth justice proposals are to be funded and operationalized. Each plan has to be submitted to the Youth Justice Board for approval (Gordon et al., 1999, p. 27). To put these plans into local action, every local authority had established, by April 2000, Youth Offending Teams (YOTs), consisting of, on a statutory basis, representatives from each of social services, probation, police, health and education authorities. YOTs are empowered to co-ordinate provision throughout youth justice to ensure that all agencies act in tandem and deliver a range of interventions and programmes that will ensure that young people 'face up to the consequences of their crimes and learn to change the habits and attitudes which led them into offending and anti-social behaviour' (Home Office, 1997, pp. 27–8). Such interventions include supervising community sentences, dealing with parents, organizing reparation and curfews, providing school reports to the courts, providing careers advice, giving advice on drug and alcohol issues and so on. To co-ordinate this work a new managerial position of YOT manager has been created; the manager's central skill is that of being able to meet key measurable objectives and standards, rather than necessarily having prior professional experience of working with young offenders. It is a role that might be particularly onerous, given:

- the mandate to act as 'agents of transformation';
- the ambitious time-scales;
- the disappointing and chaotic outcomes of previous multi-agency partnerships;
- the inequalities of power, influence and knowledge between the different agencies;
- the problem of coping with the multitude of organizational reforms flowing through the different partner agencies.

What is noticeable in this gamut of management restructuring and evaluation is that all aspects of young people's lives are now potentially open to official monitoring and scrutiny. Moreover it is a scrutiny which penetrates not only deeper, but also more broadly by targeting younger children and those below the age of criminal responsibility. As Haines and Drakeford (1998, p. 238) warned, this 'repressive intent' may not fail to prevent offending but instead will amplify and distort young people's misbehaviour 'by drawing them ever earlier and ever closer into a system which cannot but do more harm than good'.

2.3   Responsibilization and remoralization

New Labour's preferred identification of crime causation lies primarily with a lack of discipline and order in particular families and communities (Home Office, 1997, p. 5; see also Farrington, 1996; Audit Commission, 1996, pp. 60–2). The phrase 'parental responsibility' had already become something of a watchword in many aspects of British social policy (Allen, 1990). An image of wilfully negligent parents colluding with, or even encouraging, misbehaviour as the inevitable result of a 1960s permissive culture was popularized by the Conservatives in the 1980s. A breakdown of the nuclear family unit, high divorce rates and increases in single parenting, it was argued, were the root causes of a moral decay epitomized by increased crime rates, homelessness and drug taking. In addition, excessive welfare dependency had encouraged families to rely on state benefits rather than each other. In the process children's moral development had been eroded. However, as New Labour's approach reveals, the idea of a 'parenting deficit' need not be confined to those on the right of the political spectrum. Amitai Etzioni's communitarian agenda, for example, also emphasizes that the root cause of crime lies within the home and that it is in the domestic sphere that the shoring up of our moral foundations should begin (Etzioni, 1995, p. 11). A communitarianism which speaks of localism, community responsibility and moral obligation lies at the heart of New Labour's youth crime agenda (Hughes, 1996, p. 21).

Concerns over irresponsibility and lack of discipline underpin many of the powers introduced by the 1998 Act. For example, courts may impose a parenting order requiring parents to attend counselling or child guidance sessions and to ensure that their children are not absent from school. Failure to comply can lead to a fine of £1,000. The order may also be given alongside a child safety order which may require children under the age of 10 to abide by the conditions of a local child curfew. This imposes bans on unsupervised children being present in certain public areas between 8p.m. and 6a.m. The dominant objective is to encourage and, if necessary, compel parents to take 'proper' care and control of their children. For those aged over 10 an anti-social behaviour order may be brought into force requiring any person causing alarm, distress or harassment to one or more people to be subject to a series of residence, movement and association prohibitions. Breach of this civil order is a criminal offence punishable by five years' imprisonment. Collectively these provisions reflect New Labour's conviction that low level public disorder, which may not necessarily be criminal, should be a priority target. The rhetoric of 'nipping it in the bud' is not only preventive but supportive in tone. However, enforcing the sustained policing of people who are 'acting irresponsibly' or who are 'out of place' or who are simply different in outlook and style also adds a significant moral and coercive dimension to matters of achieving social control through legal recourse.

In other respects the legislation also makes individuals of every age responsible for their actions. In England and Wales the principle of *doli incapax* ensured that before anyone under the age of 14 could be prosecuted it was incumbent on the prosecution to show that they acted wilfully and with full knowledge of their wrongdoing. The doctrine was first placed under review by the Conservative government following the High Court ruling in 1994 that it was 'unreal, contrary to common sense and a serious disservice to the law'. Three years later, the new Labour Home Secretary announced that the ruling would be abolished in order to 'help convict young offenders who are ruining the lives of many communities' and on the basis that 'children aged between 10 and 13 were plainly capable of differentiating between right and wrong' (Muncie, 1999a, p. 256). This was in direct contradiction to the United Nations' recommendations that the UK give serious consideration to raising the age of criminal responsibility to bring the UK countries in line with much of Europe. Notwithstanding the fact that the move was in contravention of United Nations' stipulations on the Rights of the Child and likely to be severely tested by the 1998 Human Rights Act, the Crime and Disorder Act abolished the presumption that a child over the age of 10 was incapable of committing a criminal offence. As a result an important principle which (in theory at least) had acted to protect children for hundreds of years from the full rigour of the law was removed. Once more individual rights were forfeited whilst individual responsibility was strengthened (Bandalli, 1998; Haines and Drakeford, 1998).

3 Conclusion

Of all public sector agencies, those of criminal justice long seemed immune to the new public managerialist requisites of fiscal audit, performance indicators and measurable effectiveness. Nothing, particularly costs, could stand in the way of delivering a safer and more secure electorate. However, by the late 1980s this orthodoxy slowly unravelled with a growing penetration of managerialist philosophies and strategies into an area that had previously been considered to be solely demand-led.

To the consternation of many commentators, when New Labour was returned to government in 1997 the processes of managerialization were not only warmly embraced, but under the rubric of 'modernization' also significantly extended. The criminal justice system has been subjected to an unprecedented expenditure review and now operates with strategic and business plans with specified aims, objectives, performance measures, efficiency targets and clearly defined outcomes. League tables on various aspects of the performance of criminal justice agencies are now commonplace. Local authorities are required by law to audit their crime reduction strategies and budgets to comply with the new 'Best Value' ethos. Courts have been ordered to reduce the time taken between the prosecution and sentencing of offenders. New penal establishments are to be built with private money and run by the private sector. It has also been proposed that the prison system should regularly publish prisoner recidivism rates so that the 'best' could be distinguished from the 'worst'. All of this is intended to raise levels of organizational performance within a new conception of criminal justice purpose based on crime reduction. As a result, in place of 'old' criminal justice bureau professionalism New Labour hopes that a series of 'new' operational agencies will emerge whose performance is dominated by a 'what works' philosophy and the requirement to produce measurable and quantifiable outcomes. The practice of criminal justice is being shifted more and more towards a technical process and, to date, those working within the system have been remarkably supportive of the new highly managerialist approach. However, whilst at this level the primary rationale for the system is contained within a seemingly non-ideological and apolitical logic of evaluation/re-evaluation and audit/re-audit, at another it is also under-pinned by an ongoing moral crusade of responsibilization and remoralization.

For criminal justice professionals, the 'tough on the causes of crime' part of New Labour's soundbite seemed to herald a shift in emphasis away from an exclusionary punitive justice and towards an inclusionary restorative justice capable of recognizing that a comprehensive approach must address the social contexts in which crime occurs and should be dealt with. This is the reason they have been so uncritical of New Labour's 'tough on crime' statements, hoping them to be nothing more than rhetorical in meaning. In fact it enables New Labour to look both ways at once. The repeated claims that previous law and order policies had failed, that 'enough is enough', and that there can now be 'no more excuses' allows New Labour to hold out the promise of a 'new' era of rational policy making and good practice. But it is a future that is marked by the past. For example, running through much of the Crime and Disorder Act, 1998, is a legitimating rhetoric of restoration, reintegration and responsibility, of ensuring that offenders make amends and pay their debts to society. It is made clear that these goals are best achieved through community 'ownership' of the problem. Yet this communitarian rationale is constructed by and works within a series of authoritarian populist discourses.

While the legislation claims to be supportive of parents and protective of children its preventive rhetoric is backed by coercive powers. By equating 'disorder' with crime it significantly broadens the reach of criminal justice to take in those below the age of criminal responsibility and the non-criminal as well as the known offender. Above all, New Labour has remained silent on the place of prison in its vision for safety and justice. The numbers incarcerated continue to grow to unprecedented levels, thereby undermining any policy commitment to promoting rehabilitation. By implementing the Conservatives' plans for a network of secure training centres for 12–15-year-olds the extension of custody to young children is confirmed. Indeed since the passing of the 1998 Act, New Labour has moved further to substantiate its authoritarian populist credentials in the face of Conservative Party allegations that it is failing to respond to public concern over law and order.

All of this seems more designed to fulfil New Labour's electoral contract with 'Middle England' than to promote social inclusion. Whilst there have been important shifts in micro discourses and practices, the dominant terms of the political debate over crime and punishment have not been disputed. New Labour's proposed modernization holds authoritarian populist discourses firmly in place. Various statements emanating from the Home Secretary indicate that there can be no 'Third Way' on New Labour's promise to be 'tough on crime'.

Because of these contradictions it will not be possible to assess the full impact of New Labour's criminal justice modernization programme for several years. It is certainly not clear how the strains within and between managerialism, communitarianism and authoritarian populism will play out. The unfolding regulatory framework has the potential to empower local authorities, but the new multi-agency partnerships could also develop into highly unaccountable forms of administration. Pragmatism, efficiency and the continual requirement to 'get results' by any means necessary may well come to override any commitment to due process, justice and democratic accountability and inevitably favour situational over social crime prevention strategies. The success of restorative justice initiatives must also rest on an adequate support of health, housing and social services, yet it is these very agencies that are subject to financial under-resourcing. Moreover the commitment to be 'tough on crime' is quite capable of devaluing any fundamental purpose of criminal justice, whether that be conceived as 'justice', 'welfare', 'human rights' or indeed 'evidence based' approaches. It is not surprising that managerialization, audit and pragmatic efficiency have taken on a life all of their own within New Labour's attempt to manage its competing and conflicting philosophies.

References

Addison, N. (1998) *Modernizing Criminal Justice: Opportunities for Labour*, London, Fabian Society.

Allen, R. (1990) 'Punishing the parents', *Youth and Policy*, 31, pp. 17–20.

Allen, R. (1991) 'Out of jail: the reduction in the use of penal custody for male juveniles 1981–88', *The Howard Journal*, 30 (1), pp. 30–52.

Anderson, P. and Mann, N. (1998) *Safety First: The Making of New Labour*, London, Granta.

Audit Commission (1996) *Misspent Youth: Young People and Crime*, London, Audit Commission.

Audit Commission (1998) *Misspent Youth '98: The Challenge for Youth Justice*, London, Audit Commission.

Audit Commission (1999) *Safety in Numbers: Promoting Community Safety*, London, Audit Commission.

Bandalli, S. (1998) 'Abolition of the presumption of *Doli incapax* and the criminalization of young people', *The Howard Journal*, 37 (2), pp. 114–23.

Blair, T. (1993) 'Why crime is a socialist issue', *New Statesman and Society*, 29 January.

Blair, T. (1994) 'Preface', *Partners Against Crime: Labour's New Approach to Tackling Crime and Creating Safer Communities*. London, Labour Party.

Blair, T. (1996) *New Britain: My Vision of a Young Country*, London, Fourth Estate Books.

Bowring, B. (1997) 'Law and order in the "New" Britain', *Soundings*, Special Issue on the Next Ten Years, pp. 100–10.

Brownlee, I. (1998) 'New Labour – New Penology? Punitive rhetoric and the limits of managerialism in criminal justice policy', *Journal of Law and Society*, 25 (3), p. 313–35.

Crawford, A. (1997) *The Local Governance of Crime: Appeals to Community and Partnership*, Oxford, Clarendon Press.

Edwards, A. and Stenson, K. (1999) 'Crime control and liberal government: the "third way" and the shift to the local', paper delivered at the Crime, Neo-Liberalism and Risk Society conference, John Jay College of Criminal Justice, New York, 14–16 April.

Etzioni, A. (1995) *The Spirit of Community*, London, Fontana.

Farrington, D. (1996) *Understanding and Preventing Youth Crime*, Social Policy Research Findings 93, York, Joseph Rowntree Foundation.

Feeley, M. and Simon, J. (1992) 'The new penology', *Criminology*, 30 (4), pp. 452–74.

Fowles, A. (1990) 'Monitoring expenditure in the criminal justice system', *The Howard Journal*, 28 (2), pp. 82–100.

Garland, D. (1996) 'The limits of the sovereign state: strategies of crime control in contemporary society', *British Journal of Criminology*, 36 (4), pp. 445–71.

Goldson, B. (ed.) (1999) *Youth Justice: Contemporary Policy and Practice*, Aldershot, Ashgate.

Gordon, W., Cuddy, P. and Black, J. (1999) *Youth Justice*, 2nd edition, Winchester, Waterside.

Haines, K. and Drakeford, M. (1998) *Young People and Youth Justice*, Basingstoke, Macmillan.

Home Office (1991) *Safer Communities: The Local Delivery of Crime Prevention through the Partnership Approach* (The Morgan Report), London, HMSO.

Home Office (1997) *No More Excuses: A New Approach to Tackling Youth Crime in England and Wales*, Cm 3809, London, HMSO.

Home Office (1998a) *Guidance on Statutory Crime and Disorder Partnerships*, London, Home Office.

Home Office (1998b) *Reducing Offending: An Assessment of Research Evidence on Ways of Dealing with Offending Behaviour*, London, Home Office Research Study 187, London, Home Office.

Home Office (1999) *Criminal Justice System: The Strategic Plan for 1999–2000 to 2001–2002*, London, Home Office.

Hough, M. and Tilley, N. (1998) *Auditing Crime and Disorder: Guidance for Local Partnerships*, London, Police Research Group, Paper 91.

Hughes, G. (1996) 'Communitarianism and law and order', *Critical Social Policy*, 16 (4), pp. 17–41.

Hughes, G. (1998) *Understanding Crime Prevention: Social Control, Risk and Late Modernity*, Milton Keynes, Open University Press.

Johnson, G. and Bottomley, K. (1998) 'Labour's crime policy in context', *Policy Studies*, 19 (3/4), pp. 173–85.

Jones, C. (1993) 'Auditing criminal justice', *British Journal of Criminology*, 33 (3), pp. 187–202.

Labour Party (1996) *Tackling the Causes of Crime: Labour's Proposals to Prevent Crime and Criminality*, London, Labour Party.

McLaughlin, E. (1994) *Community, Policing and Accountability*, Aldershot, Avebury.

McLaughlin, E. and Muncie, J. (1994) 'Managing criminal justice', in Clarke, J., Cochrane, A. and McLaughlin, E. (eds) *Managing Social Policy*, London, Sage.

Muncie, J. (1999a) *Youth and Crime: A Critical Introduction*, London, Sage.

Muncie, J. (1999b) 'Institutionalized intolerance: youth justice and the 1998 Crime and Disorder Act', *Critical Social Policy*, 19 (2), pp. 147–75.

Straw, J. (1998) 'New approaches to crime and punishment', *Prison Service Journal*, 116, pp. 2–6.

Straw, J. (1999) 'Home Secretary's preface to the government's crime reduction strategy', London, Home Office. http://www.homeoffice.gov.uk/crimprev/crsdoc.htm.

Tuck, M. (1992) 'Community and criminal justice', *Policy Studies*, 12 (3), pp. 22–38.

Warner, N. (1998) 'Interview with Norman Warner', *Safer Society*, 1, pp. 2–3.

11

Leisure: Managerialism and Public Space

Alan Clarke

Contents

The purpose of this chapter is to explore the changing approaches to management which have informed the provision of leisure within the social policy framework of the United Kingdom. It is a localized study of particular practices within one section of welfare provision within one country and is necessarily limited by the social and political specificities which are inscribed in the provision of leisure. Some of these issues will be explored through an extended analysis of one form of provision within the leisure services portfolio: public open spaces. Indeed it is a part of the portfolio which is often overlooked in discussions about direct service provision because it is so often taken for granted as a natural part of our social environment. This would not be the case were we to discuss other aspects of leisure provision, such as municipal leisure centres – which are an obvious construction of direct intervention and provision – or even such aspects of municipal provision as art galleries and museums. Parks seem natural because they appear as though they have been there a very long time and also because it appears that for most of the time no one does anything with them – they become at best a form of indirect provision and possibly a form of non-provision.

Parks can stand as a metaphor for the tensions in managing public services. They are instantly recognizable and yet easily overlooked. They are a focus for public activity and open displays of management – just imagine the numbers of parks departments that have given thought to their floral displays over the years. Yet they are also a representation of those areas where there has been almost no management – there has been little change and little positive sense of managing the space which they bound. Moreover the rules – the by-laws – which govern the parks provide an interesting inscription of the dominant values of respectable behaviour in our society. They are a representation of the hegemony of the ruling classes through the organization of everyday life. In these ways the metaphor helps us to take the parks as a focal point for the discussion of the broad issues which underpin this text.

1 Leisure as welfare

Given the context of this chapter and the total neglect of leisure within much – if not all – of the literature on social policy, it is worth briefly stressing the connections between leisure and social policy and leisure as social welfare. (There are fuller accounts of these connections in Clarke, 1992 and 1994.) The arguments for the inclusion of leisure on the social policy agenda derive from two sources – first, the position that leisure holds within a full and rounded life and therefore as a part of the citizenship agenda; and second, from the custom and practice of central and local government in the UK of intervening directly in the sphere of leisure, which exhibits many of the tendencies of the managerial state (Clarke and Newman, 1997). For evidence that these temptations are still prevalent, doubters should look no further than the 'discussions' generated by the New Labour government in 1998 and 1999 on the 'right to roam' and access to the countryside.

Leisure has become an 'integral part of living a full and rounded life. Leisure must not be seen therefore as an appendage in the context of local authority service – indeed, it is being increasingly regarded as a respectable and essential service' (Benington, 1988, p. 259). Leisure can be seen as a form of social cement which can help to bind a society together. Leisure opportunities are a matter for every citizen and a part of their rights within a civilized society. As a result the state feels the need to have policies which set out the framework for this aspect of citizenship.

This citizenship argument allows for a recasting of one of the oldest rhetorics which permeates public policy on leisure, namely 'recreational welfare' (Coalter, 1990). Recreational welfare defined a role for leisure provision in combating urban deprivation and contributing to the physical health and moral welfare of the population. Leisure, properly managed, would contribute to self-improvement and to social integration for the benefit of the individual, the local and the national good.

What we see in the current debates about access and inclusion is the recreational welfare rhetoric recast from the 1890s for the 1990s as the basis for the vision of leisure in the new millennium. The full flowering of this newly polished recreational welfare rhetoric can be seen in the provision of the Millennium Dome, which has to be a national spectacle but which politicians appear to be unable to allow to be presented simply as a pleasure dome. Because of the rhetorics of recreational welfare, particularly those elements of self-improvement and moral welfare, there has been an insistence that there must be an educational and improving section within the experience. Hence the intense debates about the 'zones' and the almost complete lack of public discussion about the entertainment to be provided in the Dome.

The move to include leisure within primary health care has also shown that there is still a place for leisure at the heart of welfare provision. GP referral schemes allow local GPs to work with local leisure centres and fitness clubs to offer their patients the opportunity for preventative interventions or remedial activities. These links have had some success in working on the lifestyle awareness of leisure within a healthy regime.

The provision of leisure opportunities has been dominated by the public sector within the UK since the 1900s, when local authorities set out to provide 'serious' leisure for the local people as an alternative to what were seen as dangerous and decadent leisure pursuits. As the state moved further and further into regulating leisure pursuits, so it matched the regulation with attempts at providing an approved alternative. Banning traditional pursuits such as cock fighting and limiting the numbers of public houses and the times at which these licensed premises could be open was matched with an extension of the provision of local museums, galleries, swimming pools and parks. This provision was inspired by the rhetorics of recreational welfare and implemented with a rigorousness not always found in local provision. Leisure managers had a niche role which they defended with great tenacity – the Head of Libraries was often a key position at the heart of local debates on censorship and indeed in setting the local parameters of what was socially acceptable. This was extended when new technology introduced the need for local panels to issue certificates for local display of cinema films. The role of a Fabian, paternalist sense of duty will be looked at later in this chapter in the context of the change in the management structure for local parks, which have been moved away from the horticulturist to the managerialist, although issues of public decency and safety have always been present.

2   Public open spaces

Amongst the landmarks of British cities are the parks, the patches of green which appear on the city maps. The parks themselves represent a major development in the provision of public leisure. Coming into being at the time of urbanization and industrialization, they are now enshrined at the centre of British leisure provision. The parks will be used as an exemplar of the pressures on the public provision of leisure within the United Kingdom as they hold a unique position within the provision of leisure opportunities. To understand this position, it is worthwhile considering the origins of the parks movement within British local government. They are amongst the oldest expressions of civic identity, often pre-dating the powers given to local authorities to provide social leisure facilities as many are the product of the generosity of a local patron. These altruistic origins can be rooted within the motivations of leisure provision which still underpin the leisure framework – the contradictory dichotomy between care and control. Often the land that was donated helped to provide a 'green lung' for the expanding cities, but parks also often served to divide the city with a green corridor separating the working-class houses on one side from the affluent areas on the other.

They modelled a form of behaviour which the donors thought would greatly enhance the lives of the poorer city dwellers. The parks were sculptured landscapes, designed to include a variety of greenery and vistas that could be enjoyed by a public promenading through the leafy avenues. These same design features also designed out other behaviours which were to be discouraged – a study of local by-laws governing the parks reveals the parks to be riddled with constraints, such as no ball games, no music, no alcohol and often no animals. This twin agenda of care and control can still be found in the 1990s policies which advocate increasing leisure opportunities to enrich or rejuvenate the old parks which are drawn from a 'safe' list of 'sensible' leisure activities.

The parks occupy an open space which is statutorily guaranteed within the planning frameworks for development. Moreover they appear to be guaranteed because of the significance attached to the parks by local communities in a way which is not necessarily true of local swimming pools or leisure centres. No one seems able to dare to suggest that parks should be realized, even though they have a considerable economic value if converted into real estate. That no one has done so speaks to a cultural value attached to the parks which also marks them out from other forms of leisure provision.

Moreover, parks have served to construct the definition of the 'public' as well as that of the open spaces. The codes of behaviour which were inscribed within the parks constructed a sense of respectability and propriety within the notion of the public. Although targeted at the urban poor – the disenfranchised – the parks sought to promote appropriate behaviour within their boundaries. What is interesting is how the extension of the franchise has not changed this role for the urban park, where there are still strong elements of the disenfranchised to be found. The use of parks by the youth of the urban areas has created an alternative and sometimes challenging space but has also redefined the 'escape' which the parks offered.

3 Managing parks

The history of local parks management has been dominated by senior horticulturists who have created parks in their own images. Because of the centrality of parks in the local authority register, many authorities looked to the senior parks managers to lead them into the leisure revolution of the 1970s and 1980s when multipurpose (sports) halls were being created throughout the country. The expectation that gardeners could lead multipurpose leisure developments led to some serious problems, which not only influenced the nature of local authority provision but also shaped the way that the professional body – the Institute of Leisure and Amenity Management – shaped itself and its professional syllabus. The opportunities to use the park as a multipurpose venue were seriously restricted by regimes which consistently put horticultural welfare before social welfare.

The 1980s also presented a different challenge to the management of parks with the advent of fiscal shortages, which threatened even the core maintenance budgets for parks. The nature of the crisis was used as a way of importing a solution in the form of economistic interpretations of managerialist thought. As Mackintosh argued:

> The economic framework of the reforms has not only generated a new organisational model of public services, it has also offered a new vocabulary with which to think about it. There has indeed rarely been such a startling case study of the attempted transfer of a new vocabulary into an existing set of organisations. From markets and competition, through business units and contracts, to prices and customers, economists and management consultants have quite literally sought to put words into people's mouths. (Mackintosh, 1995, p. 4)

Other work speaks of how successful this total immersion language programme has been:

> It was also evident that key aspects of the Chief Executive's cultural change initiative had been widely disseminated amongst these middle managers. Key terms such as 'Ready, Fire, Aim', 'risk taking' and 'entrepreneurialism' were readily defined by many managers when asked, and were often mentioned spontaneously as well. A significant number of them were able to provide examples of the adoption of these in practice, and such ideas had clearly affected their management practices. (Keen and Scase, 1996, p. 183)

One of the victims of this economistic reductionism has been the traditional symbol of authority in the parks. The park keeper or park warden was a resident guardian of the park and all its features. Wardens were infamous for the sharp ways they had for dealing with 'delinquents' who threatened the order of their park but they were a clearly identified symbol of local management and control. As budgets contracted, so the money available for full-time staffing, and subsequently even part-time staffing, was reduced and the presence was lost. One London borough budgeted for shedding park keepers and used the saving to replace them with a smaller number of mobile wardens on motorcycles – only to find that the Council accepted the saving and then did not approve the 'new' expenditure.

This removal of a local presence has led to a change in the image of parks. In many areas they have moved from the representation of safe and supervised recreation into dangerous outposts of civilization, frequented by those on the fringes of legality and threatening to the local law-abiding community. There have been two responses to this – 'trustification' and 'compartmentalization'.

Trusts have become one of the primary means of delivering local leisure services. Trustification has been seen in the creation of neighbourhood trusts that have taken over the responsibility for the day-to-day management of the parks. These trusts have the power to negotiate with staff over the scale and scope of maintenance, and the programming of the parks is often left to the trust to organize. In some cases, the trust has been delegated a budget with which to do business with the local authority or its chosen service providers. This has returned parks to the community in ways which some of the original donors could not have foreseen but which can have enormous benefits for the local community and those sections of the community which most directly use the parks. However, there are limits to how innovative trusts can be as they must remain within the rubric laid down by the local authority.

Compartmentalization has proved less beneficial as this represents a change in usage for parks by segregating areas by patterns of usage. It is therefore possible to 'police' the children's playground area within the park to ensure that it is safe for children – and their parents – whilst leaving other open areas to more fringe activities. Dog walkers have complained that some of the parks now exclude them – and their dogs – from areas where they previously exercised their rights to ensure the safety of other groups: for instance by banning dogs from the play areas or paddling pools. However, they also note that some areas of parks are formally open but are too dangerous to be considered for use. Park managers have responded to these claims by seeking to reassert their control over the areas and reimpose established patterns of traditional usage. This has often meant removing groups of 'users' from the parks, thereby denying them their rights of access. The groups most often on the receiving end of these warnings are adolescent groups seeking somewhere to go, quite often just to do nothing. They are constituted as a threat because they can be noisy and boisterous, which presents itself as challenging to the order of the park and to the other users of the park. Official reactions are often addressed to the fear that such groupings will encourage the use of illicit substances and become a focus for other dangerous activities. The recreational welfare rhetoric clearly still binds the provision and the response of park management.

These institutional definitions are encapsulated in a gender-based agenda for public space, which often deters an important part of the 'public' from making full use of the provision. Gender issues surrounding the use of public space require separate consideration but it should be noted that some sections of the female public find the provision unhelpful and experience the uses which other groups make of the parks as threatening.

4   Shifting definitions

The parks provide a defining site for the construction of the relationships involved in public policies on leisure. From the original provision of the open spaces, it is possible to see them as the encapsulation of the rights of the urban citizen – bound to the local authority but benefiting from the provision of a structured openness. It is a relationship which inscribes the citizens' opportunities within a precise code of responsibilities. The space is open and the citizen is free, yet it is an openness and a freedom which is clearly circumscribed by local guardians of public decency. The donation of land to the people of an area, in trust to the local authorities, also structures the relationship. There is a gift relationship involved, which positions the recipients within it. The expected response is one of grateful thanks and courteous acceptance. Campaigners trying to change the use of open spaces have not only met resistance through regulation but also accusations of churlishness – how dare you criticize the park which has been so graciously given to you? There is little sense of park users being constituted as active consumers. They are positioned as passive recipients, structured in their presence and defined by the constraints of the space. There is no obvious entrance to the cash nexus to allow the importation of any market relationships, except for the provision of exceptional aspects of leisure such as golf or boating.

The parks were planned by the professionals – the design and layout of parks is a study in its own right and cannot be fully elaborated here, but it is important to note that the parks benefited from the professional knowledge of leisure providers of what a park should be. Drawing on the classic landscapes of great houses and country estates, urban parks were designed to provide a valuable and meaningful experience to the local people. The professionals were influenced by the design of the large gardens and pathways surrounding the great houses and transferred this desirable order from the private domain into the public. The notions of leisure which inspired the formal designs were of passive and pacified leisure notions – the introduction of 'active' activities followed on later from increasing pressures to maximize usage of urban space. The original intention was to create a landscape of tranquillity. When these designs are revisited and seen through the lens of professional discourses, it is apparent where the influence and intention was derived from. The local people were seen as passive recipients of the benefits of the 'park experience' – if their social betters enjoyed such pastimes then it would surely be of benefit to the emergent working classes to share the experience, as they had no opportunity to own or access private open spaces. Again the pressure to produce houses with gardens came after the parks movement had established the pattern of the parks – public provision was the obvious way forward.

The parks have lived within this tradition of a fixed register of leisure offering and were little changed by the consumerist demands which impacted on other local services. They have become enshrined as a fixed resort, with fixed boundaries and a fixed stock of resources within those boundaries. Public consultation about the nature of park development in the 1980s and 1990s revealed a very fixed, almost predetermined, notion of what was meant by a 'park' and therefore what a park had to offer to the public was also a fixed register. Even where authorities were seeking to challenge this preconstructed notion of the park, the feedback from public consultations returned them to it. There was no ability – or perhaps just no desire – to think outside the established definition.

The challenge to the traditional usage came through the extension of transport – initially horses, then bicycles, then motorcycles, then mountain bikes and finally off-road vehicles. The urban park has managed these changes through an almost universal proscription of such activities within the regulated boundaries of the public park. Where they are allowed, they have been allocated particular routes or trails which largely separate out the 'new' users of the park space from the 'traditional' users. This can also be seen in the ways that 'fads' such as skateboarding have been dealt with by the creation of specific arenas for such activities to be played out in. Where there has been the greatest impact is in the more deregulated open space of the countryside where the patterns of regulation are less clear and there is less chance of enforcement. Here the competing uses have become a battleground. The management of this contest has been taken back within the state and the new access bodies will find these debates at the heart of their agenda. Access is no longer simply about the right to walk across open space; it is about creating it as a terrain of active participation in a form of leisure.

The parks offer a site for many public behaviours – both celebratory and transgressive. The celebratory is witnessed by the use of parks for religious and political gatherings to celebrate the experiences of local people. These rituals can be both confirmatory, such as the Whitsuntide parades of church groups, and oppositional, such as the use political demonstrators make of parks as meeting grounds.

The confines of civil society also push people into the search for an alternative space to express their own sexuality. The parks are both convenient locations for heterosexual encounters – couples perhaps seeking the expression of the private where there is no privately owned alternative – and for gay and lesbian people. Such alternative usages of public space challenge the dominant definitions of appropriate behaviour and demonstrate the potential of the park as a public space for exploring alternative social practices.

5   Contract compliance

For many areas of public provision, one of the most significant indications of the arrival of managerialism was the introduction of contracts – contracts both within the local authority and with organizations outside the local authority. The primacy of economics in determining the terms of the contractual relationship is very important in this context. It promotes a construction of social policy in economic terms which reduces the implications of the policy to an easily understood bottom line for the operation. In leisure, this was most obviously felt in the introduction of compulsory competitive tendering (CCT), which led to the reorganization and reordering of provision across leisure departments. With the notion of contract came the necessity to specify the content of the contract and the criteria on which the contract could be monitored. This contributed to a rethinking of the role of leisure within local authority provision. It forced authorities to question – and answer – to whom they were responsible. The answer to the question was often split between customers and clients, positioning the leisure services in an awkward hinterland between being a profit-centred business and being a public service provider. The compromise definition was seen in the attempts to write social conscience criteria into the contracts to create customer-focused business units with a clear obligation to certain sections of the local communities.

The problem with the compromise became apparent with the further specifications which were required in the contracting. The more authorities specified within the contract, the more power was removed from localized management and from local communities to influence what was provided within the contract. However, the freedom which was left within the contract was used not necessarily to further local social policies but to create space to manipulate the local market to increase the return on the bottom line for the business unit. Where there is a commitment to the values of recreational welfare and the role of leisure in social improvement, market research undertaken to increase the profitability of the cost centre may work to further the exclusion and denial of those groups targeted by the social policy initiatives.

The parks offer a particular example of the dangers in contract specification. In many authorities, parks suffered from a divided responsibility. Contracts for maintenance were given to direct service organizations (DSOs) or private contractors and specified in terms of the number of times grass would be cut, the amount that was to be spent on replanting, etc. The management contract for the park would be specified separately but would be difficult to fund. Staff employed to maintain the parks had a single focus to their employment and the contract limited their remit to maintenance. Any observation about patterns of usage or changing users would not be fed back into the parks office but would stay with the maintenance contractors. The management function became distanced from the day-to-day realities of the parks. As a result, parks became a non-developing area, with the funding committed to maintaining the existing product and with management charged with overseeing the compliance of the maintenance contract. There was no room within the specificity of the contracts to allow for the cross-subsidy of these areas of activity. The usage of the park slipped from the agenda for two reasons which were mutually reinforcing – firstly that park usage is sporadic and spontaneous (with the obvious exception of fixture-listed pitch bookings), and secondly that usage does not contribute to the financial bottom line. Parks are free at the point of usage and difficult to charge extras for. As staffing levels have been reduced, even the opportunities to raise additional income through retail sales have been forfeited. Specific activities which are used on a pay-as-you-play basis have been identified and staffed specifically.

6   Best Value

The limitations of economistic evaluations of efficiency and effectiveness have led to demands for a more open way of reviewing local authority provision. The debates about introducing Best Value into service provision could prove to have direct implications for the future development of parks within the leisure portfolio (ILAM, 1998). Best Value commits local authorities to three key elements within the provision: benchmarking, continuous improvement and public consultation (Barony Consulting, 1997). A clear attempt is being made in the policy debate to show how Best Value offers local authorities more flexibility and scope for development than did the CCT model, but it is also clear that what is being introduced is yet more fashionable management-speak (Filkin, 1997a, 1997b, 1997c). In adopting the buzzwords of the 1990s textbooks, Best Value subscribes to a model of management which sees change as inherent within the provision and, as a corollary of that, as a necessary good within the system. This cannot be accepted unquestioningly, especially in relation to a part of the leisure portfolio which has such heritage connotations and is shrouded by so many constraining forces.

Benchmarking is a crucial part of the Best Value scenario and draws on a comparative methodology often criticized in practice. The benchmarking process begs several key questions, without suggesting answers to them. Most importantly it does not specify which aspects of provision should be benchmarked. For instance, with parks it will be tempting for authorities to benchmark the amount of space contained within the park boundaries rather than to look at benchmarking usage of the parks. To be truly helpful in shaping the future of the parks the benchmark should not only be about usage but should be informed by a notion of what the park is intended for. Is diversity of usage sought? Is the park a focus for a single type of activity? Does it cater for a variety of people, ages, genders, ethnic groups – or is it directed to a single audience? The benchmarks must be selected in such a way as to allow a critical debate about the park to be undertaken. If they are not, benchmarking will be used as a simple means of affirming the park's success in being itself.

Another issue arising from the benchmarking process will be the choice of comparators – which other types of provision should parks be benchmarked against. Even if the debate is confined to parks, there are important differences between the performance of authorities which primarily provide neighbourhood patch parks and those which offer parks of regional significance, let alone those who share responsibilities for a country park. To be effective, the benchmarking will have to take place at the level of the individual park and the comparators will have to be parks located in similar contexts. If benchmarking is going to inform the social policy debate about provision this context must include the demographic nature of the surrounding area and the political aims of the leisure providers. The collection of such indicators will prove too costly, which will rule out this level of benchmarking.

The notion of 'continuous improvement' also raises contentious issues. There are no absolute standards available for the nature of parks provision. There are guidelines which rest on an understanding of the amount of provision for certain levels of population, but they do not specify what standard that provision should reach. The nature of the park – as an activity centre or as an open space – will set the expectations for what improvement should be considered. However, if these definitions are set in the current state of the provision they will never involve the issue of continuous improvement towards a different type of park provision or service level.

Continuous improvement has been used as a vehicle to smuggle the debate about quality into the appraisal of local authority provision. The days of formulaic quality systems appear to be numbered. One hears less and less about BS5750 and ISO 9002 and more about flexible responses and continuous improvement, but the old quality systems remain at the heart of the discussions. There will have to be a clear statement about the current state before any work can be undertaken on the notion of continuous improvement, for if there is no starting point how can improvement be identified? Moreover there has to be a sense of direction which recognizes whether changes from the given current state are positive ones, meriting the term 'improvement'. Dealing in the area of leisure services, it is not clear where such prescriptions of direction come from. Managerialism has introduced the terms as a way of driving a process forward, but it has not recognized the void which lies at the heart of the suggestion if no politics – or values – underpin the movement. The economistic comparison cannot accommodate this debate and has no way of introducing values into the equations. What the reductionist terms imply is that the performance indicators are value free and objective, but there has to be a recognition of the values and direction of the implementation. This makes the clustering of comparators even more important than the initial comments made under benchmarking suggested. For here, we can see that the notion of continuous improvement demands comparators from within the same frame of political reference. If it does not, the model of Best Value will stand condemned of introducing a framework of national standards which have to be addressed and adhered to by local authorities. It will be a clear infringement of local autonomy and extend the range of central state control further into areas of leisure provision than it has ever gone before.

7 Managerialism and the political agenda

The drive to infuse local service provision with a sense of managerialist professionalism is partly a drive to eliminate the political from the process of local service delivery. This sits oddly with the sense of values which has to be included in the definition of 'improvement' and with the necessity for public consultation. Those of us with long memories will have recollections of senior figures in local government arguing ferociously against the need for public consultation because they had been elected by the local population and therefore were the democratic spokespeople for them. Local democracy had allowed for and given a physical embodiment to local public consultation. The officers' job within the local authority was therefore simple: all they had to do was find the most efficient and effective ways of implementing what the local democratic voice told them to do. With Best Value consultations, the situation is reversed. The policies of the authorities are to be resubmitted for public comment and presumably approval. The officers now find themselves located within two versions of the public voice – the one given through the local democratic mandate and the other through the local consultation process in which they play a key role. This is the, surely unintended, consequence of putting managers into a political situation from which they have always been seen to be at one remove.

The issue of which mandate will have the greatest power remains to be tested. Some authorities already use local referenda or opinion polling to gather local opinions but this is usually only within a given policy framework. For public consultation to be meaningful in informing Best Value, the agenda for consultation has to be constructed differently. The agenda has to be one about local Best Value, which will necessitate probing opportunity costs, relative priorities and specific project proposals with the local communities. However there is no reason, given the nature of Best Value work, to consult the whole electorate or even limit the consultation to the electorate. Within leisure provision there are clearly advantages to consulting with and hearing from the youthful disenfranchised. The question remains to be answered about how such opinions will be ranked against other voices in the consultation. The landscaping and demarcation of our parks could look very different if the parks were redesigned according to the wishes of users under the age of 18.

The assumption within the managerialist position that the only values are those of the professional manager can be seen to be tested by this construction of a managerialist solution to Best Value. The technicist definitions of efficiency and effectiveness which underpin much of the writing on Best Value cannot help the manager in selecting the direction the organization should follow. As Head (1990, p. 5) has argued, 'Performance indicators are an aid and not a substitute for judgement in decision taking.' To elaborate further, performance indicators in themselves do not provide a means of evaluating the effectiveness of provision, rather they provide signposts or guides to aid judgement. The gap in the managerialist portfolio can be seen in the writings on strategic management and the role of the mission statement in shaping the organization. These simple statements about the outline mission of a company translate uneasily into the public service domain, because the value statements of public sector organizations are more complicated than those of the private sector. They are complicated by the dimension of politics which underpins them in two crucial but distinct ways. Private sector organizations are, of course, riven with political factions – different professional discourses can be seen in the private sector just as readily as in the public sector – and differential power distributions. The context of local government however requires that there is an explicit statement of political difference between contenders for the overall control of the authority. The mission of the authority has therefore to be differentially constructed by the parties competing for dominance and this construction has to become a matter of public record and public debate. It is a tangible pressure on the actions of the authority after the democratic election process has been completed. This is not the case within the private sector organization – the value systems remain internal to the organization rather than necessarily being made explicit within public statements by the company.

The second difference in the political conditions of the private sector relates to the double accountability which the authority has to the public. The managerialist model is based upon a system of market relations, assuming a rational company and a rational consumer. This leads to a simple process model of customer relations in which the company makes an offer, the customer makes a decision, the 'purchase' is evaluated as satisfactory or not and the process moves on. For the local authority, the relationship is fundamentally different as the market is not free but structured by local boundaries. The local citizen may not ever be a consumer of some of the services offered by the authority – for instance, there is a differential pattern of usage of libraries, museums, sports centres and, another area which often comes under the Leisure Committee, cemeteries. However even if there is no direct consumption – and therefore no 'purchase' decision to review – there is still an accountability to the local citizen. This relationship cannot be escaped, even where the responsibility is devolved to a trust or a partnership. The authority can always be held accountable for its provision by the citizenry. Rather than being a simple model, this suggests a sequential process which cannot be interrupted or disrupted. The political values are therefore more pertinent here and cannot be subsumed within the technicist rationale of efficiency and effectiveness as these fail to address the central political question of what should be done efficiently and effectively.

8   The price of social inclusion

The urban parks offer one perspective on the public policy of open spaces and allow for the discussion of the localized effects of national policy frameworks. The debate about social inclusion which has been raised in the context of the parks can also be seen in the government's attempt to formulate policy on the countryside. In order to address the social exclusion of groups from the countryside the government has launched a series of integrated initiatives to encourage the usage of the countryside. This blending of transport, interpretation and facilitation is to be welcomed but it assumes that the value of the countryside is one which is shared across all groups. What we are seeing at the end of the century is a rewriting of the Fabian myths of the open space transferred to the countryside. Where the parks were designed to re-create the experience of landscaped gardens, so the countryside is being used as a way of enhancing the quality of life for groups living outside the countryside and who lack the benefits of living in the countryside. There are a number of ways of questioning this assumption but three are particularly pertinent here. Why is it assumed that the beauty of the countryside is inherently valued? As one beneficiary of an early intermediate treatment project volunteered, 'it is only fucking scenery'. The value placed on the scenery comes from a cultural system to which the excluded are not necessarily privy and are not necessarily clamouring to share. The cultural capital of the countryside has value within a particular register of cultures and this is not readily exchanged.

Secondly there is an assumption that what takes place in the countryside is of value, and because it is enjoyed by a minority of the population should be available for the enjoyment of all of society. Whilst this notion of inclusion is laudable, the question of leisure literacy must be raised. Leisure literacy is a term used to mean confidence and competence in a leisure activity, which can range from basic recognition of the opportunity to a more advanced level of reading where the person is fluent enough to take an active part in the process. Leisure literacy comes from a familiarity with the experiences and with the opportunity to try them. Where there is no familiarity there may be a reluctance to travel to the countryside because the experiences available there are meaningless and have no relevance. The desire to include people because it would be good for them harks back to the earliest forms of Fabian paternalism.

A more challenging approach to inclusion would be to look at the countryside and ask how it would have to be adapted to allow for participation in existing activities within the new setting. This would change the managerial agenda from getting more people to do the existing activities more efficiently and effectively and require managers to seek out the groups and ask them how they can cater for their needs within the constraints of their countryside locations. This use of public consultation as prospecting would challenge the paternalistic notion that providers and policy makers know what is best for the rest of us.

The price of this more challenging agenda would be to pressurize the existing provision with requests for new uses of the spaces available. Before this is ruled out, the experience of urban parks in Calderdale should be remembered. With a changing population, local planners wondered about the relevance of the formal parks to their new, mainly Asian, constituency. What they found, however, was that the space had been colonized by the new residents and was extensively used, but used for different purposes from those for which the park had originally been designed. The Asian communities used the park for social gatherings and re-created neighbourhood customs within the park – discussion groups and card schools were located in the park because the street design and traffic flows did not permit them by the houses. By transporting the example a little further, different agendas for public consultation can be constructed and the relevance of the offer made the centre of the debate.

What public consultation should ensure is the representation of cultural diversity in the usage of public open spaces. It should drive policy makers and deliverers to accept that recognizing and valuing diversity is a more central tenet of local management than the pursuit of economistic definitions of efficiency and effectiveness. The diversity will drive the provision of leisure only if the system is open to diversity and open to accommodating that diversity within its provision. Recognizing the key value at the heart of public leisure provision will strengthen and enhance the quality of the provision more certainly through usage and discussion than any narrow plan with predetermined performance indicators.

The options available for public open space are considerable and their determination should not be simply a matter of economics. The option of paving paradise and putting up a parking lot – or in this case, a multipurpose income-generating leisure unit – will not meet the requirements stemming from a commitment to Best Value in a multi-cultural context, let alone one inspired by the rhetorics of recreational welfare.

References

Barony Consulting (1997) *Best Value for the Public Sector*, London, Barony Consulting.

Benington, J. (1988) 'The need for a new strategic vision for leisure services', in Benington, J. and White, J. (eds) *The Future of Leisure Services*, London, Macmillan.

Clarke, A. (1992) 'Citizens and consumers: leisure after the welfare state', in Sugden, J. and Tomlinson, A. (eds) *Leisure after the Welfare State*, Leisure Studies Association Conference Papers 46, Brighton.

Clarke, A. (1994) 'Leisure and the new managerialism', in Clarke, J., Cochrane, A. and McLaughlin, E. (eds) *Managing Social Policy*, London, Sage.

Clarke, J. and Newman, J. (1997) *The Managerial State*, London, Sage.

Coalter, F. (1990) 'The mixed economy of leisure', in Henry, I. (ed.) *Management and Planning in the Leisure Industries*, London, Macmillan.

Filkin, G. (1997a) 'Taking Best Value to heart', *Municipal Journal*, 4 July, pp. 14–16.

Filkin, G. (1997b) 'Meeting the duty', *Municipal Journal*, 11 July, pp. 18–19.

Filkin, G. (1997c) 'Getting started now', *Municipal Journal*, 18 July, pp. 16–18.

Head, P. (1990) 'Performance indicators: quality assurance', unpublished paper, Asper Consultants, London.

ILAM (1998) *Best Value for Leisure Services*, Reading, Institute of Leisure and Amenity Management.

Keen, L. and Scase, R. (1996) 'Middle managers and the new managerialism', *Local Government Studies*, 22 (4), pp. 167–86.

Mackintosh, M. (1995) *Putting Words into People's Mouths? Economic Culture and its Implications for Local Governance*, Open Discussion Paper in Economics 9, Faculty of Social Sciences, Open University.

Welch, D. (1995) *Managing Public Use of Parks, Open Spaces and Countryside*, London, Pitman.

12

Modernizing Managerialism in Education

Ross Fergusson

Michael Freeden (1999) has argued that New Labour is located ideologically between neo-liberalism, conservatism and socialism, though not equidistant from all three. This positioning is reflected in pronouncements and policies that are sometimes ambivalent in their intent, and sometimes contradictory. Freeden argues that the choices Labour has to make 'may yet lead to the land of pluralist social democracy, but others may set down a once evolutionary socialist party in a very strange terrain' (p. 51).

There could be no better illustration of this than Labour's education policies since 1997. From neo-liberal roots they embrace the marketizing reforms of the outgoing administration. A distinctive but inherently conservative brand of ethical Christian remoralization that influences criminal justice and social security policy is also visible in education. And the managerialism that became the distinctive legacy of the New Right now serves new purposes in education. In many respects New Labour's education policies could be summarized as using broadly similar means to the New Right to achieve ostensibly different ends. And it is in the objective of improving schooling for those who gain least from it that Labour's policies retain some claim to social democratic (if not socialist) values.

It is hard to foresee whether this untested admixture of ideological sources will lead to a land of renewed social democracy, or to Freeden's 'strange terrain'. Second-guessing the social intentions of ministerial statements, Green Papers, or even legislation is exceptionally difficult, because of the sometimes deeply countervailing tendencies of means and ends. Markets for example are not celebrated for their propensity to deliver equitable outcomes. Managerialist methods and modes of governance are too much the creatures of the New Right to be easily separated from its projects. Yet both, it is claimed, alongside the remoralization project, deliver social democratic values that make sense of the commitment that 'education, education and education' are the keys to modernization, global competitiveness and greater social justice respectively. The question is: which education policy gives primacy to which aim?

Such claims strain against the critical analyses of marketization and managerialism of the last ten years. On the face of it, New Labour in education, as in other spheres, has adopted wholesale most of the premises of neo-liberalism, many of its objectives, and almost all of its methods of delivering them. Competition, choice and performance indicators remain the unchallenged totems of policy, not in overt policy statements but simply by being left untouched by New Labour reforms. Structurally, little that is fundamental is changing in the ways in which schools and colleges are run. Markets and managerialism hold sway. Structures and methods remain largely unaltered. Only the rhetoric of what schools and colleges can and should produce changes. The commitments to excellence and diversity are softened in favour of raising standards for all. The projects of the New Right and of New Labour begin to look ideologically consonant. The point of difference is not whether schools should be better, but which ones should be made better first. And what counts as 'better' remains largely locked inside the black box of the National Curriculum, testing, and how to teach more effectively.

From an 'old' socialist standpoint, the logic and surface evidence of the 'plus ça change' argument is compelling. At best the reforms look like tinkering at the margins which goes as far as it can without offending the class interests of Middle England by higher taxation, greater regulation, the limitation of choice, or the predetermination of deliberately social ends. The hegemonic forces of globalized capital, the unassailable power of the discourse of markets, and the deep permeation of the culture of managerialism all seem to have overwhelmed the forces of democracy, and leave elected governments as mere executives of UK plc operating under the thin blessing of popular mandate.

But understandings of power which view the great projects of capital as unstoppable and treat resistance as useless offer little analytic purchase. Their determinisms and grand narratives massively neglect both the fine grain and the immense complexity of institutional practices and the possibilities of political power 'on the ground'. Outcomes cannot be read off from the intentions of policy makers, even if they were explicit and unambiguous. They have to be understood and interpreted in context, with contradictions acknowledged, and the exercise of power analysed not inferred.

Applying these injunctions to understanding the workings and effects of managerialism in New Labour's key education project means answering two major questions about managerialism:

- Does New Labour's modernization agenda require managerial methods to deliver it?
- Is managerialism only capable of delivering neo-liberal objectives, or is it an adaptable and value-neutral cluster of practices and instruments?

These of course are larger questions for this book as a whole, and require analysis based on more than just education policy. This chapter attempts little more than a mapping of what they might mean and some preliminary responses. Tentative as this is, it may contribute to understanding the powers and limits of managerialism, and the powers and limits of a new government to realize ideological goals that are distinct from those of its predecessors.

1 Modernizing managerialism

One source of the managerial revolution of the 1990s was the claim that managerialism had the capacity to simulate inside public sector institutions what the market did in the private sector. The absence of properly constituted consumers was always an obstacle to bringing the claimed rigours of the market to institutions of the welfare state. The absence of choice, spending power, consumer rights and sanctions was difficult to make good. But because the mechanisms by which such disciplines were introduced came closer to mimicking than to replicating market conditions, the power they exerted within public service institutions was considerably reduced. The freedom of empowered welfare consumers to take their custom elsewhere, demand better service, or prevail against backsliding providers was highly circumscribed. The absence of shareholders and chief executives limited managers' ability to prevail over staff. The addition of autonomous professionals to the equation further limited these powers. The culture of managerialism therefore grew out of the need of would-be market-oriented public sector institutions to find ways of making good their structural 'deficiencies' as marketized providers.

New Labour's commitment is not to marketize but to modernize. In Chapter 3, Janet Newman marks the clear distinction between New

Labour's modernizing agenda, and the priorities of the New Public Management (NPM). The commitment to update NPM gives new emphasis to the pursuit of Best Value and long-term effectiveness over narrow conceptions of economy and efficiency. Collaboration is valued before competition. Public consultation and partnership qualify executive power in the pursuit of effective management. Modernization is to be achieved in full cognizance of the forces of globalization, the knowledge economy and the information society, requiring particular forms of innovation and flexibility (both already prominent in the discourses of NPM), but also giving new emphasis to creativity (see also Finlayson, 1998, for a fuller analysis of modernization).

Alongside these adjusted managerial and economic priorities New Labour's commitment to modernization includes a supplementary set of priorities which is at least partly social in character. The drive to inclusionary policies, the idea of stakeholding, and efforts to secure democratic renewal all assign a new priority to the social consequences of modernization, so long as they are accompanied by risk sharing and responsibilization. Some of these give social objectives parity with economic and management objectives. This of course is consistent with the broad thrust of the politics of the Third Way, which seeks to dissolve old oppositions of left and right, social and economic priorities, and so on (see for example Giddens, 1998). In the 1980s and 1990s the pursuit of old NPM objectives of enterprise, efficiency and effectiveness gave precedence to economic success and cost-saving management. The social consequences were at best of secondary concern. Fostering economic success meant unapologetically favouring business interests and leaving others to the market, or to residual welfare provision. Increased socioeconomic polarization became the price of international competitive success.

In contrast, New Labour's modernization agenda has sought to construct some complementarity between its economic and social priorities. According to this agenda, the choice which New Right policies posited between national economic success and social justice or equality of opportunity was misconceived. Partnership, stakeholding, consultation and democratic representation are inductive-inclusionary measures which at minimum allow all citizens some sense of ownership of decisions and projects, and at best allow them to become both contributors to and direct beneficiaries of new measures. So, for example, the power and potential of the forces of globalization, of e-commerce and of the knowledge economy could mean intensively training a new business elite ready for hyper-trade, or it could entail garnering the power of mass computer literacy to exploit the potential of information technology. The former approach is a more targeted strategy for short term success. The latter has some real potential to unleash an irresistible force of long term participants into a future key trading milieu, while also allowing maximum talent to rise from the largest possible pool. Both are versions of human capital approaches, but base themselves on very different principles of investment. More broadly, fostering innovation and making the UK a 'beacon of creativity' in service industries as well as cultural production is more likely to occur through extensive than intensive modes of development. The stress placed on the talent of the population in the 1997 election campaign was a powerful signifier of an inclusive approach, and a commitment to equalizing opportunity, marking a belief in developing the skills of 'the many not the few' as both economically sound and socially just.

Both these examples have clear and profound implications for an inclusive education system which provides an education of quality for all. And both elide economic interest with social good. What's good for the modern economy is good for the modern citizen. But to make a system geared to extensive development of human capital work, rather than concentrating energies intensively, the state requires something approaching the involvement of the whole population. This is needed both to ensure that the optimum development of talent occurs, and to minimize the 'unproductive' costs of a population of inactive non-participants. Mandatory-inclusive measures become essential as back-up to inductive measures. Responsibilization and risk sharing are the pay-back for the privilege of being in the pool for development.

It is in this sense that modernization has twin agendas: global economic success with a measure of social justice. This reflects New Labour's ideological positioning between neo-liberalism and social democracy. And completing Freeden's ideological triangle is the moralizing duty to participate owed by every (reconstructed) citizen, which makes the equation of economic advancement and social justice add up.

With such major political, economic and social principles at stake, and with such precariously poised ideological positioning being played out, the sole measure of how the balance is struck will be the letter of specific policies and the fine grain of their outcomes. The results of battles over method, priority and resource, not the struggles of an explicitly ideological nature, will mark the position where New Labour's modernization policies are 'set down'. And this in turn will partly depend on the means that are selected to deliver reform and the ways in which they shape the processes of reform.

The New Labour mission to modernize the institutions of state welfare faces comparable problems to the intractable ones faced by the New Right in its efforts to marketize the institutions of state welfare. Diverse institutions, diffuse chains of command, complex tiers of control, autonomous professionals, officers and executives, politically committed council members make it no easier to impose a modernization agenda than it was to impose the disciplines and processes of the market. The culture of managerialism that grew in credibility because of its promise to create market-like conditions appears equally promising for modernizing welfare institutions. The common strand is the need to drive new objectives down through the institutions. But the resemblances go further. Many of the objectives of modernization are inflected extensions of market-inspired policies. The pursuit of Best Value and long term effectiveness, in place of cost reduction and short term efficiency gains continues to give priority to performance and target-setting, albeit with adjusted criteria. What has changed more significantly is the ideological commitment to make a social agenda a complement to the economic agenda of modernization as New Labour tries to weld the pursuit of equal opportunity to the market, rather than reject the market as an inherently discriminatory and inequitable mechanism for allocating welfare.

The new task for managerialism is to adapt itself to modernizing objectives, and ensure their percolation through every institution. But this does not simply mean that managerialism switches its allegiances from the priorities of marketization to those of modernization, however similar. Just as it shaped the (sometimes idiosyncratic) forms which markets took within public institutions, so it will fashion and perhaps delimit what kinds of modernization are possible. Even if managerialism as a set of practices can be released from its ideological origins, it does not follow that it is a 'neutral instrument' capable of delivering any set of objectives, unalloyed by its inherent propensities to favour what can be measured, monitored, and encapsulated in pithy expressions of mission and priority.

In education as in every other sphere of social policy, then, two linked sets of tensions are being played out: between the objectives of modernization and the managerial methods used to achieve them; and between the conflicting ideological sources of the twin agendas of modernization.

2   Performance and targets

In its market-based form in the 1980s and 1990s managerialism promulgated a conception of performance founded in competition and the claimed pursuit of excellence. League tables and a system of funding in which high-performing schools were intended to prosper and those which fared badly were doomed to languish set a key framework. Decision making and resource allocation became anchored in these considerations, and managers were empowered within the inexorable logic of leagues and funds. Selective schools, specialist schools and publicly funded places in private schools were seen as central means of maximizing both performance and choice.

New Labour's modernizing agenda has different emphases. Setting standards and performance targets has priority, but with the spotlight on effective teaching for children in historically poorly performing schools. Education Action Zones are at the forefront of this drive, set up with the express aim of improving standards in a cluster of schools in areas of socio-economic deprivation (see Gewirtz, 2000).

The stress on performance has not supplanted the competitive model of separate self-managing schools with devolved budgets and incentives to expand. Nevertheless, there are important distinctions between the two modes. The focus of the New Right model was on outcomes, as end-products of a black box process that benefited some pupils but not others. How those outcomes were achieved and who benefited was of little concern to government. The skill of individual teachers in improving pupils' achievements was implicitly viewed as a kind of enterprise, fostered by a market system of promotions and demotions for schools. New Labour's version is more interventionist, and considerably more managerialist. Outcomes remain the focus, but they are now constituted as targets and benchmarks, rather than just comparisons with other institutions. And once criterion referencing has eclipsed norm referencing in this way, externally determined performance indicators are necessary. Furthermore, while the way in which those outcomes are achieved remains primarily the responsibility of managers and teachers, the 'black box' of learning/educational processes is being partially opened. For example, the imposition of numeracy and literacy hours is an attempt by government to shape the processes that improve performance.

In what ways is the managerialism of the modernizing approach different from the market approach? It appears to have greater immediacy and force. For schools in impoverished areas, the pressure of competition is contained. Schumpeterian notions of the best flourishing, the weakest wiped out and standards being driven up are refuted by the research. Menter et al. (1997) found that primary school heads knew that the prospects of increasing enrolment were small, and insignificant for funding purposes. Several studies have shown that education markets polarize rather than equalize opportunities (Gewirtz et al., 1995; Whitty et al., 1998). A five-year study of marketized provision in New Zealand (Lauder and Hughes, 1999) shows that the effectiveness of schools serving working-class areas and those with high concentrations of Maori children is diminished, not enhanced, as a direct result of the imbalanced social and ethnic mix, itself the product of the social segregation caused by free markets in access to schools. On this evidence, the supposed rigours of the market do not necessarily 'deliver the goods'.

In comparison, omnipresent targets that take reasonable cognizance of the social composition of schools, measure value added, inform inspections, and live in the consciousness of senior staff may prove more penetrating as a mode of securing changes in teachers' behaviour. OFSTED teams inspected the performance of schools, guided by Standard Assessment Tasks, before Labour came to office. But their powers have been considerably sharpened, to identify 'failing' schools, require timetabled improvements and place schools under 'special measures'. To the OFSTED machinery of inspection and evaluation, New Labour has attached new powers for the Department for Education and Employment (DfEE). These may all be preludes to a school being returned to the direct control of the local education authority (LEA), being run on contract for the LEA by a private consortium, or ultimately being taken over by another school, or closed. When Secretaries of State promise to resign if targets are not met it is clear that iron determination combined with sharpened managerial instruments have far greater force and precision than ineffective or counterproductive markets.

In some theories of institutional change, this permeation of a culture into thinking by making its devices omnipresent is the paramount process. The discursive power of targets, improvement and performance is great, and even where it is not embraced positively, it provokes defensive adaptation that is in itself tacit acknowledgement of a new regime of truth. But reliance on this mode of inculcating change would be politically rash. The discourse of marketization gained only a limited foothold in the thinking of teachers. Other tools are required. Linking pay to performance (see Chapter 14 by Waine) is one. But enforced responsibilization is a key mechanism. Once again, the shift from marketized managerialism to its current modernizing mode is marked by intensified rigour.

3 Responsibilization

Market discourses construct markets as responsibilizing institutions for framing social relations and the conduct of transactions. The pursuit of self-interest and the acceptance of the outcomes of exchange are inherent in the discourse of markets and their dynamics. New Right managerialism therefore had consumer sovereignty, and the devolution of controls to institutions, as core axioms of responsibilization. In the absence of direct consumers, parents were constructed as the proxy consumers of education, and were represented as empowered and responsible service users. The reciprocity of the 'bargain' of normal market relations lay in the supposed power of parents to choose and shape schools, to be matched by their irreducible responsibility for securing an education which matched their wishes. A range of policies aimed to allow choice of schools, through systems of supposedly open enrolment, assisted places in private schools, specialist schools to foster excellence in particular curricular areas, and a conducive environment for private schools. At the same time, parents exerted stronger collective influence over schools, by their increased presence on governing bodies, the transfer to schools of key controls over budgets, staffing, and so on. In return parents were made implicitly responsible for their children's education, as the new discourse shifted the boundaries of where the state's responsibilities stopped, and parents' began. For those parents with the necessary means, possibilities for influencing the place, and quality, of their child's education increased. However, the extent of parental choice was highly circumscribed. Similarly, how far the Conservative arrangements of governance amounted to creating 'parent power' is also in question (see Deem et al., 1995). But the 1988 reforms undoubtedly empowered managers, repositioning headteachers and college principals as the key locus of power, running budgets, steering governors, determining staffing, promoting and marketing their institutions, and striving to optimize public representations of performance.

The consequences of the new forms of managerialism that emerged in the Conservative reforms are well documented. At the heart of market-managerialism is the remaking and deprofessionalization of teachers and lecturers. Teacher autonomy was eroded on a number of fronts (see for example Lawn, 1996; Hextall and Mahony, 1998). Their curricular control was subordinated to the National Curriculum, and their adherence to it was policed by regular testing. More democratic forms of institutional decision making gave way to centralized prescription, and to positioning in the local educational market. The authority of heads and principals was sharpened by new structural divisions which positioned them unequivocally as managers, accountable to newly responsibilized governing bodies (Fergusson, 1994). These extended to financial liability that helped further shift the locus of power. Collegiality which constructed heads and principals as 'first among equals' was eroded (Menter and Muschamp, 1999). Professional autonomy to manage time and resources was compromised by imposed fixed-hours contracts. Governing bodies coped with cuts or pursued efficiency gains by making 'flexible' appointments. The lay membership of governing bodies was heavily dependent on the advice of heads and principals to make decisions on pedagogy, curriculum, staffing, and to deal with legal and regulatory complexities. This further empowered managers, by locating them at a critical point between disempowered professionals and newly empowered but inexperienced lay governors.

The modernizing version of responsibilization is a distinctive reworking of the form of managerialism based on market relations. New Labour modernization injects a key social element into market relations, by requiring that they be inclusionary. The New Labour approach takes the social relations of market transactions, entered into by supposedly free actors, and cements them as absolute requisites of social citizenship. In place of the sovereign power of the consumer balanced by acceptance of the consequences of choice, the modernizing agenda offers rights for all, notionally irrespective of means, balanced by inescapable responsibilities in exchange. The voluntarism of market relations, which leave some marginalized or excluded, is supplanted by a form of mandatory and statist inclusion, from which escape is difficult. In this sense, rights are conditional on accepted modes of participation, rather than inalienable features of citizenship. Efforts by the

state to improve welfare are counterbalanced by a reciprocal requirement of participatory citizenship, discharged by taking employment,
exercising parental responsibility, accepting legislated behavioural
norms, and so on.

In the market, the condition of securing personal advantage is that it be
reciprocated through exchange at a value acceptable to the other party. In
the modernized state of participatory citizens, the condition of securing
personal benefit from collective endeavour is to meet prescribed social
criteria. Mutuality in the market is negotiated and, in the last instance,
consensual. Mutuality guaranteed by the state is pre-determined and
ultimately imposed as an absolute choice between participation and
exclusion. The logic of self-interested individuals pursuing their maxi-
mized benefits reciprocated by others doing the same underpins both
versions. But in the market version options are reserved for different
degrees of engagement on both sides, and diversity is possible (in
principle at least). In the modernizing version models of permitted
engagement are centrally prescribed, with little room for variation in the
pursuit of some objectives to give every citizen a 'stake' of some kind. A
supposedly virtuous circle of citizens' rights, state responsibilities, state
rights and citizens' responsibilities secures interdependency and is
substituted for the negotiated mutuality of market relations.

Inspired by its inclusionary social objectives, the modernizing process
of responsibilization by the state takes the pursuit of improved performance much further than the marketized version. In schools and
colleges, this is manifest in the target-setting, goal-oriented approach. It is
supported by a number of measures, ranging from enticement to
coercion. At one end of the spectrum, the pursuit of performance-related
pay rewarding teachers whose pupils achieve targets is under way (see
Chapters 13 and 14 by Ozga and Waine), and schools in Education Action
Zones are already permitted to apply to opt out of the teachers' national
pay and conditions scheme. Other systems of prizes and awards celebrate
teaching that has demonstrably 'added value'. At the other end of the
spectrum a range of measures is in place or mooted to provide deterrents
to or removal for underperformance. Fast-track dismissal of 'failing'
teachers overrides procedures which previously deterred managers from
sacking staff. Formalized staff appraisal is intended to signal discontent
with indifferent performance, specify required improvements, and
contribute to pay determinations. Regular OFSTED inspection, publication of reports, identification of failing schools, and required timetabled
improvements assess institutional performance. The 'naming and
shaming' of failing schools, the new powers of school take-overs and
the threats of closure become the sharpest end of responsibilization.

The modernizing responsibilization of the citizen takes distinct forms
in education. For the most part it is parents who are responsibilized. The
normative and facilitative pressures on parents to maximize their
involvement in schools have been stepped up. Communications between

schools and parents are now extensive. Home–school contracts or agreements specify what parents and teachers may expect of one another, and what both expect of young people. Family learning schemes aim to cement this triangular relationship and build on work done at school. National guidelines for homework have been established. The creation of homework clubs and summer schools is intended to rebut those explanations of educational underperformance that point to unconducive circumstances for some young people trying to work at home. Finally, coercive power is now contemplated as a further route to responsibilize parents. Persistent truancy attracts heavier fines and the possibility of imprisonment for parents.

4   Short-circuiting the market

On this account, then, some answers begin to emerge to one of the questions with which we began: the modernizing agenda is clearly employing managerial methods of delivery. Indeed, the managerialist disciplines of the modernizing approach promise to be considerably more rigorous than those of the market approach. It is as though the very difficulties of mimicking the market had prompted efforts to attain some of its claimed superlatives by regulating them into existence. Much of New Labour's modernizing managerialism endeavours to short-circuit some key processes of market-replicating managerialism. Some of the more direct attempts to simulate markets by means of vouchers or control by regulators were quickly abandoned as unworkable in the context of predominantly state-provided education. Those forms that were adopted palpably failed to deliver across-the-board efficiencies and improvements in standards and had divisive and counterproductive effects for those who had always been worst provided for. Market-based managerialism was therefore unsuitable for meeting the social objectives of New Labour's modernizing agenda. A revamped version of managerialism was needed in its place.

One of the paradoxes of the move from the New Right to New Labour is that the drive to modernization has conjured up a number of centralist, statist, interventionist and prescriptive measures. The effect is to make it appear that the New Labour education reforms select the most socially acceptable prognoses of market theories, and try to regulate them into existence as institutionalized procedures in their own right. So the quest for perpetually improving performance becomes the trigger for practices, procedures and systems which can be monitored and evaluated to achieve just what a hypothetical perfect market would achieve, but by more controlled and predictable means. Similarly, the market's pursuit of efficiency becomes reworked as the quest for best value specified against clear benchmarks, codified, and heavily audited. Compulsory competitive tendering re-emerges as a new culture of bidding for ring-fenced money to advance particular modernizing objectives, with all the contractualism that such piecemeal allocation of resources implies. In a regime where meeting targets, demonstrating improvement, and institutionalizing sanctioned practices are ends in themselves, managerial methods have become unassailable as the sole means to secure modernization. Managerialism has achieved discursive supremacy within a hybridized system where market processes continue alongside the new and extended control processes of government.

5 Partnership and collaboration

In this vein, many current manifestations of managerialism are continuations of its New Right forms, but what is changing is their reach and intensity, and the vigour of their application. Such changes reside, in the last instance, in the ways in which managers and teachers imagine their tasks, conceive their priorities, reconcile their own educational principles to those of the modernizing agenda, and cope with the everyday contradictions this generates. It is in the fine grain of which tasks get done best and first that managerialism is most manifest. For example, a further education lecturer in Shain and Gleeson's research (1999) comments:

> Quality is defined by management in ways which are completely different from how teaching staff would define quality, and there is an awful lot of resentment about this. As teachers who are doing the teaching, dealing with the students every day, we know what constitutes quality. We know that if we spend five minutes marking an essay the student is going to get lower quality feedback than if we spend twenty. . . . There is this kind of smokescreen that we can somehow maintain quality because quality is a very high profile word in all of this. [Management define it] purely statistically, in terms of achievement figures. (p. 456)

Their research found lecturers who embraced the business values of newly independent colleges, keen to demonstrate the flexibility prized by management. But even those who felt they had been subjected to management bullying, particularly in relation to the enforced switch to tougher contracts, were in some degree 'strategically compliant'. In schools, target-watching, looking over the shoulder at past and prospective inspections, and adjusting to approved practices begin to infiltrate everyday thinking. As Menter and Muschamp (1999) note in the context of their research into managerialism in primary schools, 'what was occurring was a fundamental redefinition of schoolwork' (p. 81).

But the modernized and modernizing version of managerialism also has some new manifestations. Their connecting thread is partnership, along with collaboration and networking (see Chapter 5 by Ling).

Partnership has its own logics, of co-operation, effectiveness, efficiency and public service. But a key premise is that there should be sufficient commonality of purpose and explicitness of objectives to make systematic forms of reciprocity work for both parties. Partnership has the potential to supplant the rampant institutional individualism fostered by market-managerialism. But it does tie its participants largely to the modernizing agenda around which it is constructed. Perhaps the most striking instance is the tentative rehabilitation of local education authorities (LEAs) in the new governance of education. Under the New Right reforms, power to shape local provision was largely transferred to governing bodies at the institutional level. Only a small rump of LEA staff with responsibilities for very specific aspects of provision (special needs, transport, admissions) remained. At the same time, some central government powers were increased, particularly with regard to the funding of some institutions, the curriculum, assessment, and inspection.

Labour is remaking local–central relations, in a very different mould. LEAs have a key role in the pursuit of improved performance, through development planning, target setting and performance monitoring, with reserve powers of inspection, intervention, replacement of governors and direct financial control over institutions, on the principle of 'intervention in inverse proportion to success' (Singleton, 1998, p. 1). Emblematic of this modernizing managerialism is that LEAs are themselves inspected by OFSTED and monitored by the Audit Commission, which has already set parameters regarding costs and performance (Audit Commission, 1999a).

Labour also moved to breathe new life into the faltering Private Finance Initiative (PFI), by announcing that one of its key purposes would be to make good the estimated £3 billion backlog in school maintenance costs (Dean, 1997, p. 11). A large number of schemes are now agreed or planned. The legal and control complexities of PFI schemes are considerable, and the Audit Commission (1999b) has warned LEAs to ensure that they are getting Best Value, and can discharge their public service responsibilities under PFI arrangements. A key criterion for the award of PFI contracts is that there be a transfer of risk from public to private sector. Contracts assign responsibility not only for capital costs, but also for revenue costs – IT for facilities and non-teaching staff, for example. As Whitfield (1999) indicates, the possibilities of maintaining a clear separation between public ownership of core services and private contracted responsibility for infrastructural and support services are limited. PFI consortia have 'a vested interest in ensuring that [their] schools . . . perform well' (p. 8), and this is likely to extend to academic performance. Some have been awarded contracts for improving the performance of failing schools. In the process the distinction between public and private sectoral responsibilities becomes increasingly blurred.

In the case of LEAs and PFI, partnership is possible only because there is codified common purpose. These are partners in pursuit of highly prescribed centralized projects. In both cases partnership gives the senior partner a controlling hand in projects which it lacks the means to control directly, because the institutions are too numerous and dispersed, or the full cost of them is too high to countenance politically. Partnership here is necessitated by modernization, and necessitates the intensification of managerialism.

6 Managerial modernization

To complete the answer to one of the key questions of this chapter, then, the New Labour modernization agenda does indeed require managerial methods to deliver it. It is inherently dependent upon much that managerialism can offer. This includes driving the programme of modernization through the structures of dispersed institutions, and shaping the consciousness of the professionals who staff them. Modernization needs managerialism's capacity to reach into corners of long-entrenched practice and its capacity to present itself as an incontrovertible logic, because its referents are so all-pervading in discourses about how public institutions should work. Given New Labour's pledges, self-sacrificing injunctions, and the missionary zeal for improving provision for those with the bleakest prospects, nothing less than a tightly regulated regime could deliver. Modernization has required dispersed controls that acknowledge the diffusion of power in so huge a system; that can deliver the objectives of the centre; and that can govern by appeal to dominant discourses on the one hand and to the quasi-scientific paraphernalia of measuring progress on the other.

In one sense, there is an inevitability about these connections between the modernization agenda and enhanced managerialism. But the logic of arguing that modernization would have had to invent managerialism if it had not been in place pays no attention to the archaeology of ideas. Modernization would not and could not have been conceived as it is without the marketization which preceded it, and the forms of managerialism which marketization required to mimic market conditions. In that sense modernization does inevitably depend on a reinvented or new variant managerialism. But modernization *could* have taken other forms. The logics of managerialism are no more unassailable than those of any dominant discourse – that is, they are a collection of widely held beliefs that things are to be understood in this way and not that. Managerialism is not monolithic or irresistible, and it does not have hegemonic force. To take just one important illustration, many features of the New Right's restructuring of education were diluted or rejected in Scotland, particularly with regard to deprofessionalization and the competitive institutional individualization of schools. And as Ozga (1999) argues, in Scotland many of New Labour's modernizing conceptions of performance, inclusion/exclusion and responsibilization take forms that diverge from neo-liberalism. This is partly because of the public service culture and the social aims of Scotland's separate system, and partly because the Scottish Office and now the Scottish Assembly have discursive spaces within which to rework or amend the dominant (English) discourse.

7 Managerialism and ideological affinity

Another of the paradoxes of New Labour's modernizing managerialism is that one of its key objectives is to undo some of the core outcomes of marketized managerialism. Modernization actively embraces some aspects of markets but eschews others. The voluntarism of markets, their socially selective capacity to exclude, their indifference to outcome, some of the greater extremes of inequality which they cause, their narrow bases of calculating costs, their deleterious uncosted consequences, and their inherent incapacity to equalize opportunity are variously criticized. Modernizing practices and procedures must be inclusive, they must not systematically disadvantage identifiable groups, they must reduce socio-economic polarization, they must be aware of their indirect and external effects, they must widen opportunity as well as deepening it. But paradoxically the instruments by which these new objectives are to be pursued are fashioned from those which delivered marketization.

It is in this refashioning that the vigour of modernizing managerialism is clear, in the three Zs of the quest for the radical centre: zeal, zones and zero tolerance. Zero tolerance of institutional failure is the key antidote to social exclusion and polarization. Zealous self-sacrificing commitment in pursuit of targets is the means to secure adequate provision for all. The removal of bureaucratic obstacles to innovation, rapid change and the targeting of resources in the Education Action Zones all strive to raise standards where student achievement is lowest. Requiring joined-up projects which link departments into co-operative projects is designed to bring back excluded students into mainstream provision.

Criticisms that New Labour's policies are no more than a continuation of New Right marketization policies, in education at least, are unsustainable on these grounds alone, despite the continuation of the structures which attempted to marketize schools. The three Zs represent broadly social democratic aims, and they are being pursued with a very particular modernizing managerialist application. But can the instruments of managerialism be turned to very different social ends from the ones they were originally designed to achieve? On this reading, managerialism is no more than a coherent collection of techniques which can deliver any objective it is set. Empowered, mission-guided head-teachers and principals can as readily use their offices to prioritize the support of the weak as the strong. The discourses that can permeate the thinking of a school staffroom to ensure competitive performance are easily converted to supporting slow learners towards pre-set targets. The preoccupation of this year's inspection with sixth-form retention rates becomes next year's focus on disguised absenteeism, and so on.

This position is open to challenge on two grounds. The first concerns the ideological compatibility of the twin agendas of modernization, and the propensity of managerialism to assume that they can co-exist indefinitely. The economic thrust of modernization towards global economic success, by means of creative, innovative development of human capital towards the knowledge society remains irreducibly neo-liberal in character. The social agenda of modernization which stresses inclusion, equalization of opportunity (and in some versions stakeholding) is principally social democratic. As was noted earlier, New Labour has worked hard to make the case that delivering the social agenda is also a means to delivering the economic agenda. The brilliance of New Labour's project to make itself re-electable and resilient has been to harmonize the rhetoric of performance and responsibilization with that of inclusion and reduced social polarization. Targets which deploy the techniques of effectiveness and Best Value simultaneously meet the aspirations of Middle England for quality state education and promise to raise the poorest performing pupils to acceptable levels. But the underlying ideological forces of the economic and social agendas of modernization are nevertheless in conflict. Such conflicts can be disguised or managed in their presentation, but the substantive differences cannot be wished away. Priorities of resourcing, balancing competing social aims, and unanticipated obstacles to improvement may mean that the honeymoon of pleasing a wide electoral spectrum cannot endure. So far, some of the most intractable sources of political conflict in education have been circumnavigated. By placing deliberate stress on 'standards not structures' from the outset (Labour Party, 1997), deeply contentious issues over selective secondary schools and the continued isolation of 'foundation' schools from local control have been contained. The immensely deep-rooted challenges posed by racism, disadvantage, poverty and cultural exclusion which have failed so many young black men, for example, have yet to be met. Resource crises driven by economic cycles may yet have to be faced. Behind the harmonized rhetoric are likely to lie some stark choices, between those voteless students whose need is greatest, and those voting parents whose skill at extracting the best from the system is most highly developed.

The second ground for challenging the capacity of managerialism to deliver any agenda concerns how far some key values hitherto associated with managerialism are intrinsic to it. Notions of the empowerment of leaders, the pursuit of individualism, systems of extrinsic reward and penalty, chains of command and lines of responsibility, are so much of the stock-in-trade of managerialism as to make alternative understandings difficult. All are deeply associated with its neo-liberal and some corporate conservative origins. Their disjuncture with social democracy is palpable. Of greatest significance is the apparent anti-collectivism of managerialism, its antipathy to democratic decision making, its leanings towards executive modes of management, and its stress on extrinsic values. But these substantial differences do not of themselves demonstrate that managerialism is fundamentally inimical to social democracy. They concern its ways of working, not its purposes.

Of course, such 'ways of working' are no less part of a value-system or a set of social objectives than the express purposes of a project, and they are as likely to further its values. The medium of managing remains central to the message. But it is not yet clear that managerialism remains bound to employ only the devices which have historically been associated with stratified, hierarchical and rule-bound organizations. Certainly, managerialism gained hold because it offered to bring new forms of control to the cultures of welfare institutions which the New Right recognized were beyond the reach of enforced policy changes or the exercise of power through established chains of management command. This historical association, though, risks caricaturing managerialism as *nothing more than* the reassertion of some traditional powers of top-down management and control structures. Ironically, such ways of working were characteristic of the high-water mark of post-war UK social democracy. The bureau-professional axis of power and control demarcated strict domains of autonomy for professionals, based on collegiality, common values and self-regulation. In contrast, the classically hierarchical traditions of public service administration were built around structures of control, chains of command and the responsibility of leaders. In other words, there is nothing inherently collegial, collectivist or democratic about the management methods historically associated with social democracy, however central these values may have been to its political project. Two things made the 'golden years' of social democracy different, which do not prevail now: the relative unassailability of professionals, and high levels of consensus on social and political aims. In comparison, modernizing managerialism gives every appearance of being inherently hostile to these social democratic ends.

Self-evidently, any mode of managerialism which attempted to construct ways of working that embraced the political values of social democracy, around collectivism, collegiality and democracy, would have lost its claim to be managerialism. The two are indeed contradictory, to the extent that managerialism was partly born out of the perceived inadequacies of social democracy. But that does not make managerialism, even in its modernizing mode, inherently incapable of delivering social democratic ends, any more than was the case in the 'golden years'. So long as it is advancing broadly acceptable ends, by means which are not actively hostile to the political values of social democracy, managerialism may be tolerated. To the extent that it is now being used to give higher priority to policies which reverse some of the socially divisive effects of the New Right regime, managerialism may be positively embraced as a purposeful and determined approach to greater social justice by those with a commitment to social democratic ends. Acceptance by teachers and lecturers of the importance of improved educational performance in areas of social disadvantage, for example, is almost certainly extensive – although the consensus on what constitutes better performance, how it can be achieved and if it is remotely possible within existing resources is of course much more limited. But where the educational benefits are in question, or where there is disjuncture between highly managerial means and little-valued ends, tolerance becomes strained. Measures which further delimit professional autonomy without demonstrating that they add educational value are likely to prompt resistance. Forms of pupil assessment which are partly attempts at monitoring *teacher* performance, for example, heighten hostility to managerialism.

In support of these points, Shain and Gleeson's (1999) observations of 'strategic compliance' found that the vast majority of lecturers accepted the broad thrust of managerialism, but found ways of resisting some aspects, by refusing to allow competitive imperatives to override professional advice, for example, or by minor subventions of funds to support educational purposes which accounting rules precluded. The authors refute claims that managerial control is complete, identifying more complex professional cultures at work. Flynn (1999) argues that 'whatever the power of management, there is an irreducible core of autonomy which dependence on professional judgement bestows' (p. 34). Halford and Leonard's research (1999) suggests that managerialist discourses cannot and do not have unlimited powers to take over the identities of public sector professionals.

So to answer the second question with which this chapter began, managerialism may indeed be capable of delivering objectives other than the neo-liberal objectives with which it was associated. The social aspects of New Labour's modernizing agenda may well be within reach of some managerial methods. There may nevertheless be a tendency for managerialism to revert to its neo-liberal type when the tensions between the twin economic and social agendas of modernization come to the fore.

In many respects, modernizing managerialism has much in common with New Labour's 'tough love'. So long as the benefits of treatment are sufficient, some toughness is tolerated. The pragmatics of 'what works' hold sway over 'purist' arguments of principle, especially if what works does so quickly and cheaply. The contradictions become sharper where tougher treatment achieves a lesser response. Tougher methods confer weaker love, until they become irretrievably counterproductive. Managerialism which can modernize because the objectives are shared, and the normative methods are accepted, has little need of the coercive instruments of old management in new-managerial clothes. But these conditions are far from being satisfied in schools and colleges. Resistance which goes beyond marginal strategic compliance can and does arise. It is a reasonable speculation that this will intensify as the performance regime tightens towards the promised points of delivery on targets, as rehabilitated LEAs explore the political limits of their new brief, and as the bond between pay and performance is forged. Clashes over priorities and the limits of professional compliance look set to throw into sharper relief profound tensions which could disrupt the uneasy co-existence of managerial methods and the social democratic ends carried by the social facets of the modernizing agenda. Freeden's 'strange terrain' of New Labour's mixed ideological affinities will then have been reached.

References

Audit Commission (1999a) *Held in Trust: The LEA of the Future*, London, The Audit Commission for Local Authorities and the National Health Service in England and Wales.

Audit Commission (1999b) *Taking the Initiative: A Framework for Purchasing Under PFI*, London, The Audit Commission for Local Authorities and the National Health Service in England and Wales.

Dean, C. (1997) 'Firms urged to prop up crumbling schools', *Times Educational Supplement*, 4426, 27 June, p. 11.

Deem, R., Brehony, K. and Heath, S. (1995) *Active Citizenship and the Governing of Schools*, Buckingham, Open University Press.

Fergusson, R. (1994) 'Managerialism in education', in Clarke, J., Cochrane, A. and McLaughlin, E. (eds) (1994) *Managing Social Policy*, London, Sage.

Finlayson, A. (1998) 'Tony Blair and the jargon of modernization', *Soundings*, 10, Autumn, pp. 11–27.

Flynn, R. (1999) 'Managerialism, professionalism and quasi-markets', in Exworthy, M. and Halford, S. (eds) *Professionals and the New Managerialism in the Public Sector*, Buckingham, Open University Press.

Freeden, M. (1999) 'The ideology of New Labour', *Political Quarterly*, 70 (1), pp. 42–51.

Gewirtz, S. (2000) 'Education Action Zones: emblems of the 'third way'? in Dean, H. and Woods, R. (eds) *Social Policy Review*, 11, Luton, Social Policy Association.

Gewirtz, S., Ball, S. and Bowe, R. (1995) *Markets, Choice and Equity in Education*, Buckingham, Open University Press.

Giddens, A. (1998) *The Third Way: The Renewal of Social Democracy*, Cambridge, Polity.

Halford, S. and Leonard, P. (1999) 'New identities? Professionalism, managerialism and the construction of self', in Exworthy, M. and Halford, S. (eds) *Professionals and the New Managerialism in the Public Sector*, Buckingham, Open University Press.

Hextall, I. and Mahony, P. (1998) 'Effective teachers for effective schools', in Slee, R. and Weiner, G. with Tomlinson, S. (eds) *School Effectiveness for Whom? Challenges to the School Effectiveness and School Improvement Movements*, London, Falmer Press.

Labour Party (1997) *New Labour: Because Britain Deserves Better* (1997 General Election Manifesto), London, Labour Party.

Lauder, H. and Hughes, D. (1999) *Trading in Futures: Why Markets in Education Don't Work*, Buckingham, Open University Press.

Lawn, M. (1996) *Modern Times? Work, Professionalism and Citizenship in Teaching*, London, Falmer Press.

Menter, I. and Muschamp, Y. (1999) 'Markets and management: the case of the primary school', in Exworthy, M. and Halford, S. (eds) *Professionals and the New Managerialism in the Public Sector*, Buckingham, Open University Press.

Menter, I., Muschamp, Y., Nicholls, P., Ozga, J. and Pollard, A. (1997) *Work and Identity in the Primary School*, Buckingham, Open University Press.

Ozga, J. (1999) 'Two nations? Education and social inclusion–exclusion in Scotland and England', *Education and Social Justice*, 1 (3), pp. 44–50.

Shain, F. and Gleeson, D. (1999) 'Under new management: changing conceptions of teacher professionalism and policy in the further education sector', *Journal of Education Policy*, 14 (4), pp. 445–62.

Singleton, D. (1998) 'Do LEAs have a future? An OFSTED assessment', *Education Review*, 12 (1), pp. 22–5.

Whitfield, D. (1999) 'Private finance initiative: the commodification and marketization of education', *Education and Social Justice*, 1 (2), pp. 2–11.

Whitty, G., Power, S. and Halpin, D. (1998) *Devolution and Choice in Education*, Buckingham, Open University Press.

13

Education: New Labour, New Teachers

Jenny Ozga

This chapter looks at the impact of managerialism on a particular group of public sector workers, namely teachers. Although it is argued elsewhere in this volume that the operation of managerialism is not hegemonic in its processes and effects, there is, perhaps, scope for suggesting that in education its impact is particularly strong and the scope for modification and mediation especially limited. It is important to recall the long process of reform and restructuring to which education was subjected under Conservative administrations from 1979 to 1997, and which have turned out to be a mere rehearsal for New Labour modernization. Conservative attempts at modernization were always mired in contradiction, and others have illuminated the tensions between economic liberalism and the cultural restorationist project (Jones, 1989).

New Labour's modernization of education, which uses managerialism as its vehicle, seems less contradictory. It pursues modernization in education in order to create an enterprising culture of the system, the institution and the self. It privileges waged work as the passport to inclusion, as well as the creation of wealth (common and individual) and in so doing it seeks to remove the need for separate recognition of the social and cultural work that education does, because that is now encompassed within programmes that promote achievement. The pursuit of achievement is the route to employment but it is also the means of ensuring appropriate socialization and cultural integration.

Teachers present a particularly informative case of the operation of managerialism not only as a consequence of the scope of changes in their work, in their management, and in their professional formation and development, but also because teaching is the key occupation in New Labour's key service. Education is charged with the production of competitive, flexible, skilled workers who attract global capital, but it is also the site for the construction and accumulation of social, as well as economic, capital. Teachers, accordingly, are not only required to promote achievement and enterprise, they must also mirror the culture of enterprise in their self-management. Thus managerialism in teaching is attempting a fundamental transformation.

This chapter looks at the New Labour project for teachers first through a historical lens, reviewing the cycles of teacher control in England, and the more immediate past of specific initiatives that provided the regulatory framework within which managerialism is now operating. It then considers some apparently intractable problems, for example in retention and recruitment of teachers, and considers managerialist strategies for dealing with them. It moves on to consider the ways in which the management of the teaching force is rendered more complex by devolved government within the UK, before concluding with arguments about the damaging effects of managerialism on teachers and on education more generally.

The historical discussion is intended to illuminate the extent to which teachers have always been a policy problem for government. This permits us to look more closely at the definition of the problem that is currently being invoked and so helps identify the questions in education to which managerialism is taken to be the answer. It also enables us to consider whether managerialism is a stage or event in an inherently tense relationship between teachers and their employers, or whether, as indicated above, it represents an attempt to achieve a more fundamental shift.

1   Teachers as a policy problem

The construction of teachers as a 'problem' is not new. The plans for modernizing the profession set out in the Green Paper (DfEE, 1998) *Teachers: meeting the challenge of change* (in lower case, to express the simplicity and user-friendliness of the proposals) are the most recent expression of policy in a history that involves the more or less explicit attempted design and redesign of teaching, through changes in the training, development and career structures of the occupational group. Current models are distinguished by their reliance on managerialism, for example in the control of career progression and reward (see Waine,

Chapter 14 in this volume). However, there have always been attempts to use teachers as a vehicle for the transmission of particular messages into the system (for example of Christian morality, or imperial power, or meritocracy). These messages have not been absorbed by teachers without mediation or resistance.

The failure of these models to deal with the intractability and complexity of education systems and the teachers working within them points to the difficulty of relying on prescriptive policy solutions to achieve designed change. The current managerialist agenda for teachers denies the complexity of the work that teachers do and that education is expected to do. Education – or perhaps more accurately education systems – have complex social, economic and political purposes and tensions between those dimensions are endemic. They cannot easily be held in equilibrium, and the privileging of one area (for instance the economic), and its current use as a transmission mechanism for selected aspects of the others is likely to produce tension in the profession that will test the disciplinary mechanisms already in place or in progress. In the past in England the teaching force has been managed through emphasis either on direct controls that stipulate the content and process of teaching and regulate entry and career development (direct rule) or through indirect means, including fostering professionalism as a way of co-opting and regulating the profession (indirect rule). Neither management strategy is stable. In the past direct regulation has led to militancy in the workforce and inefficiency in the system (Grace, 1985; Lawn, 1987; Ozga, 2000) while the promulgation of an ideology of professionalism creates the potential for teachers to extend the terms of their licence to an unacceptable degree, as they did in the 1970s in England (Dale, 1981).

The playing out of those different modes of control is connected to the wider context of economic, social and political development. Periods of economic retrenchment or remodelling, and concern about competitiveness, combined with associated moral panics about, for example, 'national' character/identity, declining standards (of performance and behaviour), and threatened masculinity (male teachers for boys), have tended to produce attempts at more direct regulation whether they occurred in the 1860s, the 1920s, the 1960s or the 1990s. The playing out of the different modes of control is also affected substantially by the extent to which hierarchies of provision are secure or threatened, especially in English education, where, as Johnson (1989) has pointed out, differentiation, and its constant re-formation, is the enduring hallmark of English provision.

Teachers have been involved in challenging hierarchies of provision (and implicated in sustaining them). Where they successfully organize in support of redistributive measures (e.g. comprehensive reorganization in England in the 1960s and 1970s) and for recognition of cultural injustice (for example in the 1960s and 1970s around gender, 'race' and class inequalities) they challenge economic, cultural and social hierarchies that are sustained by hierarchies of provision.

2   System redesign before New Labour

Before moving on to explore the working of managerialism in policy for teachers before 1997, I would like to review the main trends in reforming teaching before New Labour, because those trends made possible the rapid implementation of the modernization project. There was, of course, extensive encroachment on the work of public sector professionals in general, in ways that undermined their claims to expertise and their legitimacy as authoritative allocators of resource and opportunity. In the case of teaching it is significant to note changes in professional formation. The reform of training is important because it produced new cohorts of teachers who have been socialized into the profession through school-based or school-led 'partnerships', which may accentuate the trainee's focus on the practical, the immediate and the approved institutional practice. It has also encouraged new teachers to receive prescribed curricula and assessment packages and deliver them, with a keen awareness of the need for successful pupil outcomes, as measured, and publicized, through national assessments. For teachers in service, managerialism was installed in education institutions in order to support the redefinition of professionalism through legislative controls and internal institutional mechanisms, notably performance indicators and inspections. Devolution of financial management to schools greatly enhanced the capacity of managerialism because it installed surveillance of the workforce at the level of the institution, and not through any intermediate arena, such as the LEA.

As well as the formal mechanisms of inspection, assessment and appraisal, there is a whole repertoire of assumptions and relationships that changed the nature of teaching in England. These have been extremely significant in establishing management's 'right to manage'. The loss of influence and unity in the teacher unions is a reflection of this, as is greater flexibility in the workforce, and a more fragmented internal labour market. The various policies that used the discourse of decentralization and devolution of financial management apparently promoted lay influence but actually developed a management cadre that took responsibility for the schools' performance against their externally published targets. In a variety of ways, teachers' work became subjected to control from, and influence by, the school manager, who in turn became an agent of accountability to the central department. These processes are readily apparent, but there are also more insidious and highly significant effects surrounding them. The practice of 'active' management by headteachers produced substantial changes in work practices in teaching, and a major shift towards committed team membership, good organization and effective co-ordination as the manifestation of reprofessionalized teacher identity. These processes 'manufacture consent' to change, because they operate through interdependent work relations, which may be experienced as coercive rather than collegiate (Menter et al., 1997). The consequence for some teachers is a fragmentation of professional identity in which there is a

> gap between the responsible, accountable professional on public display, and the private experience of bitterness, anxiety and overload. [This] is also indicative of the covert coercion of the new management. It is also significant that these teachers should internalize their responses to that coercion, and thus live out the consequences of change in terms of fractured and fragmented identities. (Menter et al., 1997, p. 115)

Studies of business organizations suggest that some of the most undesirable characteristics of the new managerially driven work cultures are their lack of trust, their refusal of complexity and their denial of values and motives other than those of self-interest. The absence of trust combines powerfully with the appearance and invocation of teamwork and empowerment to produce a state of alienation or ambivalence about work and the new work culture (Casey, 1995). The ambivalence comes from the close 'sociality' of teamwork, together with a feeling that, despite the apparent closeness and supportiveness of the team, the social relations of work have become artificially 'social' and conceal competition and manoeuvring, as well as surveillance, under a veneer of concern and support (ibid.). Workers are disciplined by teamwork, which exploits their rational knowledge and their technical or interpersonal skills, but excludes or denies characteristics such as nurturance or patience, Casey argues (1995, p. 194). These characteristics were part of the traditional and valued repertoire of teachers.

This, then, is the terrain on which New Labour hoped to build its modernized teaching force.

3   New Labour's managerialism

So in what ways does the redesign of the profession as the expression of New Labour's managerialism differ from those earlier processes of professional restructuring? Firstly there is the very heavy emphasis on the economic function of education and on education's role in preparing people for work (through skills, competences and attitudes). Work has a greatly increased significance in New Labour policy because of the government's anxiety to modernize in order to compete effectively in an unstable global environment, and because its policy responses to the problem of social exclusion that has been exacerbated by marketization are almost completely focused on waged work (Levitas, 1998). Education is tightly bound to work and hence to the economy; and preoccupation with the education–economy relationship extends into the adoption of business-derived management practice in education institutions on a larger and deeper scale than hitherto (for example performance related pay). Flexibility was encouraged in the 1980s to provoke insecurity and challenge the rather homogeneous and undifferentiated character of the occupation. In its New Labour form it is apparently driven by pragmatic concerns – in particular about recruitment and retention issues. However there are also continuing anxieties about the role of higher education institutions (HEI) in socializing teachers, which help explain the continued effort to support non-HEI providers of initial teacher training (ITT) through rewarding them with status and money.

The regulatory framework for teachers in formation or in professional development is best understood as operating outside the HEI process and culture. Both the content and process of teacher training is prescribed by the Teacher Training Agency. The establishment of the National College for School Leadership is part of the same process. In all of this there is a policy design that excludes the fostering of autonomy, judgement, reflexivity; instead there is adherence to the technical/managerial precept that one size fits all in successful teaching and successful school leadership. The standardization of practice is perhaps most explicitly illustrated in the performance pay arrangements, for example in the use of 'national standards' against which school assessments of teacher performance are to be checked by external assessors. New Labour's managerialism also involves encouraging business into education in a range of initiatives of which the Education Action Zones are the most visible. There the injection of cash resources may not be as significant as the rhetoric suggests since much of the business support is being offered 'in kind'; so that, for example, headteachers are mentored by business managers.

There is a further element in the education–work–economy relationship which in fact frames these developments and explains New Labour's preoccupation with the modernization of education and its determination to use the managerial repertoire to achieve that. This element is the shift to the knowledge economy in which knowledge and information become enormously significant in determining production and in driving competition (Castells, 1998). As Seddon (1999) points out, the knowledge that is a generative force in production is not the institutionalized knowledge currently at the heart of education, but 'knowledge in practice', 'an alive mix of information and concepts, coupled with the understanding necessary to apply them in everyday work' (Field and Ford, 1994, p. 4 quoted in Seddon, 1999, p. 4).

Seddon goes on to suggest that this shift in the nature of the knowledge that is valued reduces the status and value of the teaching profession. Instead the teacher is replaced by 'the manager as hero, leader and visionary' (ibid., p. 4).

4 The three Rs: recruitment, retention, rhetoric

Some of the initiatives mentioned above are driven by pragmatic considerations, as well as attempted modernization. This is because the teaching profession in England is not in a buoyant and healthy state. The situation is different throughout the UK, as recruitment and retention are problematic only in England – indeed Scotland is a net exporter of teachers. Comments below about low status, morale and standing with the public are also applicable more to England than elsewhere. For some, myself included, this is not unrelated to the processes of restructuring reviewed above, which have been pursued energetically in England. For New Labour, the explanation lies more in the incompleteness of the modernization process, and the resulting survival of inappropriate attitudes and dispositions among members of the occupation. The interdependent strategies of 'pressure and support' (DfEE, 1997a) are designed to address this issue.

The problems, however, are quite substantial. If we look at the supply issue it is apparent that recruitment to ITT courses has become difficult in some areas. There are shortfalls of around 17 per cent in the recruitment of secondary teachers, while the priority subjects (a list that revealingly includes all of the following: mathematics, science, religious education, information technology, modern foreign languages and music) continue to under-recruit; mathematics by as much as 35 per cent (DfEE, 1997b, 1999). There has been some improvement recently because of the introduction of incentives (payments of £5,000) in some areas, but it is not yet apparent that these incentives will keep people in the profession beyond the period in which they pay off their student loans.

Primary recruitment has always been more buoyant than secondary, but the trend is downwards, and there are concerns about the impact of tuition fees on four-year undergraduate routes. The difficulties in recruitment are interesting because they prompt discussion of underlying causes. Teaching seems more vulnerable than other occupations to the shifting graduate labour market; economic upturn has produced a swing away from teaching for graduates with marketable degrees. Explanations of this differ. My view is that the routinization of teaching, the excessive paperwork and the homogenization of content have made the profession unattractive to imaginative graduates. Graduates indicate that they seek work that offers intellectual challenge, but in teacher training much of that challenge has been stripped out, while in teaching there are pressures towards standardized pedagogies. The training process rewards conformists, and school-based training is a very conservative process of professional formation.

Problems in retaining teachers are also indicative of difficulty in the modernization project. Over 20 per cent of vacancies were found to be difficult to fill in 1999 (STRB, 1999). There are particular difficulties in recruiting to primary headship, where the character of the work has been profoundly altered by managerialism, which has removed those pastoral and 'leading professional' characteristics that made it attractive to good teachers (Menter et al., 1997). Redundancy levels doubled between 1989 and 1996. Retirement levels have also risen. There is some evidence of increased sickness and stress in the profession. At the time of writing, the picture is not one of a vibrant occupation. Nor is the public image of teaching very positive, and nearly two decades of relentless criticism of teachers have established a media perception of inadequacy. It has also undoubtedly had a negative impact on teachers' own perceptions of their work and its value. High profile recruitment campaigns by the Teacher Training Agency ('nobody forgets a good teacher') tend to highlight the gap between the rhetoric and reality, as the Select Committee report on teacher recruitment comments:

> improving the image of teaching requires more than a concerted advertising campaign, however good . . . if the nation as a whole can recognize the value of teachers, this will help reduce the apparent stigma which is currently attached to the profession. (House of Commons Education and Employment Committee, 1997, p. xxii)

The government's response to these indicators of difficulty has been to make some positive statements about the profession:

> The Government values teachers and will celebrate good practice and excellence in our classrooms. Pressure to succeed will be matched by the support that teachers need to do their job well. . . . Raising standards is the Government's priority and good teaching is key to high standards. A mark of the Government's commitment to teachers' professional standing will be the establishment of a General Teaching Council. (DfEE, 1997a, p. 33)

At first sight, this proposal seems at odds with managerialism. It looks more like the 'support' side of the 'pressure and support' equation that summarizes policy. However, there is little substance to the support, and this can be well illustrated by looking more closely at the proposals for a General Teachers' Council (GTC). The consultation document, *High Status, High Standards*, issued in July 1997, promised to establish a GTC by the year 2000 (DfEE, 1997a). There was very little indication of what the body would do, and how it would function. Stephen Byers, the then Minister of State, said in the introduction:

> We are not interested in a talking shop for teachers or a body to defend the way things are. An effective GTC must be an engine for change and a powerful driving force behind our new deal for teachers: high expectations and pressure to succeed, matched by support and recognition of achievement. (DfEE, 1997a, p. 3)

The GTC was thus from the outset co-opted into the modernization process and 'managerialized'. The remainder of the document sets out ways in which the body can assist in monitoring the profession, in disciplining incompetent or unprofessional teachers, and in regulating entry to the profession. This is an instrumental document, which says nothing at all about the purposes of education or the nature of teaching. It asserts that what is being established is a General Teaching rather than a General Teachers' Council. The two are apparently incompatible.

The other substantial policy text that provides insights into New Labour's managerialism is the Green Paper mentioned earlier: *Teachers: meeting the challenge of change* (DfEE, 1998). This document encapsulates a view of teaching that denies the social aspect of the teaching role absolutely, and also excludes knowledge-based formations of professional identity. In constructing a career hierarchy for teachers in which pay and performance are linked in a particular way it is apparent that government really does see the educational workplace as an enterprise. The policy assumes that improvement in education will follow from a system that treats teachers as careerists, as entrepreneurs of the self. The provisions of the Green Paper may be divided into two broad sections: those dealing with pay, and those dealing with professional formation and development. I will review these, discussing evidence of managerialism, and starting with performance related pay (PRP).

The introduction of PRP was contemplated by the last Conservative government but not acted upon. There had been moves towards it in the form of much greater use of incentive allowances, but these remained largely tied to responsibility rather than performance. The School Teachers' Review Body, established in 1991, was supportive in principle of PRP but concerned about the complexity of linking pay and individual performance. The Green Paper and, in particular, its technical annexe, suggest that these complexities are no longer an issue. Teachers are to have a performance threshold set for them at £23,000 beyond which they need to perform successfully in a rigorous annual appraisal that subjects them to a threefold assessment, by their headteacher, and against national standards of performance and external validation. Teachers must prepare and submit a portfolio that provides relevant information about their performance, and that gives data of pupil performance. Those who perform well and demonstrate their willingness to meet 'higher professional expectations' will go through the threshold and enter a process of 'salary uplift'.

There are some obvious difficulties with this plan. A major one is that of matching teacher performance and pupil performance – both in disaggregating pupil performance and in demonstrating a causative relationship between improvement or deterioration – and teaching. This is before we consider the impact of such individualized calculations on the overall culture and climate of the school. Then there are the issues of gender and the performance of competence or excellence. Research on appraisal in education and elsewhere indicates that women consistently undersell themselves in such self-promoting systems, and also draws attention to the gendered division of labour in teaching, where women are more likely than men to spend time and effort on unremarked tasks that do not carry weight in the appraisal process. This system of performance appraisal may well exacerbate already existing tendencies towards discrimination, and it is interesting that the Green Paper also contains fast track proposals for promotion that claim to have no implications for equal opportunities but will inevitably benefit more mobile teachers. It is also worth noting that the policy text has revisited nineteenth-century concerns about the feminization of the profession and the detrimental impact of this on boys.

If we consider the meaning of the Green Paper for wider issues of professional formation and development in the teaching profession, then again it is possible to interpret the proposals as shaping the redesign of the profession away from an undifferentiated and relatively flat hierarchy into one that is much more internally stratified and subdivided. There are different forms of entry proposed, some of which permit the strengthening of flexible part-time training for categories of teacher who can start as auxiliaries and move into full professional status. There is an interesting combination of disciplinary control over development through compulsory induction and professional development within a highly specified framework, along with rhetoric that echoes the status and attributes of the private sector. This is a very ambitious and far-reaching project of redesign.

5   Beyond Westminster and Whitehall

Before summarizing some of the fundamental issues that are raised by the application of managerialism to education there is a need for a comparative (UK) perspective on the 'problem' of teachers and their attempted refashioning by New Labour. In part, this is a necessary corrective to assumptions (made equally by policy makers and policy analysts) that any English pattern is reproduced throughout the UK. These assumptions are inaccurate, and fail to recognize the impact of the different contexts in which education systems have evolved, in England, Wales, Scotland and Northern Ireland. Nor do they recognize the different administrative and political frameworks within which they operated, even before the establishment of separate Assemblies in Wales and Scotland in 1999. Those Assemblies provoke interesting considerations about the nature of managerialism and managerial solutions. It is possible to see Devolution (with a capital D) as a paradigm of managerial policy: solving the problem of political representation in a technical way but failing to comprehend that separate Assemblies would reflect separate political and administrative cultures, and could not be relied upon to act as a conduit for New Labour's project to modernize governance.

In the sphere of education, the resistance of Scotland to Thatcherite redesign was quite marked, and more recent indications of difference can be seen in the different public responses to the Private Finance Initiative. Yet the managerialist insistence on standardized solutions (indeed standardized definitions of problems) produces initiatives such as those in the Scottish Office (1999) consultation document *Targeting Excellence: Modernising Scotland's Schools*, which reads like a somewhat uncomfortable translation of DfEE school standards-speak into the Scottish context. For example, in relation to teachers, the section 'Targeting Excellence in Teaching' contains loud echoes of English preoccupations with leadership and with site-based management as 'solutions' to the 'problem' of changing organizational cultures in education. It proposes more school-based responsibility for the management of teachers and is evidently unhappy with the corporatist approach of the current arrangements through which the Scottish Joint Negotiating Committee for Teaching Staff in School Education (SJNC) brings together representatives of the employers (education authorities) and the teacher unions to settle issues of pay and conditions.

The document states that 'the Government believe that changes in pay, promotion structures, and terms and conditions is needed if teachers, the most expensive and important resource available in education, are to continue to make a fully professional contribution' (Scottish Office, 1999, p. 64). This is undoubtedly the view of the UK government, but may not be that of the Assembly. The concluding discussion of teachers looks at the 'teacher of the future' and ties itself in knots in its attempt to produce justification for change in a group with few recruitment or retention problems, fairly high status, high levels of parental support, and operating with considerable autonomy and with an established and influential General Teaching Council. This is the resultant paragraph:

> In the Scotland of the 21st century just as throughout this century the teacher will be central to the health of our society. Teachers are role models for children and young people at all stages of development and all walks of life. The position and status of the Scottish teacher should be improved and enhanced; they should be, as in the past, members of the local community whose values, attitudes and views are sought and respected. Their central role will remain the development of knowledge, skills and values in children and young people. The profession must be modernized without losing the traditional values of the Scottish teacher . . . .
>
> . . . the Government's vision for modernization is of a teaching profession founded on the strengths of the past and present, and adapted to meet the challenges of the future. (ibid., p. 68)

This exemplifies the operation of managerialism in policy for teachers, and also illustrates some of its shortcomings. Because managerialism is impatient with the non-standard, it seeks uniformity and homogeneity in order to permit the operation of its auditing and benchmarking procedures. However it is hard to see why uniformity in education policy and in policy for teachers between England and Scotland was assumed to be unproblematic post-1999. Differences in national politics (in the constituent nations of the UK) may well produce difficulties for the managerial solutions to political problems, and raise considerable possibilities for conflict where the model or template for improvement is not understood in the same ways in the constituent parts of the UK. The reform/restructuring of the public sector is probably not perceived in quite the same way in Scotland and England, for example, for historical and political reasons. The place of teaching in civil society and its public value are also different, as the backward-glancing references quoted above indicate. Managerialist strategies for the diagnosis of problems and development of solutions in education (broadly) and in the specific area of teachers and teaching show little sign of acknowledging the significance of these differences.

6 Beyond managerialism

I tried earlier to set the reprofessionalizing agenda within a broader picture of economic change. The shift towards 'informational' capitalism is accompanied by very significant social and political changes. The social changes include fragmentation and uncertainty; the political changes include new forms of regulation of social life. Policy makers in England are focused on the economizing agenda, and are neglecting the work of education in the production of citizens, and in the codifying and disseminating of knowledge and culture which have valuable social functions. The missing social and political dimensions in policy indicate a failure to recognize the importance of education as 'a significant region of social practice', a place where people learn how to be as well as how to labour (Seddon, 1997).

This is not a romantic and nostalgic perspective; rather it is a recognition of the ways that education mediates contradictory and destabilizing forces, and provides stability in times of flux and pressure for change, such as these. As Seddon argues, in a world in which innovation, change, and constant consumption hold sway, education is a social institution that offers some counterbalance to the 'post-modernizing fragmentation of social life, fuelled by radical individualism and the erosion of social capital' (Seddon, 1997). Current policy understands education as a social institution that can serve informational capitalism. But education is also a place where people develop essential capacities for social interaction and for political practice. It is a place where people learn to engage with social life and to try out and construct identities. Education thus contributes in a fundamental way to creating social infrastructure. That it often reproduces conservative political and social relations illustrates its significance for stability. But this does not mean that education is inherently conservative. Indeed part of my argument has been that it is inherently contested. Connell (1995) has described the work that teachers do in the formation of active citizens, not just as a consequence of embodying formal authority, but through the development of power relations based on negotiation, dialogue and co-operation. These ideas, which draw attention to some of the complexity of the work that education does for society and its considerable progressive potential, are intended to highlight the emptiness of current policy directions and their inadequacy as solutions to problems that are themselves incorrectly defined. Managerialism, and the vision it works for, is limited. If morale and status are to be restored, the profession needs to have restored to it the right to claim service to the public good and to demonstrate it in ways that extend beyond the narrow, economistic version currently offered to them. Teachers need to be recognized for the educational work that they do that helps learners learn how to learn, that is embedded in interpersonal relations, and that is full of content and skill, rather than empty, bureaucratic and utilitarian (Seddon, 1996).

References

Casey, C. (1995) *Work, Self and Society after Industrialism*, London, Routledge.

Castells, M. (1998) *End of Millennium*, Malden, Mass, Blackwell.

Connell, R. (1995) 'Transformative Labour: theorising the politics of teachers' work', in Ginsburg, M. (ed.) *The Politics of Educators' Work and Lives*, New York, Garland Press.

Dale, R. (1981) 'Control, accountability and William Tyndale', in Dale, R., Esland, G., Fergusson, R. and Macdonald, M. (eds) *Education and the State*, vol. 2: *Politics, Patriarchy and Practice*, Lewes, Falmer Press.

DfEE: Department for Education and Employment (1997a) *High Status, High Standards: General Teaching Council – A Consultation Document*, London, DfEE.

DfEE: Department for Education and Employment (1997b) *Written Evidence to the School Teachers' Review Body*, London, DfEE.

DfEE: Department for Education and Employment (1998) *Teachers: meeting the challenge of change*, Cm 4164, London, The Stationery Office.

DfEE: Department for Education and Employment (1999) *Written Evidence to the School Teachers' Review Body*, London, DfEE.

Field, L. and Ford, B. (1994) *Managing Organisational Learning*, Melbourne, Longman.

Grace, G. (1985) 'Judging teachers: theoretical and political contexts of teacher evaluation', *British Journal of Sociology of Education*, 6 (1), pp. 3–17.

House of Commons: Education and Employment Committee (1997) *First Report: Teacher Recruitment: What Can be Done?* London, The Stationery Office.

Johnson, R. (1989) 'Thatcherism and English education', *History of Education*, 18 (2), pp. 91–122.

Jones, K. (1989) *Right Turn: The Conservative Revolution in Education*, London, Hutchinson Radius.

Lawn, M. (1987) *Servants of the State: The Contested Control of Teaching*, Lewes, Falmer Press.

Levitas, R. (1998) *The Inclusive Society?* London, Macmillan.

Menter, I., Muschamp, Y., Nicholls, P. and Ozga, J. with Pollard, A. (1997) *Work and Identity in the Primary School: A Post-Fordist Analysis*, Buckingham, Open University Press.

Ozga, J. (2000) *Policy Research in Educational Settings*, Buckingham, Open University Press.

Scottish Office (1999) *Targeting Excellence: Modernising Scotland's Schools*, Edinburgh, Scottish Office.

Seddon, T. (1996) *Pay, Professionalism and Politics: Changing Teachers? Changing Education?* Melbourne, Australian Council for Educational Research.

Seddon, T. (1997) 'Education: deprofessionalized? Or reregulated, reorganized and reauthorized?' unpublished paper, Monash University, Melbourne.

Seddon, T. (1999) 'A self-managing teaching profession for the Learning Society?' paper presented to the European Education Research Association Conference, Lahti, Finland, September.

STRB: School Teachers' Review Body (1999) *Survey of Vacancies and Recruitment in Schools*, London, Office of Manpower Economics.

14

Managing Performance through Pay

Barbara Waine

Contents

While attempts to measure the performance of public sector services are in no sense a new phenomenon, their operation in the 1980s and 1990s has a number of distinctive features: their scale and pervasiveness; the significance attributed to measuring the performance of provider units such as schools, NHS Trusts and Executive Agencies; and the attempt to link the performance of such units to the pay of individual employees with schemes of performance related pay (PRP). With PRP the assessment of an individual's performance may either be quantified and act as a direct determinant of pay or may combine quantitative and qualitative objectives, with their achievement judged via appraisal. Examples of the former would be the payment by results system for elementary school teachers introduced by the 1862 Revised Code, whereby a fee per pupil was linked to a minimum attendance level and examination results in reading, writing and arithmetic (Cutler and Waine, 1999, p. 56). A more recent example of a target-based PRP scheme is that of the 1990 General Practitioners' contract which linked part of the remuneration of GPs to the achievement of immunization and cervical screening targets. Examples of PRP combining quantitative and qualitative measures can be found with senior managers in the National Health Service (Dowling and Richardson, 1997) and the scheme proposed by the Labour government for headteachers and teachers (Department for Education and Employment, 1998, 1999a).

This chapter focuses on PRP in the public sector. It is divided into five sections: the first traces the emergence of PRP in the 1980s and 1990s and its relationship with public sector managerialism; the second focuses on the way in which New Labour is developing PRP as a key aspect of a 'modern' managed public sector; the third section discusses the difficulties posed for PRP by problems of performance measurement; the fourth section discusses the claims of PRP to be an equitable pay system; while the fifth section considers certain limits and tensions of this New Labour project.

1   PRP and public sector managerialism

A central political assumption under Conservative governments in the 1980s and 1990s was that the public sector was inefficient and represented a drag on overall economic performance. An obvious strategy, given such a stance, was to cut the size of the public sector. However, while privatization was pursued vigorously in relation to public utilities it was much less significant in social welfare (for discussion of the reasons for this see Cutler and Waine, 1998, Ch. 1; Pierson, 1994). Consequently the government remained a substantial employer of labour (Hogwood, 1998; Salford and MacGregor, 1998) and policy on public sector pay became a significant element in the 'reform' of the public sector.

This involved challenging many of the institutions and practices of public sector pay determination which the Conservatives had inherited – national pay bargaining, comparability, rate for the job, automatic annual increments (Employment Department, 1998, para. 3.5). The preferred alternatives were decentralized pay bargaining, pay related to market forces, and pay linked to performance in the job, that is, PRP. While all of these alternatives allowed a greater element of pay flexibility and discretion for employers, it was PRP which was most closely linked to the project of transforming the management of the public sector services.

A central critique of public services was that they lacked specific objectives and thus the means of evaluating whether service goals were being attained. For example, this criticism was made of the organization of the health service in the Griffiths Report (1983), of the universities in the Jarratt Report (1985), and in the *Next Steps* Report on management in the Civil Service (Jenkins et al., 1988). One effect of the acceptance of such arguments by government was the belief that an effective organization needed to have explicit targets designed to secure improvement. It followed that organizations must be structured to ensure that these targets were achieved and that elements of the organization not directly focused on such targets had to be changed. Thus PRP could be seen as a managerial tool which allowed the use of the pay system to achieve goals regarded as appropriate by government. Such schemes, it was argued, were more characteristic of the private sector than the incremental and non-performance-related systems characteristic of the public sector. Thus support for PRP was also part of the process of seeking to reconstruct public sector services on private sector lines.

With the Citizen's Charter, the government announced its intention to pursue PRP vigorously (Prime Minister's Office, 1991, p. 35). A further development of this process came when, at the request of the relevant government departments, the Review Bodies on Doctors' and Dentists' Remuneration, for Nursing Staff, Midwives and Health Visitors and for Schoolteachers all considered the case for introducing PRP for their professional groups (Cutler and Waine, 1994, pp. 124–30). PRP came into operation for all civil servants, other than the most senior levels, and for senior managers in local government (Income Data Services Report, 1996, pp. 20, 31) and in the NHS (Dowling and Richardson, 1997, p. 349); for general practitioners via the 1990 GP contract; in universities (Jackson, 1997) and for headteachers and deputies (Cutler and Waine, 1999, pp. 58–9). However, by the time the Conservatives left office, they had secured only modest changes in introducing PRP into the public sector.

2   New Labour and performance management

The Labour government has not sought to distance itself from the managerialism of its predecessors; like them, it has recognized that tight public expenditure limits offer a negative message, while in contrast, managerialism offers a positive one: thus, it can be argued that goals can be attained with the use of existing resources if only the appropriate management approach is adopted. However, Labour has sought to distinguish itself by pursuing a reformed managerialist agenda. A key example of this is the way in which it has characterized performance. For Conservative governments improved performance would be delivered by market and quasi-market mechanisms, reinforced by performance measurement. For Labour, while such market mechanisms are still relevant, there has been an attempt to limit their use. Thus decreased reliance on quasi-markets has been paralleled by a more salient role for both performance measures and performance management. Labour has also taken up the criticisms that the Conservatives' performance measures focused excessively on narrow 'efficiency' indicators. Part of the Labour project is that performance measures should be based on a more rounded set of measures with a greater emphasis on quality. The 1997 White Paper *The New NHS* was accompanied by the consultative document *National Framework for Assessing Performance*, which argues that it is by 'comparing standards and best practice' that 'standards of performance' will improve (NHS Executive, 1998, p. 2); and in June 1999 a new 'performance assessment framework' for the NHS was issued (NHS Executive, 1999) which includes a set of indicators designed 'as the basis for benchmarking performance of NHS organizations' (ibid., p. 6). Similar trends can be seen in education. Circular 7/97 (Department for Education and Employment, 1997), on information on secondary school performance, states that 'the Secretary of State supports the development and publication of value added measures which will help schools to analyse their performance more closely and set targets for improvement' (p. 5).

What have been claimed by the government to be enhanced performance measures have been constructed to facilitate the achievement of government-determined objectives – the raising of standards and improvement of quality – in public services (Treasury, 1998, p. 1). The link between objectives and measures is via performance management. For example, the White Paper *Modernising Social Services* argues that only if 'performance systems are in place can high quality and good value services be achieved' (Department of Health, 1998, para. 7.1). Similarly, under the 'Best Value' policy, the White Paper on Local Government proposes that it be obligatory that local authorities have a performance management framework (Department of the Environment, Transport and the Regions, 1998).

A more extensive discussion of performance management, which relates specifically to schools but has general applicability in the current public sector, states that:

> Systematic performance management is key to achievement in organizations. In schools it motivates teachers to give of their best and provides school managers with the tools to deploy and develop their staff most efficiently. It should encompass a robust system for appraising staff against clear objectives and outcomes and ensure that proper links exist between performance, pay, career progression and professional development. (DfEE, 1999a, para. 4)

The intention of embedding PRP into performance management was outlined by the Prime Minister in a key speech on public sector pay. He argued that ensuring improved performance and results in public services would partly come from the government 'making better use of the pay bill' and considering 'the lessons of performance pay' and where it should be used in the public sector (*Bargaining Report*, 1999, p. 7). Plans for a new pay system for the NHS include a possible development of PRP to give 'more flexibility on how staff move up the pay spines in place of the current automatic annual increments' (Department of Health, 1999). However, it is in education that the government has announced its intention to introduce performance pay in its most ambitious form.

The 1998 report of the School Teachers' Review Body (STRB), which, since 1992, has advised the government annually on both the appropriate level of pay and the system of pay determination for heads and teachers, was the first produced for a Labour government. The Secretary

of State for Education and Employment continued the practice of his
Conservative predecessors by asking the STRB to consider 'what
measures might be taken to ensure that pay systems are used to relate
pay more closely to individual performance' (STRB, 1998, Appendix A).
PRP for heads and teachers was trailed on other occasions throughout
the year. The Green Paper proposals (DfEE, 1998) represent the most
comprehensive attempt by a government to change the system of pay
determination for any group of public sector employees; it has been
termed 'the world's biggest Performance Related Pay System' (National
Association of Head Teachers, 1999). The government has moved
beyond exhortation by outlining a timetable for implementation of all
elements with the final deadline of 2000 (DfEE, 1999b, p. 15).

3 The travails of performance management

A key problem for any scheme of PRP lies in the selection of appropriate
performance measures. The most obvious reason for this is that the
performance measures are supposed to capture the key dimensions of
what constitutes 'success' or 'failure' for the organizations concerned.
Quantitative measures – pupil attendance levels, exam results, immunization targets, job placement figures – frequently involve difficulties.

First, definitional problems can occur, even with the most straightforward of measures. Pupil attendance levels provide a good example.
Schools are required to take an attendance register at the beginning of
morning and afternoon sessions for pupils of compulsory school age: a
distinction should be made, in the register, as to whether the absence
was authorized or unauthorized and the latter must appear in school
prospectuses and annual reports (Department of Education, 1991, para.
6). One difficulty with the completeness of this measure is that it fails to
capture 'post registration' truancy (Hallam, 1997, p. 2). Also there is
considerable discretion as to whether a school classifies an absence as
authorized or unauthorized. Hallam (ibid.) has shown that schools differ
significantly in the extent to which they investigate the authenticity of
reasons for absence.

Secondly, the performance measures used might not be within the
control of the organization. For example, unauthorized absence from
school might be condoned by parents (Trade Union Research Unit, 1992,
p. 20), or absence is at such a low level that the scope for improvement is
limited. Variations in test or examination results from year to year will
be affected by differences in pupil cohorts (ibid.). GPs might experience
difficulties in meeting their immunization targets if their practice is in
an inner-city area which has a large number of transient or homeless
families. This, in turn, raises the question of the appropriateness of
applying a global measure of performance to practices with different
population characteristics (Elkan and Robinson, 1998, p. 1517).

Thirdly, performance indicators may be open to manipulation. In 1997, the *Guardian* ran a series of articles which revealed weaknesses in the performance related pay scheme at the Employment Service. One of the targets used in the scheme was the number of successful job placements an individual member of staff made. Evidence was found of double recording of placements or recording as definite those placements which had still to be confirmed (Marsden and French, 1998, p. 53). Similarly linking pay to examination results could lead to manipulation, such as a refusal to enter pupils for examinations unless they were likely to pass or gain good grades (Mayston, 1992, p. 25) or the concentration of resources on pupils thought capable of achieving a GCSE C grade with additional tuition, in order to boost the percentage of pupils in the A–C grade rank, a published performance measure (Gewirtz et al., 1995, p. 175). Schools could also base their selection of pupils on those likely to do well in examinations and, as there is a strong relationship between socio-economic class and success in examinations, attempt to increase their intake of advantaged pupils (Mayston, 1992, pp. 22–3). Those GPs who failed to meet their immunization targets because of the population involved could also manipulate their list to exclude problem patients (Elkan and Robinson, 1998, p. 1517).

Of course it is often argued that more rounded measures of performance are desirable in themselves and would make more acceptable the use to which they were put, e.g. PRP. A good example of such measures again is examination results. Thus the STRB always sought to distance itself from a key measure of school performance supported by the Conservative governments: the schools 'league tables' published in 'raw' attainment form, for example the percentage of pupils attaining five or more GCSE passes at grade C or above. Such league tables have been criticized for failing to take into account the standards of pupils on entry to the school (McPherson, 1993). In attempting to overcome this problem the STRB argued that improvement in school performance rather than absolute attainment levels should be used. However, improvement is not without its problems, since it raises the question: improvement in what? This is particularly pertinent when published examination results can involve a plurality of measures – passing GCSEs, passing at particular grades (e.g. A–C) or success at A Levels. A further problem is that some schools have 100 per cent success rates in examinations, so that improvement would not be possible. Finally, it is argued that the problems in respect of raw data and improvement measures could be resolved by using value added measures which utilize data on attainment to generate expected examination results which can then be contrasted with actual scores.

This has received support in a DfEE publication (DfEE, 1997, para. 17). However, it cannot be unequivocally argued that value added can be attributed to the effects of teaching; peer pressure effects, for example, could also be significant (McPherson, 1993). A similar point on the difficulty of interpreting the causes of performance improvement can be made in respect of increased take-up of the cervical screening service. A study, discussed by Elkan and Robinson (1998, p. 1517), found that in the six months after the introduction of the GP contract, coverage had increased from 78 per cent to 85 per cent. The authors of the original study concluded that this was due to the performance related pay system. However, it was also pointed out that a major contributory factor to this increase could well have been an improved call system for patients (ibid.).

An important aspect of research on attitudes to performance measurement and PRP is the extent to which employees are critical of the performance measures used in their organizations. Marsden and French (1998, p. 122) argue that while the scepticism of the headteachers and deputies in their study could perhaps be allayed by the more careful use of performance indicators, many believed that they would still not reflect those aspects of a school's performance which they (heads and deputies) believed were most appropriate. Equally, staff at the Employment Service felt that the targets they were given did not reflect the totality of what they considered to be 'good performance' (ibid., p. 54). In education this failure to measure what was appropriate was perceived as more fundamental because, as Marsden and French comment, 'education in a pluralist democracy is about values' and it might be thought that the concerns of heads and deputies 'reflect a deeper disagreement about the goals of education' (ibid., p. 122). This reflects a dilemma of performance measurement and PRP. Dowling and Richardson's (1997) study of PRP for NHS managers found that, while it was only regarded as motivating by a minority of managers, those who did find it so thought that clear-cut targets were desirable. Other groups frequently do not view performance targets in this way and are inclined to stress the crudity of reducing measures of organizational performance to quantitative targets. So one obstacle to PRP is the difficulty in finding acceptable measures even where purportedly the indicators are designed to be more sophisticated. This is also related to a broader issue, namely whether the PRP system is perceived as equitable.

4 A fairer pay system

A key feature of PRP within the context of performance management is that it should motivate individual staff to greater efforts: if this is to happen then staff must believe that the scheme operates fairly. Marsden and French's research shows that this was not the perception of the majority of staff in the Inland Revenue and Employment Service. Thus, 60 per cent of Revenue staff and 40 per cent of Employment staff participating in the research stated that management used the scheme to reward their favourites; 75 per cent of staff in both organizations believed that a quota system was in operation, limiting the opportunity to achieve the highest markings; staff also believed that the pay system was open to manipulation, with the appeals system being ineffective (Marsden and French 1998, pp. 27 and 47). Foster and Hoggett's (1999, p. 29) study of Benefit Agency staff also elicited criticism of PRP from staff who felt it was open to abuse and 'highly personalized'.

A further dimension of fairness is the connection between PRP and equal opportunities. A case could be made that PRP has positive equal opportunity effects when contrasted with incremental pay systems, divorced from direct performance links, which have dominated public sector pay. Such scales, which depend upon experience, can discriminate against women, who for family reasons either take a number of years out of their career or, if combining family with part-time work, fail to move up the incremental scale as rapidly as their male counterparts. The flexibility and discretion in PRP could overcome the limitations of traditional career routes, 'unlocking rigidities' (Newman, 1994, pp. 186–7). However, in the Inland Revenue, it was precisely 'the largely subjective nature of appraisal' (Marsden and French, 1998, p. 28) which was seen as discriminatory. An internal study by the Revenue in 1996 indicated some biases against women, especially those employed part-time, and members of ethnic minorities. Participants in Marsden and French's study themselves, especially those from ethnic minorities and part-timers, felt that they lost out. Thus the perceptions of the Revenue are reinforced by the staff (ibid., pp. 29–30).

The research on heads and deputies raised a very specific form of perceived inequity. Marsden and French (1998, p. 119) found, for example, that over 50 per cent of heads surveyed thought that PRP enhancements for heads and deputies operated to 'undermine team working in schools'; under 30 per cent of respondents disagreed. This survey was conducted in the context of a scheme limited to rewarding heads and deputies. The authors argue (ibid.) that the negative effects on team working could be related to two factors. One was that 'it is unfair that classroom teachers are denied opportunities open to heads and deputies'; the other source of difficulty was that 'it is believed hard to identify individual contributions'. Not only are results seen as the result of a collegiate/collective exercise but many teachers do not teach end of key stage or GCSE, A/AS level or GNVQ passes (NAHT, 1999). Again Marsden and French (1998, p. 120) found that over 50 per cent of respondents disagreed with the statement that 'individual performance objectives are a suitable basis for rewarding enhancements', while only about a third agreed. The rewarding of particular individuals only was felt to be both unfair and damaging to intra-school relations. Indeed in groups of employees where PRP was more widely available, research evidence points to its negative impact on co-operative working relationships because of its divisive nature (Dowling and Richardson, 1997; Marsden and French, 1998, pp. 33–51; Foster and Hoggett, 1999, p. 31).

The concerns expressed by heads and deputies about possible dis-agreement over the goals of education point to a feature of PRP experienced by other groups: its unitarist assumptions. A 'unitarist' approach rests on the view that one set of goals can be defined for an organization and that it is appropriate that the activities of the whole workforce are directed to the achievement of these goals. A corollary of such an approach is that goals are set by management and thus the approach is 'top-down' with those outside management grades expected neither to determine the goals nor to challenge them. Such an approach is not inconsistent with collective bargaining *per se* but it necessarily narrows its scope. For example, the expectation that organization goals are not to be challenged means that trade unions are not accorded a legitimate role in criticizing them and seeking to change them. Equally, unions ought not to support employees who challenge these goals since their pursuit is taken as a duty of the whole workforce. Survey evidence on performance related pay has found that its use is within such a unitarist framework. At the Employment Service, Marsden and French recorded that many staff felt that the term 'agreement' where reference was made to objectives used in PRP was inaccurate, as they maintained that they had been 'pressurized into accepting management's targets' (Marsden and French, 1998, p. 54). This, it could be argued, raises a crucial aspect of PRP, namely its use as a mechanism of managerial control, which is discussed below.

A final dimension of fairness in respect of PRP for public sector employees is the appeal to external experience, the claim that 'everyone else is tested'. This suggests that, in operating pay systems which involve either no, or a very limited, relation between pay and per-formance, the public sector is exercising an unjustified privilege. The implicit comparison here is to the private sector. It is therefore interest-ing to note how PRP works for one group of private sector employees: senior executives. Studies of PRP schemes for this group have con-cluded that their pay does not usually vary with corporate financial performance (Parkinson, 1993, pp. 223–4). Of course, central to this problem is the method used to determine the pay of senior executives: the decision is either made by the board without the corporate execu-tive present, or by a remuneration committee composed of non-executive directors (ibid.). Both methods involve conflicts of interest. Members of the board will not wish to reduce the salary of any one member because this is likely to impact on all their salaries. Similarly, non-executive directors are themselves executive directors of other companies and as such have no interest in cutting executive remunera-tion (ibid., p. 218). What is striking in such instances, at least at the top of the private sector corporate hierarchy, is the lack of an arm's-length relationship in pay determination. In effect, while a form of PRP is adopted, the pay rise is guaranteed; and there is a marked lack of testing.

The effective non-existence of the link between pay and performance for this group of employees does point to a major issue with PRP. Few organizations, in either the public or the private sector, evaluate the effect of performance pay on individual motivation or the subsequent performance of the organization. This is now being rectified in the public sector with studies by Dowling and Richardson (1997) and Marsden and French (1998). The latter, covering three diverse areas of public sector employment – the Civil Service, NHS Trusts, headteachers and deputies – concluded that most staff had doubts regarding the effectiveness of PRP as a motivational mechanism (p. 10), although line managers in the Inland Revenue and Employment Service stated that PRP had improved productivity. However, such claims about pro-ductivity have to be examined in the context of the difficulties of explaining improvements in performance. As Marsden and French (1998) point out, in both cases (Inland Revenue and Employment Service) there had been significant declines in staffing levels. This suggests an alterna-tive scenario in which productivity improvements would 'automatically' arise via work intensification, independent of PRP.

But even if we accept that PRP could function effectively as a motivational mechanism, it is reasonable to assume that the performance bonuses would have to be significant if they were to influence behav-iour. For example, offering an extra £200 per year to a professor who already earns £35,000 per year is not likely to bring about an overnight personality transformation. But if the bonuses are significant and a fair number of people get them, then the implications for the total pay bill are heavy. (If very few get them then that has obvious motivational consequences of its own.) So either the total pay bill will rise – which is unlikely in practice, as the Treasury is averse to PRP schemes being built upon increases in total pay expenditure – or the pay rises for everyone else (the non-performance-bonused) have to be lower than they would otherwise have been. In some cases they will be zero. So, looked at from a collective point of view, PRP in practice is not a pay improvement at all – it is a pay redistribution. When those without performance bonuses realize this, they are likely to be even more disaffected.

The evidence on PRP suggests there is a number of reasons why employees are suspicious of their potential for pay inequity. In the final section this theme is developed by focusing on the relationship between professional groups and the introduction of PRP systems.

5 Uncertain project

Two key features of PRP in the public sector in the 1980s and 1990s are that both Conservative and Labour governments consistently favoured its introduction, and that both favoured its application to welfare professional groups. Conservative government proposals for PRP could be seen as clearly linked with the New Right critique of professions. Professions were treated as a particular type of producer group and were accused of seeking to establish a monopoly over service provision and to insulate themselves from markets and competition. However, while Conservative rhetoric suggested a radical approach, policy was much more cautious. By the time that the Conservatives left office, little had been achieved. While the GP contract introduced a link between pay and performance, this was restricted to meeting targets in relation to cervical screening and immunization of children, which represented a limited proportion of GPs' total remuneration. After 1992, PRP for hospital doctors and nurses was not revisited. Finally, despite the supposed merit of linking pay and performance for *all* teachers in education, as early as 1993 the STRB was focusing on heads and deputies rather than the teaching workforce as a whole and this position was accepted by the government.

In its 1997 manifesto, the Labour Party committed itself to continuing a policy of public sector pay restraint but was initially silent on forms of pay determination in the sector. However, throughout 1998, the government indicated its intention of linking pay and performance for teachers and in 1999 confirmed this commitment (DfEE, 1999b). This, together with the possibility of introducing performance pay for clinical groups within the NHS, and senior civil servants (Sherman, 1999), represents the most comprehensive attempt yet by any government to extend PRP to professional groups. This final section will explore some of the tensions within this policy in the context of New Labour's commitment to performance measurement, with its emphasis upon objectives, outcomes and managerial accountability.

While there are, necessarily, important differences between professional groups, they also have certain features in common. Professionals are characterized by 'irreducible autonomy – the space within which professional judgement can be exercised and must be trusted' – and the processual nature of professional intervention which involves acting in the best interests of patients, clients and pupils (Clarke and Newman, 1997, pp. 6–7). In addition, professionals have attachments and loyalty to others than their employing organization: they have professional/occupational identities on to which are grafted 'often unarticulated notions of public service' (ibid., p. 62). Professionals have considerable discretion in the use of resources by deciding, for example, what medical treatments will be provided or how teaching should be organized. New Labour's managerialism represents a clear challenge to professional power.

First, the specification of quantified targets, for example increasing the proportion of 16-year-olds with five or more GCSEs at A–C grades (Treasury, 1998, p. 11) contrasts with the notion that professional practice contains an irreducible element of judgement and can involve challenging professional views on how resources should be used.

Secondly, there is an emphasis not only upon quantified targets but also on the setting of such targets by the centre. With public sector agreements, objectives and performance targets have been established for each welfare service (ibid.): these, in turn, will cascade down to specific units such as schools, NHS Trusts and social service departments which must meet the targets. It is a short step then to building targets into the appraisal process and pay determination of individual employees. For example, in discussing PRP for teachers, it is stated that the 'agreeing of personal objectives would be a school-based process carried out in the context of the school's development plan' (DfEE, 1999b, para. 14). Inevitably such a plan would be aligned with the public service agreements for education. Centrally determined performance targets are yet another restraint on professional practice.

Thirdly, and in parallel with a hierarchical approach to the setting of objectives, is an emphasis on leadership. It is the leader who will galvanize employees to meet the performance targets. 'Effective leadership is critical to success in schools' (DfEE, 1999b, para. 8). Part of the process of modernizing teaching involves the creation of a new leadership group in schools plus the establishment of a National College for School Leadership. Such discussion clearly links with ideas of reasserting the 'right to manage' which have been dominant from the 1980s onwards. It will be the leader (or school manager) who will decide on how resources will be used most efficiently. Concepts of leadership are inimical to professional practice with its emphasis on collegiality and team working.

The Labour government has committed itself to a strong performance management culture in the public sector: its aim is to improve both the standards and the quality of services. Improving performance is seen to require a more active use of the pay structure, in particular the introduction of PRP and the extension of its coverage to professional groups. Research evidence of the negative impact of PRP, i.e. its potential to demotivate, is ignored and there is little evidence of its beneficial consequences. No less a body than the Audit Commission has made this point: there is 'no clear evidence . . . that PRP improves staff motivation or performance' (Audit Commission, 1995, p. 43). At the same time the tensions embodied in applying PRP to the public sector are ignored (Foster and Hoggett, 1999, p. 36). So if there is scepticism about whether PRP does or does not improve the performance of an organization, the question remains as to why the introduction of such schemes is regarded as important. Research on PRP has consistently pointed out that a major reason for introducing it is the facilitation of change in the organizational culture (e.g. Kessler and Purcell, 1992, p. 21; Marsden and French, 1998, p. 1). What is crucial here is the form of change being proposed; performance management, mediated by PRP, will link the workforce into superordinate goals determined by 'the management', i.e. central government. The stage is thus set for a major confrontation between professional and managerial forms of power.

References

Audit Commission (1995) *Paying the Piper: People and Pay in Local Government*, London, HMSO.

Bargaining Report (1999) 'The perils of performance pay', 195, pp. 7–11.

Clarke, J. and Newman, J. (1997) *The Managerial State*, London, Sage.

Cutler, T. and Waine, B. (1994) *Managing the Welfare State: the Politics of Public Sector Management*, Oxford, Berg.

Cutler, T. and Waine, B. (1998) *Managing the Welfare State: Text and Sourcebook*, Oxford, Berg.

Cutler, T. and Waine, B. (1999) 'Rewarding better teachers? Performance related pay in schools', *Educational Management and Administration*, 27 (1), pp. 55–70.

DfEE: Department for Education and Employment (1997) *Publication of Information about Secondary Schools in Performance Tables in 1997* (Circular 7/97), London, DfEE.

DfEE: Department for Education and Employment (1998) *Teachers: meeting the challenge of change*, Cm 4164, London, The Stationery Office.

DfEE: Department for Education and Employment (1999a) *Teachers: meeting the challenge of change: Technical Document*, London, The Stationery Office.

DfEE: Department for Education and Employment (1999b) *Teachers: Taking Forward the Challenge of Change: Response to the Consultation Exercise*, London, The Stationery Office.

Department of Education (1991) *The Education (Pupils' Attendance) Regulations 1991* (Circular 11/91), London, Department of Education and Science.

Department of the Environment, Transport and the Regions (1998) *Modern Local Government: In Touch with the People*, London, The Stationery Office.

Department of Health (1998) *Modernising Social Services*, Cm 4169, London, The Stationery Office.

Department of Health (1999) *A Modern Pay System for a Modern Health Service*, www.doh.gov.uk.

Dowling, B. and Richardson, R. (1997) 'Evaluating performance related pay for managers in the National Health Service', *International Journal of Human Resource Management*, 8 (3), pp. 348–66.

Elkan, R. and Robinson, J. (1998) 'The use of targets to improve the performance of health care providers: a discussion of government policy', *British Journal of General Practice*, 48, pp. 1515–18.

Employment Department (1998) *Employment for the 1990s*, Cm 540, London, HMSO.

Foster, D. and Hoggett, P. (1999) 'Changes in the Benefits Agency: empowering the exhausted worker?' *Work, Employment and Society*, 13 (1), pp. 19–39.

Gewirtz, S., Ball, S. and Bowe, R. (1995) *Markets, Equity and Choice in Education*, Buckingham, Open University Press.

Griffiths, R. (1983) *NHS Management Inquiry*, London, HMSO.

Hallam, S. (1997) *Truancy: Can Schools Improve Attendance?* Institute of Education Viewpoint 6, London, Institute of Education.

Hogwood, B.W. (1998) 'Towards a new structure of public employment in Britain?' *Policy and Politics*, 26 (3), pp. 321–41.

Income Data Services Report (1996) *Pay in the Public Services: Review of 1995 Prospects for 1996*, London, Income Data Services.

Jackson, M. (1997) 'The impact of discretionary pay in the UK universities', *Higher Education Management*, 9 (2), pp. 99–113.

Jarratt Report (1985) *Report of the Steering Committee for Efficiency Studies in Universities*, London, Committee of Vice Chancellors and Principals.

Jenkins, K., Caines, K. and Jackson, A. (1988) *Improving Management in Government: The Next Steps*, Report to the Prime Minister, London, HMSO.

Kessler, I. and Purcell, J. (1992) 'Performance related pay: objectives and application', *Human Resource Management Journal*, 2 (3), pp. 26–33.

Marsden, D. and French, S. (1998) *What a Performance: Performance Related Pay in the Public Services*, Centre for Economic Performance, The London School of Economics.

Mayston, D. (1992) *School Performance Indicators and Performance Related Pay*, York, Centre for Health Economics, University of York.

McPherson, A. (1993) 'Measuring added value in schools', in *National Commission on Education, Briefings*, London, Heinemann.

NAHT: National Association of Head Teachers (1999) *Response to the Green Paper 'Teachers: meeting the challenge of change' and Technical Consultation Paper on Pay and Performance Management*, Haywards Heath, NAHT.

Newman, J. (1994) 'The limits of management: gender and the politics of change', in Clarke, J., Cochrane, A. and McLaughlin, E. (eds) *Managing Social Policy*, London, Sage.

NHS Executive (1998) *National Framework for Assessing Performance*, Leeds, NHS Executive.

NHS Executive (1999) *Quality and Performance in the NHS: High Level Performance Indicators*, Leeds, NHS Executive.

Parkinson, J. (1993) *Corporate Power and Responsibility*, Oxford, Clarendon Press.

Pay and Benefits Bulletin (1998) 'There is merit in merit pay', 445 (April), pp. 4–7.

Pierson, P. (1994) *Dismantling the Welfare State*, Cambridge, Cambridge University Press.

Prime Minister's Office (1991) *The Citizen's Charter: Raising the Standard*, Cm 1599, London, HMSO.

Salford, J. and MacGregor, D. (1998) 'Employment in the public and private sectors', *Economic Trends*, 532, March.

Sherman, J. (1999) 'Whitehall told to keep Labour promise', *The Times*, 24 August, p. 1.

STRB: School Teachers' Review Body (1998) *Seventh Report*, Cm. 3836, London, HMSO.

Trade Union Research Unit (1992) *Performance Related Pay*, London, NASUWT/NUT.

Treasury (1998) *Public Services for the Future: Modernization, Reform, Accountability*, Cm 4181, London, The Stationery Office.

15

Guarding the Public Interest? Auditing Public Services

John Clarke, Sharon Gewirtz, Gordon Hughes and Jill Humphrey

Contents

The reconstruction of public services in the UK in the last two decades of the twentieth century involved the development of processes designed to scrutinize, evaluate and regulate the performance of agencies involved in service provision. These control processes were made internal to particular organizations through requirements that they collate evidence to report on their own performance. At the same time, such processes have been embedded in functionally separate agencies that are charged with providing independent scrutiny of service providers. Organizations were created for this specific purpose, for example, the Audit Commission, established in 1982, and OFSTED (Office for Standards in Education), created in 1992; other organizations have combined the functions of evaluation with other activities, such as funding services (e.g., in the Higher Education and Further Education Funding Councils). Organizations that have had longer established responsibilities, historically defined as 'inspection', have also taken on more formally evaluative roles. We have seen partnerships between different types of agencies, for example in the joint evaluations of social services conducted by the Social Services Inspectorate and the Audit Commission under legislation introduced in 1996.

These developments pose some distinctive problems about terminology. The first – and most obvious – is simply that of what to call these processes, assuming that they represent a relatively coherent dynamic in the restructuring of the British state. Despite the variations in organizational form and method of exercising control, most studies seem to conclude that these new structures and processes represent a distinctive realignment of forms of governance in the UK's public services. For Hood and his colleagues (1998), these changes constitute a growth of 'regulation inside government' – a terminology also developed in the study by Cope and Goodship (1999). Regulation here is taken to refer to systems of control ('setting, monitoring and enforcing rules and standards', Hood et al., 1998, p. 199) that are not part of direct line management systems, but involve the exercise of powers by a separate agency. Other studies have placed a greater emphasis on processes of 'surveillance', 'scrutiny' and 'audit' (Power, 1993, 1997) in these new forms of governance, highlighting the emphasis on assessing the performance of organizations delivering public services.

For the purposes of this chapter, we have used the terms 'audit' and 'inspection' as a means of designating this concern with the processes of monitoring performance. This choice, however, highlights the second problem about terminology in relation to these new arrangements. 'Regulation', 'audit' and 'inspection' all come with acquired historical meanings that designate established practices (as the work of auditors or professional inspectorates, for example). There is a long history of audit as a process of financial accounting in relation to the provision of public services, ensuring standards of probity and fiduciary responsibility in the use of public money. The 1980s saw an intensification of such concerns, reflecting one response to the 'crisis' of public spending. But such terms remain in use despite the fact that the practices of such agencies may have changed significantly during the last twenty years. The work of the Audit Commission may have its roots in a traditional model of financial audit, but its work has gone beyond that focus into issues of organizational design; policy development and implementation and the development of 'best practice' approaches to public services management (Cutler, 1992; Humphrey et al., 1999). This is not to suggest that the fundamental concern with accounting for public expenditures has disappeared. Far from it: the processes of audit retain a concern with financial performance that provides a crucial methodological and discursive underpinning for its expanded roles. As a result, the words we use in this chapter are tentative – and need to be seen as both having their own 'careers' and having an unstable approximation to the organizations and practices that claim them.

1   Separating the public and public services

In this chapter, we will argue that this expanded view – and practice –
of audit has formed a central thread in New Labour conceptions of
public service provision and its programme of 'modernization'
(Newman, Chapter 3 in this volume). However, it has its roots in the
earlier New Right onslaught on public services, understood as services
that were provided to the public by public institutions. Most accounts of
the new patterns of audit and regulation have stressed their relationship
to the new organizational forms and problems of exercising control at
'arm's length' over fragmented systems of public services (e.g., Hood et
al., 1998, explore their relationship to the rise of a 'New Public Management'). We want to suggest that the emergence of audit as a central
practice of new patterns of governance also rests on the ideological shifts
accomplished by the New Right. In particular, it is important to examine
the ways in which New Right politics redefined the relations between
the public, public services and government in the 1980s and 1990s.

The New Right sought to destabilize a set of assumptions embodied
in the post-war social democratic (or Labourist) welfare settlements
about the homological relationships between the public, public services
(and their characteristic organizational forms) and the state (Clarke and
Newman, 1997, Ch. 1). In this social democratic ideology, the state,
through processes of political representation, both expressed and acted
to defend and enhance the 'public interest'. Public services, organized as
professional bureaucracies, were socially neutral agencies through
which the public good could be pursued. As a consequence, the public's
needs and interests were understood as being represented within service
organizations and through parliamentary and local government processes (Hughes, 1998). A number of different political challenges dis-
located these once comfortable assumptions. However, it was the New
Right that played the dominant ideological role in reconstructing the
way in which the relationship between the public and public services
was thought about. The New Right also instigated the organizational
reconstruction of those services.

While most accounts of New Right politics have emphasized their
prioritization of market processes over state bureaucracies, we think it is
important to recognize how neo-classical economic models were also
used to prise apart the naturalized alignment of public, the public
interest and publicly provided services. Where social democratic
ideology treated 'public servants' as a neutral social force, motivated
by an ethos of public service, the New Right construed them as motivated by self-interest, seeking to expand the power or resources over
which they could exercise control (du Gay, Chapter 4 in this volume).
Public choice theory became a means of dislocating the presumed
affinity between the public and public servants (Dunleavy, 1991;
Niskanen, 1971). 'Professionals' and 'bureaucrats' came to be denigrated

in the New Right attack on state provision. The New Right developed the dislocation of the public and public service into a 'crisis of trust'. Where professional ethics, bureaucratic impartiality or the ethos of service could not be relied on to discipline those providing services to the public, the public could not be expected to trust service providers. The New Right treated claims to such ethics of service as a smokescreen intended to obscure venal self-interest, organizational imperialism or, worst of all, the pursuit of ideologically motivated ends (see also Skocpol, 1997, on the US attack on 'big government').

Something had to fill the vacuum created by this dissolution of identification and trust between the public and public services. Of course, describing this as a dissolution overstates the case: the process was more partial and uneven in its practical effects, for example in the perception of different sorts of 'public servants'. Nevertheless, Conservative reforms sought to use market mechanisms as one new 'guarantee' of public service. For a range of reasons, this was only ever partially achieved. Market mechanisms themselves may promote outcomes other than good public service (competition can 'incentivize' bad behaviour as well as good). Markets were introduced into the co-ordination of public services in very specific and limited ways (Bartlett et al., 1998; Clarke, forthcoming). The limited development of markets also reflected the contradictory issues of political control over services.

Audit was developed in this space, offering the prospect of *an independent evaluative practice* that would both safeguard 'taxpayers' money' and provide a countervailing influence to the problem of 'producer domination' of service provision. By laying such producers open to scrutiny, audit could preserve the public interest. It could do so because it is itself the product of other forms of mistrust, having been developed to resolve problems about the validity, reliability and trustworthiness of information within and between corporate organizations (Armstrong, 1994). This conception of audit thus combined two distinct political and ideological trajectories in the reconstruction of public services. First, it represented a new embodiment of the public interest, which could be trusted because of its 'independence'. There is a variety of overlapping types of independence or autonomy to which audit and inspection agencies lay claim: *professional* independence, where a distinctive knowledge base (or ethical and regulatory systems) underpin autonomy; *technical* independence, where the techniques and practices used by the agents are seen to produce neutral or impartial results (Power, 1993, p. 5); and *organizational* independence, where the agency's separation from the business or service being evaluated is the basis for its claims. In practice, the expansion of audit has been legitimated by reference to all of these. Secondly, it offered a mode of control that would enable government to exercise supervision and direction of services that were increasingly being provided in new devolved, decentralized and dispersed organizational forms. In the process of reconstructing public services, the issue of how to control dispersed service providers emerged as a central focus for 'reinventing government'.

2 Audit and the dispersed state

Although various terms have been used to describe the process – fragmentation, decentralization, marketization, mixed economies and dispersal – it is clear that the organizational forms of public service provision and control underwent major structural changes in the 1980s and 1990s. The dis-integration of state professional bureaucracies and systems of control created a more complex and dispersed network of 'provider organizations'. These were repositioned in new fields of relationships whose vertical axis ran from central government to service consumers, and whose horizontal axis typically placed individual service providers in a competitive – or quasi-competitive – relationship with other providers (Clarke and Newman, 1997). Most service organizations were expected to take on devolved managerial responsibilities and freedoms and were expected to behave in a 'businesslike fashion' (Pollitt et al., 1998; Hoggett, 1996).

The development of a new state form, different from the relatively integral professional bureaucracies of the post-war state, implied new issues of control for the centre. To some extent, of course, some established control processes were continued and even intensified: the financial and other resource frameworks remained centrally determined as did a whole array of policy objectives, guidelines and instructions. In some cases, control became increasingly centralized (as in the case of the National Curriculum in education). Nevertheless, dispersed service-providing organizations with a degree of autonomy over 'operational management', with instructions to compete, become more flexible and adapt to local or consumer interests, posed new problems of control 'at arm's length' (Hoggett, 1996). As Power has argued, 'The great attraction of audit and accounting practices is that they appear to reconcile these centrifugal and centripetal forces better than the available alternatives' (1993, p. 16). He suggests that audit 'symbolizes a cluster of values: independent validation, efficiency, rationality, visibility, almost irrespective of the mechanics of the practice and, in the final analysis, the promise of control. All of these apparent virtues have come together to make audit a central part of the "reinvention of government"' (1993, p. 17).

Audit has emerged as a generic feature of this new state form in the UK although it combines in complex ways with a variety of 'arm's length' control systems and practices: inspection, accounting, regulation, performance review, and processes of organizational development. Audit has historically designated the practice of scrutinizing financial control processes and financial decision making, as in the work of the National Audit Office (NAO; see also Pollitt et al., 1998). However, the practice of audit in relation to public services has come to include a wider range of evaluative and normative functions, most evidently in the work of the Audit Commission. As Cutler and Waine have argued, the Commission's work has seen

> a major extension of the role of audit, which traditionally has been mainly concerned with the accuracy of accounts and ensuring that public bodies were acting within their legal remit. VFM (value for money) audit, however, involves an assessment of service performance, an area which, of course, intersects with professional judgements that were of limited or no relevance to the narrower financial and legal concerns of traditional audit practice. (1997, pp. 30–1)

This rise of audit has had a number of significant consequences for the restructuring of public services and the co-ordination of the dispersed state. Here we will explore two dimensions of change in which audit has been influential: the creation of auditable organizations; and the relation between audit, performance and competition, which has implications for the changing role of auditing organizations.

3   Accounting for achievement: the construction of auditable organizations

Considerable time and energy have been devoted to creating service organizations that can be audited by, or on behalf of, central government. It has been a consistent point of criticism that public services were poorly documented, producing little reliable information about their performance other than accounting for 'inputs'. As a result, organizations have been required to produce auditable information about their activities, with a steadily increasing emphasis on outputs and outcomes (the effects produced by the organization's activities). Such information allows the organization to be evaluated both intrinsically and comparatively (i.e., is it efficient and is it more or less efficient than similar organizations?). These demands for auditable organizations have been framed by discourses of accountability and transparency – against the suspicion of 'producer domination' of organizational choices (see Rouse and Smith, 1999; and Walsh, 1995).

This concern with producing evaluative information creates a number of subsidiary dilemmas (at the intersection of the organization and the auditing agency):

- To what extent can the objectives of the organization be clearly and simply specified? (E.g. what is a school for?)
- To what extent can those objectives be transformed into outcomes that are measurable? (E.g. do exam results measure school success?)

- To what extent is organizational performance a closed system in which outcomes reflect the effect of organizational activity? (Who or what else contributes to 'results'?)
- To what extent can comparability be guaranteed between organizations? (What unmeasured or unmeasurable factors within or outside organizations may differentiate organizational performance?)

There is a growing literature that explores the political, organizational and methodological problems associated with evaluation (e.g., Cutler, 1992; Newman, forthcoming; Pollitt, 1995; see also Humphrey et al., 1999). We do not intend to pursue it here beyond noting that each stage of evaluation involves potentially contested processes of social construction. There are potential conflicts over the definition of objectives; over the choice of indicators; over the attribution of causal effects; and over how comparison is effected. More substantively, however, the construction of these scrutinizing processes requires an organization that produces auditable information. Power (1993, 1997) talks about this in terms of a shift of organizational resources from 'first order functions' to 'second order functions' – that is, organizations must divert resources from what they do to processes of accounting for what they do. The costs of audit are not only the cost of producing and maintaining auditing organizations, they are also the internal costs of service organizations making themselves auditable. In business, this category of spending is referred to as the 'compliance costs' and it is routinely calculated (Hood et al., 1998).

Audit has come to play a double function in the control of public services. Its primary or original purpose was to ensure compliance with the requirements of good government. The demands of accountability meant being able to account for the use of public resources ('the taxpayers' money'), demonstrating that appropriate control and accounting systems existed to prevent fraud, misuse or incompetence. These are relatively formalized concerns, and underpin the idea that audit is a generic or abstract process that can be applied irrespective of service or product context (Power, 1993, pp. 19–21). At the same time, audit has also come to mean the evaluation of organizational performance, implying a degree of engagement with service or product specificity. There is a paradox here: it is precisely the generic formalism of audit that allows it to be deployed in service-specific contexts, because it guarantees a degree of separation from professional, expert or producer interests (which cannot be trusted).

Audit appears to have shifted from issues of procedural compliance to a growing involvement in performance evaluation. This development produces an engagement between audit and professional knowledges that involves their displacement or co-option. The achievement of improved organizational performance has been increasingly transformed into the province of 'good management', rather than being entrusted to professional standards. The pursuit of 'quality', 'excellence' or 'standards' means that evaluative agencies have come to colonize organizational terrain that was previously the province of professional expertise (see also Kirkpatrick and Martinez-Lucio, 1995). Different public services (as other chapters in this book have demonstrated) have seen different accommodations between professional expertise and evaluative agencies – e.g. the OFSTED, SSI, Quality Assurance Agency for Higher Education, etc. Hughes and his colleagues (1996) have suggested that the emergent audit-and-inspection regimes that operate in different welfare fields vary partly as a result of the relative power of the different professional and occupational groups (see also Cope and Goodship, 1999).

4 From compliance to competition: comparing organizational performance

The next issue concerns the shift from compliance to competition. The evaluation of performance has centred on producing comparative information ('league tables' and the like) through which organizations are judged in terms of their relative success in achieving desired results. Hood et al. talk about these processes as involving a 'hybrid' of 'oversight' and 'competition' (1998, pp. 14–17). This point emphasizes the constructed character of the competition in which organizations are embroiled (see also Clarke, forthcoming). Although many processes are used in such evaluation, there are also some common features. The first is that 'success' and 'failure' are intended to have significant consequences for the fortunes of the organization (either in direct resourcing or indirectly via affecting consumer choices). The second is that 'success' and 'failure' are necessary statistical artefacts: league tables are never anything other than tables, running inexorably from top to bottom. There will, as a result, always be a 'bottom 20 per cent' of any specific set of organizations, even if the policy goal is to improve or remove the organizations that currently occupy the bottom 20 per cent of the table. Cutler (1992) has examined how such statistical artefacts were used to establish the 'problem' of organizational inefficiency in NHS bed occupancy in an Audit Commission study (1992). Performance management is consistently framed through this methodology – as addressing the problem of bringing the weakest performers up to the average – or even top – standards.

However, the single-minded pursuit of 'success' is now understood to have both unanticipated consequences and perverse effects. Organizations will try to tell what Corvellec (1995) calls 'stories of achievement' about their success, even in the face of declining resources, because they must announce themselves as successful in competitive contexts. Organizations may concentrate only on the 'core business' that directly produces measured results, withdrawing from or downgrading other public functions. They will also try to manage their operating environments and inputs to produce success (selecting for 'good pupils' or 'good patients', for example). Where efficiency or success is calculated at the level of organizational units, organizations will be faced with incentives to improve their own, rather than overall service, performance. Such a concern with specific targets or standards of performance will have implications for the pursuit of 'joined-up government' and 'partnerships' that imply attention to goals beyond organizationally defined core business (see also Newman, Chapter 3 in this volume).

Shifts in what audit means and how it is practised raise questions about the role of evaluative agencies. We have suggested that it is possible to see differences of role between financial auditing (and compliance testing of financial control systems) and performance evaluation. Performance evaluation has taken audit into new and more complex areas of professional practice and service provision across almost the whole range of public services – policing, housing, social care, health provision, the court system, and so on. Those interventions have also been the point at which audit has taken on a more normatively managerialist role. For example, OFSTED has prescribed a range of approaches from classroom methods to the leadership style to be expected of headteachers. The Audit Commission has identified the best forms of organizational structure, culture and management practice for the delivery of various public services, from community care to crime prevention (Langan and Clarke, 1994; Hughes, 1999).

This places evaluative agencies in significant roles within two processes of the restructuring of the state in the late twentieth century. They have become part of what can be called 'the politicization of organizational design', in which normative judgements about the 'best' organizational forms for public services have been central features of the politics of reform in both New Right and New Labour variants (Clarke and Newman, 1997). Such initiatives have borrowed heavily from corporate sector images of new organizational forms (often associated with 'post-Fordist' patterns). They are 'anti-bureaucratic' (Barzelay, 1992; Osborne and Gaebler, 1992; also see du Gay, Chapter 4 in this volume). They also promote a conception of the service organization as a (relatively) autonomous 'small or medium business' (Hoggett, 1996). The imagery of the corporate sector has served as a means of naturalizing the forms of organization being promoted: they are represented as both generic (suitable for all organizations) and superior (to public sector professional bureaucracies). In the context of New Labour conceptions of modernization, an increasing emphasis on successful partnership working may form an added strand of organizational design (and evaluation).

Such a politicized view of organizational design has implications for how the co-ordination or governance of public services is understood.

Evaluative agencies have increasingly challenged the 'professional cultures' in public services and have argued the need for more, and better, management in such organizations. In these ways, such agencies have been a powerful normative force in constructing the conditions for the managerialization of public services. 'Management' in this discourse is understood as a modernizing and improving force that is free of the narrow or sectional interests of (professional) producers. Unlike bureaucrats, professionals and even (some) politicians, management can be relied upon to promote the interests of the user/consumer of public services (Clarke and Newman, 1997).

The original conception of audit had a normative component, both in relation to accounting as a set of conventions and in terms of the modelling of control systems and reporting procedures. Nevertheless, the extension of audit to these new evaluative and organizational development roles has extended the scope and significance of the norms it carries and circulates. In these respects, some audit agencies – although by no means all – have become governmental agents as much as 'independent scrutineers'. They have become evangelizers for (rather than evaluators of) the 'New Public Management' (Humphrey et al., 1999). This issue of their relationship to the politics of organizational design is separate from the question of their relationship to the implementation of specific government policies.

5   Representing the public interest

In the governance of the dispersed state, evaluative agencies play a double role. First, they are the agents of central government. In this role, they are one of the means by which 'arm's length' control may be exercised over service provision, via scrutiny, comparison and the normative drive for 'continuous improvement'. Secondly, they are the putative representatives of the public interest. Since government and the public cannot be assumed to be identical, this role for evaluation raises questions about how the public and its interests are understood and represented in the practices of evaluation. We would suggest that it is possible to see three different conceptions of the public in the work of such agencies: the public-as-taxpayers; the public-as-consumers; the public-as-communities of interest. For example, the Audit Commission has presented itself as helping local government respond to a 'call for accountability' that 'comes from all sections of the public – for the users of services, from ratepayers, from councillors themselves, and of course, from central government' (Audit Commission, 1989, p. 2).

The dominant conception of the public interest is embodied in the image of 'taxpayers' money'. Audit in public services has been driven by a strong concern for limiting the 'burden' on the taxpayer that public spending represents and for promoting the efficient use of the 'taxpayers'

money' that is spent. The Audit Commission was established to promote
the 'three Es' of economy, efficiency and effectiveness in local government in England and Wales (and subsequently in the NHS). The search
for 'Value for Money' (and subsequently 'Best Value') has been a
recurrent image in the reform of public services. This conception of the
public interest is founded on several distinctive discursive features. It
rests on the separation of the taxpayer identity from other social or public
roles: 'taxpayers' pay for rather than use or benefit from public services.
Their primary concern, then, is necessarily with their tax. Clarke (1997)
has argued that one of the accomplishments of New Right politics was to
'split' the citizen identity into three differentiated figures: the taxpayer,
the scrounger and the consumer. In the process, taxes (and their payers)
were placed in a potentially antagonistic relationship with the user/
abuser of services (the scrounger). We will come back to the consumer
shortly.

Separating out the 'taxpayers' in this way makes it possible to
attribute an interest to them. As Cooper has shown in her analysis of the
concept of 'Fiduciary Duty' in local government, 'taxpayers' interests are
equated with efficient, cost-effective services and business-like practices'
(1998, p. 83). She suggests that this equivalence rules out other social and
political orientations to public service. It also conceals a double discursive construction: the 'taxpayers' are both an abstract and universal
category and are embodied in a 'particular image of the local community as individualistic and self-interested and as abstract, conservative and male' (1998, p. 86). For example, the Audit Commission stresses
how local authority 'openness' about expenditure on communications
'can be an effective way of dispelling fears that taxpayers' money is
being used improperly to produce self-serving propaganda' (1995, p.
45). Taxpayers are both universal and particular. The 'Value for Money'
to be sought in their interest treats specific social values as if they are
transcendent, consensual and self-evident. In the process, we would
suggest, an economic calculus for the evaluation of public services has
been naturalized.

The consumer offers a second incarnation of the public and its
interest in relation to the evaluation of public services. Although there
are extensive arguments about the consumer model and its use in public
services, it is clear that the idea of the consumer has added new
dimensions to the way the public interest is being represented (Clarke,
1998). Above all, 'the consumer' is held to mark a shift from 'passive
recipient' to 'active choice maker' in relation to services. For example,
the 1998 Green Paper on Welfare Reform argued that consumerism was
a driving force for the modernization of the welfare state:

> Society has become more demanding. Consumers expect ever higher levels of
> service and better value for money. Voters want politicians who are account-
> able. Taxpayers want public agencies which meet their objectives efficiently.

The way in which a service is delivered can be as important as the service itself – as retailers know only too well.

Three trends highlight the rise of the demanding, sceptical citizen-consumer. First, confidence in the institutions of government and politics has tumbled. Second, expectations of service quality and convenience have risen – as with the growth in 24-hour banking – but public services have failed to keep up with these developments; their duplication, inefficiency and unnecessary complexity should not be tolerated. Third, as incomes rise, people prefer to own their own homes and investments. (Secretary of State for Social Security and the Minister for Welfare Reform/Department of Social Security, 1998, p. 16)

This active consumer is the force that requires modern public services to be adaptive, responsive, flexible and diverse rather than paternalist, monolithic and operating on a model of 'one size fits all'. The consumer thus forges a story about the past and future of public services. Like the taxpayer, s/he is an economic invention. Consumers know their own wants, can make rational choices and expect producers to serve them. Like taxpayers, consumers are abstracted from other social roles and positions, including the problematic and stressful conditions in which many public services may be used (Barnes and Prior, 1995). And, like taxpayers, consumers are both universal and particular: the role of consuming is universalized (and naturalized), while the wants are particularized (and individualized). Consumerism registers diversity (everyone has different wants) but does not recognize the inequalities of social differentiation. Finally, consumerism constructs the public interest as a series of specific and individualized encounters and interactions: each consumer consumes a particular bit of service. Collective consumption of public services is invisible (as is the 'enforced consumption' of services).

Nevertheless, evaluative agencies have been constructed as representatives (if not champions) of the public as consumers. They construe themselves as at least potentially adversarial to 'producer interests' in the role of representatives of users/consumers: a role most visible in but by no means exclusive to OFSTED. Despite the nominal diversity of consumerism, consumers are often practically invoked in normative ways (the 'normal family' is the template against which others may have 'special needs'). This model of rational choice implies that we would all make the same calculations about price/quality trade-offs (and are unlikely to let 'dogma', 'ideology' or other forms of unreason cloud our choices).

The collection of evaluative and comparative information is understood as making organizations more 'transparent' to consumers and making information available that will enable the exercise of rational choice on the part of consumers (or purchasers). Where the public as taxpayer legitimates the pursuit of efficiency (and economy), the public as consumer legitimates the pursuit of comparability in relation to standards or quality of services. These two images have been the dominant representations of the public and its interests in the last decade, but there are signs of an emergent third view of the public.

Where the taxpayer and consumer conceptions of the public imagine a unifying and coherent identity for the public and its interest, other pressures have shaped a more differentiated conception of the public at the end of the twentieth century. The public is being imagined as a field of differences: different 'communities', different cultures, different socio-demographic groups who may have different interests. As Humphrey et al. (1999, p. 16) indicate:

> the Audit Commission has recently begun to enumerate the groups which are likely to be hard to reach from the perspective of local authorities in their duties to resource and represent their publics . . . the Best Value document refers to 'demographic groups', such as young people, 'communities of interest' such as ethnic minorities and 'geographical communities' such as people living in isolated rural areas (Audit Commission, 1998).

A number of strands play into such conceptions of a diverse public. One thread is formed out of a variety of activist social movements and their intersection with the local state around 'equalities' struggles (see, for example, Breitenbach et al., forthcoming). A linked strand is formed by the pursuit of 'access', 'anti-discriminatory' or 'anti-oppressive' practices in different professional fields. High profile public events (such as the MacPherson inquiry into the Stephen Lawrence case) have also helped to make difference visible in the constitution of the public and public services. Increasingly sophisticated marketing and sampling processes attentive to both demographic and 'lifestyle' differentiation have also played a part. All of these have, as Newman (Chapter 3 in this volume) argues, made an issue out of the politics of representation and the 'representativeness' of public services. To some extent, this image of a diverse public may be strengthened by some elements of New Labour proposing a 'multicultural, multinational Britain' that is made 'stronger by its diversity' (Gordon Brown, *Guardian*, 6 May 1999, p. 22).

Such a view of the public raises some profound problems about the place of evaluative agencies. How is such diversity to be understood and categorized? Are formalized socio-demographic distinctions adequate to the task? Can the public interest be produced from sampling the population by age, ethnicity, gender, sexual orientation or other categorizations? How is a diverse public to be consulted and represented? Are there differences in how services are to be evaluated? If so, how can they be either accommodated or reconciled (if not by the imposition of majoritarian norms)? Should such a diverse public be consulted or represented through service organizations, their governing bodies or evaluative agencies? The beginnings of a move away from the taxpayer/consumer models of the public imply political, processual and technical problems for a practice of evaluation in defence of the public interest (see also Ellison, 1999; Fraser, 1997).

6 Dogmatic pragmatism: New Labour, evidence and evaluation

As a number of chapters in this volume have suggested, the New Labour approach to the further reconstruction of public services has continued and intensified the rise of audit and evaluation. Rouse and Smith (1999, p. 250) suggest that:

> The performance management ethos has become even more pronounced under New Labour. . . . There is every prospect that the guarantors of standards, in the form of auditors, most notably the Audit Commission, Ofsted and Social Services Inspectorate will have a busy time in promoting efficiency and high standards in many services. They will be strengthened by a new Commission for Health Improvement and a local government inspectorate attached to the Audit Commission.

These agencies will embody the concern with 'standards' and the commitment to 'continuous improvement' that are recurrent themes in New Labour policy statements. There are significant parallels between the continued development of external scrutiny (and competitive comparison as a form of discipline) and the widespread emphasis on 'evidence based practice' in a range of service areas: health, social care, criminal justice and so on (see, for example, *Public Money and Management*, 19 (1), 1999). In these developments, welfare professionals are being recruited to processes of self-assessment and continuous *self-*improvement that are disciplined by systems of evidentiary evaluation. At the same time, performance evaluation, appraisal and pay systems are being discussed as a means of disciplining service workers and promoting service improvements (see also Waine, Chapter 14 in this volume).

New Labour's approach to public services has been marked by a number of continuities with New Right politics. One central element is the populist conception of the relationship between the people, the government and public services. New Labour has made significant discursive attempts to differentiate itself from a Conservatism that is identified as being against public services: characterized as pro-market, pro-privatization and holding a residualist view of welfare, for example (Clarke and Newman, 1998). But New Labour has not tried to reconstruct a homological relationship between the public, the government and public services. Like Thatcherite populism, New Labour represents itself as being on the side of 'the people' against the state – defined as public service providers (see Hall, 1988). This antagonistic relationship is particularly strongly expressed in the mission to 'modernize' the state and its array of public services. Its stance in relation to service providers has tended to be a sceptical one: expressing concerns about 'producer domination' and the inertia or resistance of public services confronted by the need to change. In such formulations, the New Labour government has characteristically positioned itself as the champion of the public (consumer) interest. In this view, evaluative agencies represent an effective way of installing the interest of the 'sceptical citizen consumer' within 'modern' processes of governance. As the Prime Minister has indicated: 'In all areas, monitoring and inspection are playing a key role, as an incentive to higher standards and as a means of determining appropriate levels of [central] intervention. A new pragmatism is growing in the relations between the public and private sector. The emphasis must be on goals not rules, and monitoring achievements not processes' (Blair, 1997, pp. 16–17).

New Labour has celebrated this 'pragmatic' stance on the means of providing public services, refusing to make 'ideological' judgements about the relative merits of public or private sector forms of provision. The extensively quoted observation by Tony Blair that 'what counts is what works' both articulates this pragmatism and enshrines the role of evaluation as a central feature of governance in a 'modern' society. Rouse and Smith have argued that there may be a 'third way' approach to accountability which 'has also been inspired, in part, by a belated recognition of the value of some of the aspects of the New Public Management. This has been adapted to uphold accountability to users in the context of community and not as separate atomized consumers' (1999, p. 254). Nevertheless, they recognize some unresolved tensions within this 'third way' – not least that of reconciling the community orientation and its emphasis on participation with 'the centralized search to improve performance throughout the welfare state, so ardently pursued by New Labour' (1999, p. 254). Cope and Goodship (1999) raise rather different questions about the role that regulation, audit and inspection may play in furthering or hindering New Labour's search for 'joined-up government'. They suggest that differences of style and organizational competition between regulatory agencies may inhibit the development of 'joined-up scrutiny' to support 'joined-up government'. Joined-up scrutiny is also potentially problematic because regulatory agencies tend to reflect the functional divisions across which joined-up government would have to work. However, some of these problems are being addressed in the creation of new bodies such as the Public Audit Forum and the Inspectorate Forum.

To some extent, such issues are part of the tensions and contradictions that feature in New Labour's ideology, politics and policy. We would want to argue that they are also integral to the wider programme of state restructuring that New Labour inherited (and to which it has added its own initiatives). The processes of managerialization – and now modernization – have changed state forms, and reorganized flows and relations of power. But in the process of transforming the old professional bureaucracies, they have given rise to new tensions. The rise of audit and inspection agencies – the new machinery of evaluation and scrutiny – is an attempt to solve some of those problems – not least how to control a dispersed or fragmented state. But their rise is also part of the same process – one aspect of a technocratic, economistic and managerialist conception of how to order the public realm. As such, they carry with them internal problems, affecting their internal capacity to evaluate and install 'what works'. They also bear the marks of the wider social dislocations that challenge simple or unified conceptions of the public interest – the conflicts that give rise to the question of *'who counts'* in determining the public interest.

References

Armstrong, P. (1994) 'Professions of contention', paper presented to ESRC Seminar on Professions in Late Modernity, University of Cardiff, 14 April.

Audit Commission (1989) *Managing Services Effectively – Performance Review*, Management Paper 5, London, HMSO.

Audit Commission (1992) *Lying in Wait: The Use of Medical Beds in Acute Hospitals*, London, HMSO.

Audit Commission (1995) *Talk Back. Local Authority Communication with Citizens*, London, HMSO.

Audit Commission (1998) *Better by Far. Preparing for Best Value*, London, HMSO.

Barnes, M. and Prior, D. (1995) 'Spoilt for choice? How consumerism can disempower service users', *Public Money and Management*, July–September, pp. 53–9.

Bartlett, W., Roberts, J. and Le Grand, J. (eds) (1998) *A Revolution in Social Policy: Quasi-market Reforms in the 1990s*, Bristol, The Policy Press.

Barzelay, M. (1992) *Breaking through Bureaucracy: A New Vision for Managing in Government*, Berkeley, University of California Press.

Blair, T. (1997) *The Third Way*, London, Fabian Society.

Breitenbach, E., Brown, A., Mackay, F. and Webb, J. (eds) (forthcoming) *Gender Equality and the New Politics*, Basingstoke, Macmillan.

Clarke, J. (1997) 'Capturing the customer? Consumerism and social welfare', *Self, Agency and Society*, 1 (1), pp. 55–73.

Clarke, J. (1998) 'Consumerism', in Hughes, G. (ed.) *Imagining Welfare Futures*, London, Routledge.

Clarke, J. (forthcoming) 'Making a difference? Markets and the reform of public services in the UK', in Schröter, E. and Wollman, H. (eds) *Modernizing Public Services in Germany and the UK*, Basingstoke, Macmillan.

Clarke, J. and Newman, J. (1997) *The Managerial State: Power, Politics and Ideology in the Remaking of Social Welfare*, London, Sage.

Clarke, J. and Newman, J. (1998) 'A modern British people? New Labour and the reconstruction of social welfare', paper presented to the Discourse Analysis and Social Research Conference, Copenhagen Business School, September.

Cooper, D. (1998) *Governing out of Order: Space, Law and the Politics of Belonging*, London, Rivers Oram Press.

Cope, S. and Goodship, J. (1999) 'Regulating collaborative government: towards joined-up government?' *Public Policy and Administration*, 14 (2), pp. 3–16.

Corvellec, H. (1995) *Stories of Achievements: Narrative Features of Organizational Performance,* Malmo, Lund University Press.

Cutler, T. (1992) 'Sunlight later? The Audit Commission and the management of acute hospitals', paper presented to the Labour Process Conference, London, July.

Cutler, T. and Waine, B. (1997) *Managing the Welfare State,* Oxford, Berg.

Dunleavy, P. (1991) *Democracy, Bureaucracy and Public Choice,* London, Harvester Wheatsheaf.

Ellison, N. (1999) 'Beyond universalism and particularism: rethinking contemporary welfare theory', *Critical Social Policy,* 19 (1), pp. 57–86.

Fraser, N. (1997) *Justice Interruptus,* New York, Routledge.

Hall, S. (1988) *The Hard Road to Renewal,* London, Verso.

Hoggett, P. (1996) 'New modes of control in the public service', *Public Administration,* 74, pp. 9–32.

Hood, C., Scott, C., James, O., Jones, G. and Travers, T. (1998) *Regulation inside Government: Waste-Watchers, Quality Police and Sleaze Busters,* Oxford, Oxford University Press.

Hughes, G. (ed.) (1998) *Imagining Welfare Futures,* London, Routledge.

Hughes, G. (1999) 'Community safety in the age of the "risk society"', in Pease, K., Ballantyne, S. and McClaren, V. (eds) *Key Issues in Crime Prevention, Crime Reduction and Community Safety,* Aldershot, Ashgate.

Hughes, G., Mears, R. and Winch, C. (1996) 'An inspector calls? Regulation and accountability in three public services', *Policy and Politics,* 25 (3), pp. 299–313.

Humphrey, J. with Clarke, J., Gewirtz, S. and Hughes, G. (1999) 'Audit and inspection in the public sector', paper presented to Social Policy Association annual conference, July, London.

Kirkpatrick, I. and Martinez-Lucio, M. (eds) (1995) *The Politics of Quality in the Public Sector,* London, Routledge.

Langan, M. and Clarke, J. (1994) 'Managing in the mixed economy of care', in Clarke, J., Cochrane, A. and McLaughlin, E. (eds) *Managing Social Policy,* London, Sage.

Newman, J. (forthcoming) 'What counts is what works? Constructing evaluations of markets in public services', *Public Administration.*

Niskanen, W.A. (1971) *Bureaucracy and Representative Government,* New York, Aldine-Atherton.

Osborne, D. and Gaebler, T. (1992) *Reinventing Government: How the Entrepreneurial Spirit is Transforming the Public Sector,* Reading, MA, Addison-Wesley.

Pollitt, C. (1995) 'Justification by works or by faith? Evaluating the New Public Management', *Evaluation,* 1 (2), pp. 133–54.

Pollitt, C., Birchall, J. and Ritman, K. (1998) *Decentralising Public Services Management: the British Experience,* Basingstoke, Macmillan.

Pollitt, C., Girre, X., Lonsdale, J., Mul, R., Summa, H. and Waerness, M. (1998) *Performance or Compliance? Performance Audit and Public Management in Five Countries,* Oxford, Oxford University Press.

Power, M. (1993) *The Audit Explosion,* London, Demos.

Power, M. (1997) *The Audit Society,* Oxford, Oxford University Press.

Rouse, J. and Smith, G. (1999) 'Accountability', in Powell, M. (ed.) *New Labour, New Welfare State?* Bristol, The Policy Press.

Secretary of State for Social Security and Minister for Welfare Reform/Department of Social Security (1998) *New Ambitions for Our Country: A New Contract for Welfare,* Cm 3805, London, The Stationery Office.

Skocpol, T. (1997) *Boomerang: Health Care Reform and the Turn against Government,* 2nd edition, New York, W.W. Norton.

Walsh, K. (1995) *Public Services and Market Mechanisms: Competition, Contracting and the New Public Management,* Basingstoke, Macmillan.

Index